THE DYNAMICS OF RELIGIOUS REFORM IN NORTHERN EUROPE, 1780-1920
POLITICAL AND LEGAL PERSPECTIVES

THE DYNAMICS OF RELIGIOUS REFORM IN CHURCH, STATE AND SOCIETY
IN NORTHERN EUROPE, 1780-1920

Editors-in-chief: Joris van Eijnatten and Nigel Yates†

Before the last quarter of the eighteenth century there was a generally clear and remarkably uniform pattern of church-state relationships across Europe, which had emerged from the religious conflicts of the sixteenth and seventeenth centuries. In the course of the 'long' nineteenth century this firm alliance between political and religious establishments broke down all over Europe. A substantial degree of religious pluralism developed everywhere, requiring church and state to accommodate change. Defining religious reform as 'the conscious pursuit of renewal with the aim of adapting organised religion to the changing relations between church, state and society', this series examines the reforms initiated by the organised religions of Northern Europe between c.1780 and c.1920. There has been an assumption that it was the change in the church-state relationship that was largely responsible for the ecclesiastical reform movement of the nineteenth century, and that it was the state that was the principal agent of change, with the national churches seen as resisting changes that had to be forced upon them. Recent research across Europe has shown that in some parts of Europe ecclesiastical reform was initiated by the churches; and that there were times and places when it was the state rather than the church that was hostile to alterations in the status quo. This series explores this process of change from different angles, looking particularly at its impact on the question of religious reform, in England, Ireland, Scotland, Wales, Belgium, the Netherlands, Germany, Denmark, Sweden and Norway.

Financial assistance for the research programme on 'The Dynamics of Religious Reform in Northern Europe, 1780-1920' is gratefully acknowledged from the Netherlands Organisation for Scientific Research (NWO), University of Wales, Trinity St David (formerly University of Wales, Lampeter) and the Documentation and Research Centre for Religion, Culture and Society at K.U.Leuven (KADOC).

THE DYNAMICS OF RELIGIOUS REFORM IN NORTHERN EUROPE
1780-1920

LEUVEN UNIVERSITY PRESS

EDITED BY KEITH ROBBINS

POLITICAL AND LEGAL PERSPECTIVES

The series 'The Dynamics of Religious Reform in Northern Europe, 1780-1920' is a sub-series of the 'KADOC Studies on Religion, Culture and Society', published under the supervision of the KADOC Editorial Board:

© 2010
Leuven University Press / Presses universitaires de Louvain / Universitaire Pers Leuven
Minderbroedersstraat 4 bus 5602, B-3000 Leuven (Belgium)

ISBN 978 90 5867 825 6
D/2010/1869/32
NUR: 694

Contents

6

Introduction

Keith Robbins

Part I: Envisaging 'Northern Europe'

'The Dynamics of Religious Reform in Church, State and Society in Northern Europe 1780-1920' encompasses a wide field of investigation. The first task is to consider what kind of 'place identity' is being suggested by the term 'Northern Europe'. A moment's reflection or, alternatively, prolonged immersion in the concepts of cultural geography, prompts the response that there is no simple, single and universally satisfying answer. A name distinguishes a particular place from other spatial entities. Its sense may be weak or strong. Its identity, supposing we can speak confidently about identity, may be established either by some kind of internal coherence or by reference to a perceived 'Other'. These two aspects may fuse, or separate, at different points in time.

So it is with the 'Northern Europe' of this project. There is no map which tells us unambiguously where to locate it: what is 'in' and what is 'out'. Different vantage points suggest different conclusions about where borders and boundaries are and what, in turn, they signify. Historians, political scientists, geographers and ethnologists are all capable of producing their own definitions - and disagree about the appropriate starting point. The 'inclusions' of one century may be the 'exclusions' of another. So it is even the case within the long nineteenth century adopted in this project - and periodization has its own elements of arbitrariness. There is, therefore, an inescapable fuzziness about 'Northern Europe'. We cannot approach it with any confident sense of what constitute its 'core' and what its 'periphery'. It has no 'capital' and there are

'*Northern Europe*' *c.1870.*

no 'provinces'. To say that is merely to state what applies also to 'Europe' itself.[1] The 'heart of Europe' is an enigma inside a mystery. 'North' and 'South' can at least be said to have polar compasses. But no such help becomes available in defining 'Western' and 'Eastern' and whether there is indeed a 'Central Europe' which consists of 'lands in between' packaged now one way and then another. The scope for further sub-division is always there - South-East Europe or North-West Europe, for example - but it is an enterprise which still always frays at awkward edges. In the very act of assembling common 'content' to cartography, 'out of area' facts obstinately obtrude. So, the 'Northern Europe' of this project is consciously capacious, unashamedly provocative and inescapably blurred. One size does not fit all. Moreover, the delimitation has been made with particular regard to the fact that the focus is specifically on 'religious reform'. Another focus might well yield a different combination. It has meant that, taken as a whole, the church and state structures under review have sufficient commonality to be comparable, but also sufficient diversity to avoid a monochrome analysis. This is not a view of 'Northern Europe' as Protestant which is in contrast or even in opposition to a 'Southern Europe' which is Catholic. It straddles different internal confessional balances.

All that said, and much more in the same vein has been and could be said, the countries under scrutiny are England, Ireland, Scotland, Wales, Belgium, the Netherlands, Germany, Denmark, Sweden and Norway. The word 'country' is manifestly a loose one. They are not all 'states'. What their 'names' signified in 1780, from a constitutional or political perspective, was by no means always what they signified in 1920. In turn, these countries have been grouped into four blocs: the United Kingdom of Great Britain and Ireland, the Low Countries, Germany and Scandinavia/the Nordic Region. This grouping reflects the fact that we are dealing with 'countries' which had their own religious characteristics but which, in this period, constituted parts of a unitary state, perhaps even a nation-state; countries which were, for a short or substantial time, unitary states, or countries which were in the process of forming a state/empire.

The fact that all the countries concerned are, relatively speaking, 'close' to each other makes likely, to an extent, common mindsets, shared cultural formations, familiar institutional patterns and commercial exchange but does not guarantee them. They inherit a concept of Christendom and all, in different ways, wrestle with its contemporary significance and application. Proximity, however, also, makes possible a sharp sense of 'otherness', and, with it, the possibility, even the likelihood, of conflict. 'Ownership' of particular territories may be contested, metaphorically as well as physically. 'Elites' within particular countries, whether cultural, political or social, may 'position' themselves in the territory which they inhabit with their 'fellow subjects' or maybe 'fellow citizens' differently from 'the people'. The categories of thought which they employ, even the very language they use, may lead them to iden-

9

---

[1] It is no part of this project to produce a definition of 'Europe' but the following works by British, German and French historians respectively open up avenues: Davies, *Europe*; Schulze, *Staat und Nation*; Duroselle, *Europe*.

tify different 'neighbours'. If geography, in one fundamental sense, determines where a country 'locates' itself, 'culture' or 'history' or 'religion' may suggest other senses of 'belonging'. What now follows in this first Part constitutes a short commentary on the composition of those four blocs and their significance in terms of this project's agenda.

This initial exercise in contextualization places the defined blocs in 'Northern Europe' yet it also deliberately goes on to provide a modest descant to the 'bloc mentality' which may otherwise prevail. Contributors, naturally and properly, concentrate on the specific aspects of 'their countries'. It is only when placed in a wider context that what seems 'obvious' and 'normal' in the relationship between church, state and society in any given country can appear from outside to be 'bewildering' and 'exceptional'. This introduction is therefore a reminder that our blocs are porous. 'Influences' did not respect frontiers. There is, in short, a 'religious reform' which can be approached 'transnationally' as well as through a set of apparently clearly defined 'national stories'. It is not being assumed, therefore, that 'Northern Europe', in this period, is a straightforward and 'naturally' homogeneous geographical region following a uniform path of social, political, cultural and religious development. Nor is it assumed that 'religious reform' unfolds uniformly, according to a set pattern, from country to country, so that contributors to this volume merely tell the same story, but in different places. 'Reform', in each case, has an individuality which reflects the extent to which the narratives of 'nation', 'state', or 'church', in the particular countries under review, fuse or diverge. Terminology and nomenclature further complicates any interpretation of the whole. The language of this publication is English, but the outcome rests upon research which has of course been largely conducted in the languages of the countries under investigation. It has been apparent, in the interaction between the contributors, that key words in the project's title always have contextual implications and associations which risk being lost or misconstrued in the act of translation. The word 'dynamics', therefore, is not idly chosen. It emphasises that the triggers of change do not all stem from a single source: just like historians, they interact unpredictably.

The United Kingdom of Great Britain and Ireland

The United Kingdom of Great Britain and Ireland, as it had become in 1801 and which it was ceasing to be with the impending separation of the Irish Free State, and the partition of the island of Ireland, as our period concludes, would not immediately have seen itself as 'Northern'. It was normally referred to 'on the continent' as 'England'. Stewart J. Brown and this author, writing as they have done at some length elsewhere, are well aware of the complexity which attaches to any attempt to 'place' the islands, with their extraordinary global prominence, indeed pre-eminence, in this period. They faced many different directions.[2] There is no need to construct a *Sonderweg* - as

[2] Robbins, "Location and Dislocation", and critique
by Craig, O'Háinle, Jenkins and Longley, 181-213.

though there was in fact some single European, or even Northern European 'way of life' from which they particularly diverged - to observe that British peculiarities stand out conspicuously in comparison with other countries under consideration.[3] The combination of insularity and non-participation (after 1815) in wars on the 'mainland' brought a sense of detachment, brazenly if inaccurately described as 'splendid isolation'. There was, therefore, no direct cultural transfer. It scarcely needs to be said that Britain did not experience at first hand the direct impact of either the French Revolution or the Napoleonic 'integration' of Europe.[4] Whether in the Low Countries or in Germany, it is impossible, in reading the respective chapters in this volume, to avoid the multi-faceted impact of foreign occupation on subsequent internal development. The imprint of Napoleonic legislation could not be eradicated. France, of course, forms no direct part of this project. Only by severing it in two and emphasising the 'northernness' of northern France would it have been plausible to have done so. Nevertheless, it was France, in attraction or revulsion, which in effect still set an agenda in many or indeed most of the countries which do come within the project's scope. There was a sense in which France and Britain offered, or offered themselves, as competing models to show 'Northern Europe' how to bring about 'modernity'.[5]

That sense of self-containment and assured institutional adaptation which normally prevailed in Victorian Britain did not mean that there were no particular relationships beyond its shores in Northern Europe. There had been 'Scandinavian moments' in British history but they were somewhat distant. The 'British moment' experienced by the Danes of Copenhagen was more recent but no more enjoyable. In September 1807 Scottish infantry, clad in alarming kilts, were camped in the Tivoli gardens watching the city which they, as invaders, had set up in flames. The incident did not suggest friendly solidarity across the North Sea. Fortunately, relationships improved. Another more peaceful penetration occurred in 1883. The British Liberal Prime Minister, William Gladstone, set sail for a visit to Norway. He did so after receiving the freedom of the town of Kirkwall on the northern 'British' island of Orkney whose people seemed to him to be of 'Scandinavian character'. He thought the people of Christiania (Oslo) to be most courteous and happy in their separate constitution under the Swedish Crown.[6] Could not something similar happen to Ireland under the British Crown? In 1914, Britain, recognising that Denmark was in the power and sphere of interest of Germany, left the country in peace.[7] It might be said, and not unexpectedly in the light of history, that Scotland (and its Northern Isles particularly) did have a kind of Scandinavian 'feel' but that was of limited political significance. Ecclesiastically, however, Scotland was a Reformed and not a Lutheran country - Swedish bishops, in the previous century, had instigated raids on the Reformed religious practices of the

11

---

[3] Robbins, "Ethnicity, Religion, Class and Gender and the 'Island Story/ies'".
[4] Neisen, "Das Bild der Französischen Revolution in Grossbritannien"; Woolf, *Napoleon's Integration of Europe.*

[5] Aprille and Bensimon, *La France et l'Angleterre.*
[6] Matthew, ed., *Gladstone Diaries*, XI, 28-29.
[7] Kaarsted, *Great Britain and Denmark*, 209-214.

English and Dutch colonies in Stockholm. It was with the Netherlands that Scotland's ecclesiastical (as also its commercial and educational) contacts were closest, though no longer as close as they had been in the previous century. It is noteworthy that the author (1832) of the history of the Scottish Church which was established in Rotterdam published, as an appendix, a 'Brief View of the Dutch Ecclesiastical Establishment' as reconstituted in 1816. Subsequently published in pamphlet form, it was thought to be relevant in relation to debates on comparable issues in Scotland.[8]

In any case, whether the United Kingdom wished to see itself, fundamentally, as a European state was itself problematic.[9] It was clearly not itself 'Mediterranean' (though from Gibraltar through Malta and eventually to Cyprus the Mediterranean was envisaged by the British Admiralty as a kind of British lake) but did 'the islands' belong anywhere in relation to the 'mainland'? Fog in the English Channel meant that 'the Continent' was cut off - not the other way round. Besides, these islands were not just ordinary islands. They were not of the Mediterranean but they were, in other senses, potently present there. Indeed, as needs scarcely any elaboration, in that expansion and consolidation of the global British Empire which characterised this period, the British, in a geographical sense, were 'everywhere'. The United Kingdom was not 'just' a Northern European state. The same could be said of the Netherlands and even of Denmark but it was the sheer scale of the British presence across the world that made it extraordinary. Historians have long argued, and will continue to argue, over the place of accident and design in the creation of the British Empire. It is not a debate to be entered into here. The point to be emphasised, however, is that a comparison across the states of Northern Europe which fails to note, by the end of this period, the 'extra-territoriality' of most of them - massive, modest or miniscule - fails to grasp the context in which internal policy decisions with a bearing on 'church-state-society' were made. Yet, while this reminder is salutary, the United Kingdom could never be completely 'isolated', and certainly not 'isolated' from a Northern Europe of which it was a part, if a rather complicated part, and in whose affairs at governmental and other levels, it had never ceased, some might say, to meddle.

Leaving the question of Empire aside, the United Kingdom also wrestled with inter-nation issues which were analogous to those contemporaneously troubling Scandinavia. The Act of Union of 1801 had appeared to settle the relationship between Great Britain and Ireland, but it had soon become clear that this was not the case, or at least not on the basis then set out. The demand for Home Rule for Ireland became ever stronger, though whether, should it ever be achieved, it was only a stepping stone towards independence was strongly argued over. The presence of Ireland within the United Kingdom blunted any possibility that the state as a whole might think of itself exclusively in 'northern' terms, whatever Protestant Englishmen might wish. Irish eyes, predominantly Catholic, did not instinctively turn in the direction of Protes-

[8] Drummond, *The Kirk and the Continent*, 145.

[9] Robbins, *Great Britain*; Id., "L'histoire britan-nique et la 'Britishness'".

tant Scandinavia seeking solidarity. They looked for support to Rome and a 'Catholic Europe' which was not 'northern'. Ireland was sometimes referred to as 'West Britain' and, within Europe, it was the most westerly of countries.[10] 'Beyond' was America, not Scandinavia, and it was there that millions of Irish people had emigrated and created an Irish-American continuum which outweighed any sense of a 'northern' belonging. Of course, emigration from Scandinavia and Finland to the United States was also a feature and, likewise, in the movement of people, out and back, also created a kind of continuum. Emigration to, but also continuing interaction with, America, in the late nineteenth century, shaped 'Northern Europe' (though of course not only Northern Europe). It was another element which cautions against the notion that 'church-state-society' relations in any country were solely shaped by factors within that country.

The Low Countries

The Low Countries form the second bloc. They forged their politics sandwiched between the Great Powers to their east and west, both seeking safe haven.[11] Whether as a matter of legal definition, or informally, they sought to identify themselves as 'neutral', though their geographical position was likely to mean that they would find it more difficult for this status to be honoured by bigger and more powerful neighbours than would the 'peripheral' states of Scandinavia. The Netherlands and Belgium, by the end of the nineteenth century, were also unlike the Scandinavian states in that they were both substantial colonial powers, even though their respective colonial territories had different origins and related differently to the conduct of their domestic politics. Use of the term 'the Low Countries', as a composite, implies a commonality - also extending to Luxembourg, though that grand duchy is not considered here.[12] There were obvious senses in which this was the case, but it should not be overstated. The inclusion of Belgium, however, may seem altogether 'out of place' insofar as it breaks up 'Northern Europe' if it is perceived as 'in essence' Protestant. If that were the yardstick, the Netherlands would be 'in' and Belgium 'out'. It has already been made clear, however, that inclusion does not conform to a confessional divide. It would have been impossible to exclude 'Germany' from 'Northern Europe' even though inclusion necessarily means that large parts were 'in essence' Catholic (though, as our contributors make clear, even Bavaria had to 'accommodate' a significant Protestant population). They also make clear, as will become apparent, that although there have to be separate Protestant and Catholic stories to tell, they cannot individually be interpreted except by reference to the other.

The first guidebook for British travellers to the continent, produced by John Murray in 1836, did think that the inhabitants of this new kingdom could be succinctly

13

---

[10] O'Connor, ed., *The Irish in Europe*, 20-22.
[11] Renckstorf and Lange, *Niederländer über Deutsche*.
[12] Tamse and Trausch, eds., *Die Beziehungen zwischen den Niederlanden und Luxemburg.*

described. The Belgians, it was said, differed from the Dutch in two essential points, which were quite sufficient to make them a distinct nation, incapable of sustaining the union which had been imposed in 1815. The Belgians were "French in inclination, and Roman Catholic in religion".[13] There is no need to controvert the assertion that they were Roman Catholics. That they were French by inclination left many things unsaid. The complex relationship between Flanders and Wallonia and the two languages, Dutch and French, raised enduring questions about the nature, indeed the viability, of the Belgian state. It is interesting to note the assumption that 'the Dutch', in contrast, were Protestant. That, of course, was not correct. Indeed, the virtue of the inclusion of the Netherlands in this particular 'Northern Europe' lies in the way it forms a 'bridge' between 'the Far North' and Catholic culture. What that all meant in practice is something pursued by both contributors writing on the Low Countries. They write separately on the two countries but together give this bloc its starting point.[14]

It should not necessarily be supposed that 'outsiders', the British, for example, automatically found themselves 'at home' in the Protestant Netherlands and 'aliens' in Catholic Belgium. The blunt categorisation of a Murray guidebook skated over other cultural and economic factors. English Protestants, particularly, if they wanted to stress their Anglicanism, did not find Dutch Calvinism altogether congenial. Fancying themselves to be 'warm and friendly', the English could find that Calvinists had whitewashed away all the charm which had once been found in Dutch churches. In Holland, religion seemed to be 'a cold if not repellent thing'. Belgium, though Catholic, was more welcoming. Perhaps this reflected the extent to which the commercial/industrial ethos of the two countries had a very close correspondence in terms of their development. Richard Cobden, a mild Anglican, visiting Belgium in 1838 readily concurred with the view that Liège was "the Birmingham of Belgium".[15] Englishmen were to be found everywhere busying themselves with industrial machinery. It also followed that this busy Belgium also had a 'working class'. How such a class was, or was not, to be incorporated into the body politic was early an issue in these two countries, though by the end of this period 'democracy', whatever it meant, had made inroads everywhere (at least as far as men were concerned). Further, though admittedly in the context of a book published in 1915, an English author stressed the extent to which, as he believed, the Belgians, like the English, were a hybrid nation. They both stood at the meeting place between French language and culture and Low-German language and culture. In the one case, separated by the sea, these two languages fused and formed the speech in which his book happened to be written. In the other case, however, they had remained distinct. In both England and Belgium, he thought, albeit by a different route, the position was clear, "a nation was formed, and exists".[16]

14

---

[13] Morgan, *National Identities and Travel in Victorian Britain*, 88.
[14] James Kennedy's particular contribution fits into the broader picture expounded in his "Religion, Nation and European Representations of the Past".

[15] Davis, ed., *Richard Cobden's German Diaries*, 102. Liège, however, had only around a quarter of the population of Birmingham at this time.
[16] Ensor, *Belgium*, 11.

Emiel Lamberts and James Kennedy, writing respectively on Belgium and the Netherlands are well aware that the story they have to tell is to some extent 'one' yet never completely so, even during the fifteen years when there was one kingdom. The histories which they relate, in varying ways, necessarily overlap, but do not fuse. Further, to speak of a 'Belgium' in juxtaposition to 'the Netherlands' presents another oversimplification, given the scale of linguistic, cultural and socio-economic division, running along more or less clear territorial lines within Belgium and the jostling for parity (or aspirations for ascendancy) evident, with varying intensity, at different points in roughly a century of the country's existence as a state. That division, too, points to the fact that Belgium stands at the extremity of our 'Northern Europe'. That part of its population which is French-speaking together with, for long, the hegemony of French culture, makes it stand out from a 'Northern Europe' whose linguistic communities were, broadly speaking, 'Germanic', with some being, with effort, mutually comprehensible linguistically, at least in certain contexts. Use of such a term, occasional use of the language of 'cousinhood' apart, should not be taken to posit a strong political sense of alignment or even any widespread sense of a rather nebulous cultural identity amongst 'Northern Europeans'. Yet if Wallonia is to be incorporated into the 'northern world' which has thus far been delineated, it must be because of 'Belgium' not because of France. Flanders takes one into the 'northern' world of the Netherlands with its historic links into northern seas. Yet, no more than in any other 'frontier' country could there be rigid demarcation. The history of 'the Low Countries' had been so intimately shaped by their southern invaders that it necessarily had a kind of 'southern' past almost completely lacking elsewhere in 'Northern Europe'. Yet, even here there was irony. At the close of our period, the Northern Netherlands was able to stay out of the European war whereas its southern neighbour, by virtue of the violation of its neutrality, had no alternative but to be involved.

15

'Germany'

'Germany' forms our third bloc. Whilst its history has frequently been seen as a country 'in the middle', drawn both westwards and eastwards and uncertain in its vacillation between the two, it was also a country with one foot in 'Northern Europe' and another 'in the South'. Throughout the whole process of nineteenth-century unification lay the debate over where 'the real Germany' was to be found. What did Hamburg have in common with Munich? The balance to be struck between a unity that was 'national', and a particularism still strongly felt, was never easy to find (nor was it, in the event, one to be settled by academic discussion). It was still formally expressed within the new German Empire in the continued existence of distinct kingdoms (and postage stamps) - with ecclesiastical consequences of great variety. Over the period under review, therefore, the contributors are well aware that they are not dealing with a homogeneous 'Germany' but with a country struggling to come to terms with the diversity of deeply-entrenched structures and legal norms. Andreas Gestrich and Heiner de Wall, in this volume, cannot hope to describe the full complexity of the ecclesiastical/political picture in Germany in this period. There is an understandable focus on the picture in Prussia on the one hand and Bavaria on the other. There is sufficient reference, however, to the arrangements obtaining in, say, Mecklenburg, Oldenburg or Württemburg, to make one aware of many contrasts. Diversity in church affairs was, of course, only one aspect of the wider question of 'placing Germany' 'between East and West', a topic with a considerable literature.[17] Being 'between North and South', however, is a less frequently addressed geopolitical aspect. With Berlin as the capital and the King of Prussia as Emperor, the 'new Germany' also had a northern 'feel'. The fact that its imperial 'heart' was geographically close to Scandinavia did not entail, as the contested Schleswig/Sleswig question (a matter referred to again shortly) demonstrates that there was a necessary presumption of 'northern' commonality. It is not 'neighbours' who are automatically 'the best of friends'.[18]

There can be no pretence that dividing 'Northern Europe' into four blocs implied that they all carry the same 'weight' and constitute some kind of even equilibrium. What stands out most are the contrasts and similarities between the two 'Great Power' blocs and the two 'Small Power' blocs. Individual churchmen in the latter, sandwiched between the English-speaking or German-speaking competitive worlds, admired both but sought to ape neither. An underlying theme of this volume, therefore, might be described as being a British-German battle for the 'soul' of Northern Europe, a particular variant of the enveloping 'struggle for mastery' in Europe. To use such stark terminology, however, inevitably distorts relationships, to speak only at the political level, of considerable complexity and variation, one decade on another. It has to embrace phases of Anglomania and Anglophobia, and Germanophobia and Germanomania, held in different circles in the two countries at different points in the long nineteenth century. The outbreak of war in 1914, and its antecedent events, can suggest an inevitable and cataclysmic conflict, but detailed scrutiny of British-Germans relations, at many different levels, presents a picture of jealousy, rivalry and mutual admiration all mixed up untidily together.[19] It was not, however, events in Northern Europe which triggered the war, but the ensuing struggle did show the two leading Northern European powers locked in a final catastrophic conflict. It was a war into which the 'Northern Neutrals' did not wish to be drawn. The magnitude of the Great War and the creation of a 'new Europe' at its conclusion makes it appropriate to end this study of 'the last century of Old Northern Europe' in 1920.

---

[17] Winkler, *Der Lange Weg nach Westen.*
[18] See the essays in Süssmuth, ed., *Deutschland-bilder.*

[19] Stibbe, *German Anglophobia and the Great War*; Wallace, *War and the Image of Germany*; Geppert and Gerwath, eds., *Wilhelmine Germany and Edwardian Britain.*

Scandinavia/the Nordic Region

Scandinavia/the Nordic Region constitutes the final bloc. It is also apparent, as our chapter on this area demonstrates, that the configuration of 'Scandinavia' is not in fact self-evident. There were significant shifts in power-relations both between the countries of the region themselves and in their individual relations with 'non-Scandinavian' powers. There is, however, no desire here to enter into a long discussion of the proper uses of the terms 'Scandinavia' and 'the Nordic Region'. For our purposes the two terms are to be regarded as interchangeable. The fact that 'peaceful change' - the detachment of Norway from the Swedish Crown - was achieved should not, however, create a picture of imperturbable harmony. There were important differences in self-perception. Certain 'historical overhangs' in the dealings of 'Scandinavians' with each other lingered. There was uncertainty about the shape of the 'Danish realm'. Although not discussed here, Icelanders and Faroese were gradually distancing themselves from Copenhagen (Iceland gained virtually full autonomy under the Danish Crown in 1918). Yet, at the end of the period, what is notable is the fact that 'Scandinavia' did not take part in the war which engulfed 'Europe'. That abstention, which did not apply, or did not completely apply, to the other three blocs under consideration, may be taken to indicate the extent to which Scandinavia was *sui generis* within late-nineteenth and early-twentieth-century 'Northern Europe'. Liselotte Malmgart and Anders Jarlert, in their chapters, do not examine the high politics of these matters but they are well aware that internal 'church-state-society' issues cannot be detached from this broader context.

17

Scandinavia is frequently defined in terms of the region's supposed 'peripherality' (conceived, either geographically or culturally) in relation to the 'European mainstream', together with a substantial linguistic affinity and expressed, in religion, through a pervasive 'Lutheranism'. From an English point of view, for example, when Charles Wordsworth, subsequently a bishop in the Scottish Episcopal Church (Anglican), took off in 1833 as the travelling companion and tutor of a young nobleman on "an extensive tour over the north of Europe" it was certainly deemed to mean Denmark, Norway and Sweden.[20] Moving in the opposite direction, N.F.S. Grundtvig, the Danish scholar, poet and preacher paid three visits to England in 1829, 1830 and 1831. His literary enthusiasms led him to incorporate England without hesitation into the old Nordic culture. On the last occasion, spending time at Trinity College, Cambridge, he professed himself to be more at home there than he would have been at the University of Copenhagen. He formed a glowing impression of the country. Remarkably, he did not restrict his attention entirely to its bookshops. Although distressed by evidence of what he called the 'mechanical spirit' amongst the English, he became steadily more

---

[20] Wordsworth, *Annals of My Early Life*, 125.

impressed by them. England could teach important lessons which he wanted to incorporate into the many which he himself wished to impart to his fellow-countrymen.[21]

Scandinavia stood between the Great Powers to its south (and east). It was not, and could not be, a Great Power. London and Berlin (and to some extent St Petersburg) found themselves increasingly in a political and economic competition to keep Scandinavia 'on side'. Scandinavian political, ecclesiastical and social elites, for their part, mostly tilted in a cultural direction that was German, particularly given the prestige accruing to German education and scholarship. It has been argued that their historical consciousness was largely 'Germanic', though there are some paradoxes. Germany, in short, loomed larger than any other country in its impact on the Nordic region. It could sometimes be generously allowed a share of that 'Nordic spirit' about which much was spoken.

As before, but certainly after 1780, 'Denmark-Norway-Sweden' did have an overlapping political history which required, at particular points, new or renewed definitions within new borders. Their nineteenth-century historians wrote in terms which suggested that the Scandinavian *folk* apparently knew instinctively what animated them and where they were going.[22] Hans Christian Andersen, planning Christmas celebrations in Rome in 1833 wrote that in that city "Swedes, Norwegians and Danes become one nation".[23] Whatever went on in Rome apart, it was scarcely the case that 'on home ground' any such sense existed. The approach adopted to 'Scandinavia' in this volume therefore attempts to encapsulate both a kind of unity yet also acknowledges diversity. The time had passed when any Scandinavian country constituted a 'Great Power' and even as a collection of states Scandinavia scarcely matched any of the Great Powers of Europe.[24] In these circumstances, therefore, it is not surprising to find, amidst the particular differences between Denmark, Norway and Sweden alluded to by the contributors, a greater homogeneity in matters of state-church relations than exists within any of the other blocs into which this volume is divided.

It is conceded that the exclusion of Finland in this volume may raise eyebrows. After all, the contemporary visitor to the National Museum in Helsinki will find it stated definitively that the course of Finnish history has led to it becoming now part of 'Western Europe'. It is arguable, however, that it was really only from the second half of the 1930s that the idea of Scandinavia was expanded (as *Norden* or the Nordic region) to include Finland. During the period under review, however, after the 1809 Treaty of Porvoo, the territory had passed from Sweden to Russia, as a Grand Duchy, and thus became, politically and constitutionally, part of 'the East' whatever the continuing significance of Sweden-Finland's past, its strong Lutheranism and an intellectual orientation which, in some intellectual circles, was studiously 'western'. J.V. Snellman (1806-1881), Finland's 'national philosopher', studied in Germany and absorbed Hege-

---

[21] Thyssen and Allchin, "Grundtvig's Relationship to England", 22-23.
[22] Aronsson et al., "Nordic National Histories", 257. The authors also point out that Danish anti-
German national history was also being written with a distinctly German flavour.
[23] Rasmussen, "Patriotic Perceptions", 173.
[24] Salmon, *Scandinavia and the Great Powers*.

lianism. To have brought Finland into the picture, however, would in turn have raised the 'Baltic/Nordic' question - Estonia, Latvia, Lithuania - and led the project to heavy engagement with the Russian Empire as part of 'Northern Europe'. It would be foolish to deny that during this period Russia was also a significant element in the politics of Northern Europe. There are indeed legitimate questions which might be asked about church, state and society in this wider north-eastern area - but they are not asked here. Finland, arguably a quintessentially border country, tilting now one way now another, has therefore been omitted. In this period, when its separate statehood had not been achieved, and when Russian influence was necessarily so strong, it has been judged, possibly harshly, to be 'out of area' as far as this volume is concerned. It may also be noted here that similar reasoning has applied to Poland. It too is a northern country and much interest attaches to the arrangements with the Catholic Church which its foreign rulers reached, but in the end it was the fact that its division would lead one too deeply into the internal policies of Russia and Austria which led to its omission from this 'Northern Europe'.

The concept of Finland as quintessentially a border country, however, does not make it utterly distinctive. With the exception of the 'British' Isles, all the countries under consideration have land borders with one, or more than one, other country. They are borders between 'small' countries, with the exception of those which border on 'Germany', an entity, of course, as this volume reiterates, which has in turn its own protracted 'internal' wrestling, both militarily and diplomatically, with borders and 'unity', through the nineteenth century. Such borders have varied in their longevity, fragility (or durability) and mutual acceptance. They could be 'seen' differently. The realm of the Danish crown, for example, was judged by the king to include the 'German' duchies of *Schleswig* and Holstein. Denmark as the country of the *folk*, as opposed to the whole territory of the Danish monarchy, on the other hand, might end where in *Sleswig* the Danish language community ended.[25] In 1864 a few Norwegian and Swedish volunteers fought alongside the Danish army, but such modest Scandinavian aid was to no avail. In this, and other less dramatic instances, boundaries were always contested by populations which thought, or were urged to think, that they 'belonged' elsewhere, whether by virtue of language, religion or a supposed ethnicity. The period under review, of course, begins with decades in which, to greater or lesser degree, all of the countries had been caught up in the upheaval of the Revolutionary and Napoleonic wars. The decisions of the 1815 Congress of Vienna, at their conclusion, had great significance for all the territories with which this volume is concerned. It set a new pattern of states and boundaries, though both in Scandinavia and the Low Countries, in particular, that pattern was not to endure. Of course, whatever the map might say, not all boundaries produced in the traveller an acute sense of moving into a country that was 'foreign'. On the other hand, he or she could hardly fail to note, as decades passed, the extent to which travel appeared to become steadily more bureau-

19

---

[25] Bjørn, "From Danish Patriot to Patriotic Dane".

cratic - border controls, passports and documentation of many kinds. Similarly, too, with varying intensity and outcomes, states took steps to define and describe their own 'citizens' and in the process make more explicit who was and who was not a 'foreigner' and who did, and did not, 'belong' to the nation.[26]

Christian Northern Monarchies

All the countries under review were at this time monarchies, but what monarchy meant had no uniform meaning. There was a sense in which Christian kings gave Northern Europe a kind of unity. It was thought fitting that when a new one had to be installed in Norway he was crowned in Bergen cathedral. As individuals, they could be devout, or distinctly less than devout. The precise powers monarchs fought to retain, unwillingly conceded, or graciously gave up, varied from country to country, but new constitutions or political conventions constrained them. As a generalisation, however, at the end of the nineteenth century, monarchs were no longer able to do what their predecessors had assumed to be within their power a century earlier. Their ceremonial or symbolic function and the 'traditions' they sustained (or invented) also altered. The ambience of the Danish monarchy was not the same as the Dutch. 'Germany', both before and after 'Empire', was replete with monarchs, of one stature or another. The German emperor had considerably more power than the British king. The monarchs, and their 'families', generously and generally, with the exception of Romanov marriages, married across 'Northern Europe'.[27] It would be as foolish to exaggerate the political, social and cultural significance of this interlinking as it would be to dismiss it as of no importance. There was a time, for example, when Baron Stockmar, Leopold, Albert, Queen Victoria and Empress Vicky shared the view that the Coburg family might be able to bring together Britain and Germany on the basis of moderate liberalism and constitutional monarchy. 'Royal cousinhood', even if it was inclined to do so, could not stand out against policies determined by ministers and in some circumstances family frictions might precipitate inter-state crisis, but there was a subtle sense in which the monarchies of Northern Europe could still 'oil the wheels' and ride above 'national' prejudice or stereotype.[28] Yet, they could not escape ever closer identification with 'their people' whatever their own 'national' origins. A king of the Belgians (not of 'Belgium') had to become a Belgian. The others either did not have to make such a 'choice' or slipped into national mode unobtrusively. It was only the 1914 war which caused the British royal house to abandon its German family name.

Royal families married across national and state boundaries in alliances which combined dynastic, personal and national requirements to a significant degree, if

20

---

[26] Fahrmeir, *Citizenship*; Liedtke and Wendehorst, *The Emancipation of Catholics, Jews and Protestants.*
[27] Urbach, ed., *Royal Kinship.*

[28] McLean, *Royalty and Diplomacy in Europe*; Paulmann, *Pomp und Politik*; Robbins, "The Monarch's Concept of Foreign Policy".

with outcomes that were not altogether predictable. It was in fact through the 'family networks' of the crowned heads that 'Northern Europe' had some semblance of a common identity. A Danish princess married the heir to the British throne (another, the Russian). Queen Victoria was able to supply a daughter for 'Germany'. Saxe-Coburg came up with a king for Belgium, Leopold, an uncle of the British queen, Victoria, who remained a Protestant in his new country with its miniscule Protestant population.[29] The British king, Edward VII, was on hand to make sure that Norway equipped itself with an appropriate monarch in the shape of his Danish son-in-law. And so on. It is not suggested that these dynastic linkages, by their very existence, eliminated rivalries between the states over which, to one degree or another, they could be said to rule. Nevertheless, it might be said that monarchs, whatever their own personal proclivities, could not but occupy that precarious place where sacred and secular intersected and church and state came together. Their occupation of this position may not loom large in their mutual correspondence or probably in their conversation - but 'Christian monarchy' was a common aspect of 'Northern European' experience in this epoch. When royal marriages between Catholic, Protestant and Orthodox families occurred, complications inevitably ensued. In some cases bride or groom could be allowed the maintenance of their confessional allegiance (so long as children were brought up in the confession of their future family) while in other cases conversion was required. However, one estimate is that in the great majority of cases in this period, marriages were concluded between families of the same faith or of non-conflicting confessions.[30]

21

It is against this background that the chapters make it clear that the monarch's voice, in some cases, could still be decisive in determining ecclesiastical policy. Much could depend on individual whim. A Swedish king could decide to dispense with a coronation on the grounds of expense. Church and State came together in their persons. Men on the throne (and, with the not insignificant exception of Queen Victoria, they were men) knew that 'religious reform' was not an area which could be roped off and treated in isolation from other aspects of state policy.[31] The Crown was central. In Sweden, Denmark, the Netherlands but perhaps above all in the Germanies, we find evidence of the extent of royal intervention in proposing, resisting or enforcing constitutional or inner-church 'solutions'. Of course, it becomes equally clear that this is not merely a matter of formal power. The personality of the monarch mattered and sometimes, in dealing with 'religious freedom' or 'parity' monarchs brought to bear, in a wider arena, their domestic experience of living with a partner of a different confessional allegiance. Monarchs, as was the case with Queen Victoria, got used to the fact that the Crown had a relationship with 'the church' which differed across her realm. In taking the sacrament according to the rite of the Church of Scotland she upset Church of England bishops and went her own way.

---

[29] Simon, *Léopold Ier*.
[30] Schönpflug, "One European Family?".

[31] Arnstein, "Queen Victoria and Religion"; Wolffe, *Great Deaths*.

'Natives' and 'Others' in Northern Europe

Tourists moved across Northern Europe. The steady expansion of the rail networks and steamships made possible faster and more regular travel within and between states for a wider section of the population. Even in the 1880s, however, Norway was conceived in Britain to be a country inaccessible to 'all but the more moneyed classes'. It was only at the turn of the century that the 'really courageous' Polytechnic Tour brought a different British clientele. Charles Wordsworth, in the 1830s, sought an English-language church service in Norway without success. Only when he got to Stockholm did he find one - though it was provided by Wesleyans. The Edinburgh preacher, George Scott, had gathered a congregation about him (though he was to be forced to leave the country).[32] A high proportion of travellers took a keen interest in the church services and structures they encountered, inevitably taking as a norm what they were used to at home. The British travelled more than most, or at least believed that they did, and in some cases where they settled, at least for 'seasons', sought the ecclesiastical security to be found in erecting Anglican churches. How far, if at all, it was the duty of the state, through the Foreign Office, to assist in funding for this purpose was contentious.[33] 'Foreign' churches, indeed, became common, being established to serve the needs of 'working abroad' nationals. Northern Europeans, so inclined, could find an ecclesiastical 'home from home' in mercantile or other centres. Almost by definition, however, the extent to which such congregations, whether of English in Gothenburg, Norwegians in Cardiff or Scots in Rotterdam, Germans or French in London, impacted on 'indigenous' political/ecclesiastical contexts was limited.

The identification of such 'alien presences' provides a reminder of the extent to which Protestant churches in all of the countries under review presented themselves as being, and were perceived to be, an integral element in an amalgam that was 'national'. J.C. Ryle, the leading light of late Victorian Evangelicalism, was not alone in claiming that England's political liberty and religious freedom owed everything to the Protestant Reformation. It is not difficult to find comparable claims for the significance of the Reformation in the Netherlands. Any 'reform' of itself which the Church of England might attempt that tampered with this foundation of national greatness was to be resisted. It is argued that it would be a mistake to suppose that this conviction had disappeared by the end of the period under review.[34] In Germany and Scandinavia, our chapters make it evident, in considering issues of 'freedom' and 'parity', how strongly 'old' churches resisted incomers, particularly of 'Anglo-Saxon' provenance. State churches were transmitters of the national myth. 'Foreign' churches in alien lands were there in order to preserve rather than to provide a means for sharing, let alone fusing, ecclesiastical traditions.

---

[32] Robbins, *Britain and Europe*, 153; Fjågesund and Symes, *British Perceptions of Norway*; Wordsworth, *Annals of My Early Life*, 140; Black, ed., *Sweden-Britain*, 60.

[33] See essays in Robbins and Fisher, eds., *Religion and Diplomacy*.

[34] Grimley, "The Religion of Englishness".

Nevertheless, even if there were limited direct 'interventions' by 'outsiders' in 'indigenous' ecclesiastical/political issues, there were networks - that provided after 1815 by the British and Foreign Bible Society being but one example - within a kind of Protestant world which operated transnationally. It found later expression in the Evangelical Alliance. Yet there were always 'sensitivities' which were, at least in part 'national'. Nor were such sensitivities only on display between subjects of different states. In the early 1840s, at a time of great ecclesiastical controversy a well-known Scottish writer, Hugh Miller, complained of the errors committed by the British government "in legislating for Scotland in matters of religion, as if it were not a separate nation of its own [...] but a mere province of England".[35] English clergymen wrote books whose purpose was to explain that the 'Scotch Church' was significantly different from the English.[36] The contribution in this volume by Stewart J. Brown, himself a professor in Edinburgh, is in no danger of ignoring this fact. He can bring to his assessment the detached perspective of an American. Henry Mayhew, a well-known Victorian commentator, spent a year in Germany, mainly in Eisenach and Jena, in 1862. He was writing a study of German life and manners. On learning that baptism into the Protestant Church was required by law, he exclaimed "This is a form of religious tyranny that, thank Heaven! advanced notions on such matters have long ago, in England, blown to the winds".[37] It becomes clear in this volume, however, that it would not only have been in Germany that Mayhew would have found this requirement. He perhaps overstated, too, the degree to which England was 'advanced'.

Urban and Rural Life

Northern Europe, as considered here, presented no uniform 'urban' or 'rural' pattern. In particular countries the shift from the predominance of the rural to the urban took place at different rates. Population densities varied considerably - as between the countries of Scandinavia and the Low Countries, for example. In considerable numbers, continental visitors came to England, Scotland and Wales, with their intense industrial regions, to see 'the future' at work. Some them, in so far as Manchester represented it, did not like 'the future' at all and returned with a sense of foreboding. However, this revolution could probably not be avoided. There were, in turn, niches for English and Scottish instigators of industrialism throughout Northern Europe. The cities of 'our' Northern Europe, however, even their capitals, were not in the same league as the major provincial cities of the British Isles - Manchester, Liverpool, Birmingham, Glasgow. These four, together with London, had the distinction, in terms of population, of being listed in the world's top thirty cities in 1890. There were other major English cities,

23

---

[35] Cited in Morgan, *National Identities*, 106.
[36] For example, the Rev. Francis Trench, *Scotland, its Faith and its Features* (1846) discussed in Robbins, *Nineteenth-Century Britain*, 67-68.

[37] Cited and discussed in Morgan, *National Identities*, 100; Robbins, *Protestant Germany through British Eyes*; Davis, *The Victorians and Germany*.

too - Bristol, Leeds, Nottingham and Sheffield among them. The English had turned into a nation of city dwellers.[38] In some cities, however, it was not certain who these 'English' were. Liverpool was exceptional but in 1881 it contained only 81% English-born inhabitants. And London, of course, was simply a phenomenon - containing as it did in the 1890s some 20% of the population of England and Wales. It had grown from 1.1 million in 1801 to 6.6 million in 1901 (of course an increase which includes boundary changes). Berlin, over the same period had grown from 172,000 to 3.7 million. Only two other German cities, Hamburg (some 700,000) and Munich (500,000), topped half a million at the turn of the century, but others were rising quickly. The intensity and form of this urbanisation, particularly in Britain and Germany, unsurprisingly, gave rise to the most varied of reactions from gloom and despair to amazement at the dynamism of big city life.[39] Correspondingly, in 1851 about a quarter of occupied British males were employed in agriculture, dropping to about 17% in 1881 and 12% in 1901. During these decades between a half and a third of the labour force in Germany, Denmark and Sweden were still on the farm. Religion functioned still, in large measure, in these latter countries according to the rhythms and requirements of rural life.

24

Amsterdam with more than 200,000 inhabitants at the end of the eighteenth century was the only large urban centre in the Low Countries. A century later, it had only risen to some 317,000 and had yielded first place to Brussels which had risen to 421,000 in 1880. Both cities comfortably outdistanced their national competitors. What was true of the Low Countries was even more true in the case of the Scandinavian capitals and their national 'competitors'. All of this was in turn reflected in aggregate figures of national populations. The Dutch population of some 2 million in 1780 more than doubled to reach 5 million by 1900. The Belgian population grew from 3 million in 1800 to 5.5 million in 1880 and sustained a demographic lead over its neighbour. The Danish population of a million in 1800 had reached 2.5 million a century later; the Swedish grew from 2.5 million in 1800 to 5 million in 1900; the Norwegian from 0.9 in 1800 to 2.25 in 1900. There was, of course, a substantial outflow from all the Scandinavian countries to the New World - the Norwegian contribution being proportionately the largest - amounting to more than 2 million in this period. The population of England and Wales grew from approximately 8 million in 1781 to nearly 26 million in 1881 and more than 38 million in 1921; Scotland grew from approximately 1.5 million in 1781 to 4 million in 1881 and approached 5 million in 1921; Ireland had a population in 1781 of 4 million. It peaked at 8.5 million in 1845 and fell back to 4.5 million in 1900. No country in this project had had as disastrous a demographic experience as Ireland. During the famine years 1846-1851 a million people left the island and a further 3.5 million left between 1851 and 1900. The German Empire of 1914 contained a population of 68 million. Over a million people left Germany in the decade after 1850 and another 1.3 million in the decade after 1880. Such aggregates do not attempt to unpack

---

[38] Robbins, *Eclipse of a Great Power*, 57-64.
[39] Coleman, ed., *The Idea of the City in Victorian Britain*; Dyos and Wolff, eds., *The Victorian City*;

McLeod, ed., *European Religion in the Age of Great Cities*.

the extent of in- and out-movement between countries.[40] The growth of new industrial regions, particularly in Germany, played havoc with the role of 'established' cities within the historically complex particularisms which constitute so significant an aspect of the German discussion in this volume. The social and educational consequences of these developments are to be covered in other volumes. Demographic transformations and industrialisation (on different timescales), however, cannot be overlooked - as there is always a temptation to do when the focus, in the relationship between states and the churches, is on formal constitutional documents and legal enactments. These are broad-brush illustrative figures and do no more than hint at the dislocation (literally) that was happening. They are sufficient, however, to convey the extent to which behind the 'dynamics of religious reform' lay a dynamic population growth which placed stress on the adequacy of a host of civil institutions. 'Reform', whatever it meant in particular instances, was not an option but an imperative.

Conclusion

The picture of Northern Europe outlined in these previous sections should counsel   25
against any attempt to give it firm coherence and establish it as an entity whose member states - if one can even use such a notion - stood over against some other 'Europe', perhaps, for example, a Latin or a Mediterranean one. Yet such reservation should not lead to dismissing any notion of special relationships which give some sense of 'neighbourhood' within Europe and in the similarity of their engagement, occasional tensions notwithstanding, with 'worlds' beyond Europe, whether in relation to Africa, Asia and America. Of course, even where they did have acknowledged substance, such relationships were not exclusive. Northern Europe, as envisaged here, embraced in this period both such 'precocious' industrial economies as Belgium and Britain, and economies which, to a very substantial degree, retained significant agricultural (or fishing) sectors. These countries were manifestly not all 'the same'. Yet, in comparison with literacy levels in Eastern or Southern Europe, their collective attainment was substantially common and high. Until the war of 1914, the incidence of warfare on the soil of Northern Europe had diminished sharply. The likelihood of an attack by one 'northern' state, as here defined, directly on another such state, as had occurred in the not very distant past, had not entirely disappeared, but seemed much reduced. At least in comparison with the in-regional conflicts of South-Eastern Europe, Northern Europe, although 'militarised' to varying degrees, seemed 'peaceful'. Moreover, its stability and relative prosperity did not seem likely to be put in jeopardy, as was the case elsewhere in Europe, by the existence of multi-national empires - Romanov, Habsburg or Ottoman - judged to be in decline and unable to cope with the demands of peoples

---

[40] Figures derived from McEvedy and Jones, *Atlas of World Population History*.

'struggling to be free' but whose aspirations, in doing so, were by no means necessarily compatible with each other. A sense of sustainable statehood, with historic lineage, might be weak or strong, relatively newly-minted or long-established, but Northern Europe, with the independence of Norway, come to look 'settled' on the eve of the Great War. It scarcely needs to be stated that the war brought unsettlement, most specifically in the cases of the two Great Powers, Imperial Germany and the United Kingdom. The former, in defeat, becomes a grudging republic and embarks on a reworking of church-state-society. The concluding section of the chapter on Germany outlines the treatment of church and state in the 'Weimar' Constitution. It appears certain that it was only the upheaval of defeat that unsettled arrangements that, in essence, had lasted four hundred years.[41] The latter, in victory, was embroiled in Ireland in a political, military and even quasi-ecclesiastical struggle out of which emerged both a ruptured United Kingdom and a partitioned Ireland (views stressed by competing interpreters).[42] Europe as a whole, at this juncture, witnesses, or so it might appear, 'the collapse of Christendom'. In stopping, chronologically, where it does, it is not the purpose of this volume to seek to unpick the meaning and implications, looking forward, of that notion.

26

Part II: Religious Reform

It is against this conception of Northern Europe that 'religious reform' has been assessed in the individual chapters that follow. It has been defined as the conscious pursuit of renewal with the aim of adapting organised religion to the changing relations between church, state and society. It is a definition which deliberately avoids talking about 'modernisation', as if there were a simple signposted route to a manifestly 'modern' arrangement. Yet, if there is no attempt to score countries against some ideal notion of 'modernity' it is obvious that the relations between church, state and society were in flux. The religion that is being studied is 'organised', that is to say is present in society in terms of institutions and structures which, most frequently, have legal form. They can be 'adapted' to meet the needs of society. But who is taking the initiative in adaptation and to what end? 'Adaptation' may be a euphemism for emasculation, obliteration or regeneration. These are questions, in the last resort, of power.

The emphasis in this volume falls on the role of the state in 'adapting organised religion'. In having this objective, contributors are well aware that 'the state' is a necessary fiction. They have to deal with it operationally - with individuals (kings and prime ministers) or collectives (governments and ministries) - rather than metaphysically. Yet metaphysics cannot altogether be avoided. Just what the state should purport to embody and embrace in terms of 'collective will' was never far away from both private and public discussion. Should it 'have a view' or should it simply 'hold the ring'? By what right and with what mechanisms should the state 'adapt'? The state,

---

[41] Borg, "*Volkskirche*, 'Christian State' and the Weimar Republic".

[42] A recent overview is Elliott, *When God Took Sides.*

that is to say either individuals or governments, may act from mixed motives. They may be appalled by what may variously considered as waste, indolence, corruption, maladministration or other evidence of a church being not 'fit for purpose' and seek to rescue it from itself. They may be moved, in short, by 'rational' concern for the proper use of Christian resource. They may, however, be moved by quite other considerations - a hostility or indifference to all religion producing a desire to reduce the presence of ecclesiastical bodies in 'the public sphere'. In the mêlée of political life it might be hard to distinguish between malevolent and benevolent motives in considering the impulse behind particular enactments. State-directed reform, of course, inevitably starts from the top and penetrates down. Its enactments may take time, locally, to permeate and be subject to evasion or obstruction. In general, however, while local practice could be aberrant, the capacity of all the states to implement, and enforce, if necessary, the adaptations they desired, was effective.

The companion volume to this starts not from the state but from the church. It does not presuppose that the church was soporifically supine, only pushed and prodded into adaptation by intrusive bureaucrats and coercive governments. Such an approach is, to a degree, 'bottom up'. It sees a church struggling to adapt to all the pressures and forces outlined in Part I, but determined to do so 'from within' and sometimes to do so in a manner which confronted the course on which the state appeared to be set. The church was 'organised religion' and the organisation of religion was its business. There is a sense, therefore, in which many of the same issues emerge between the volumes but their thrust is different. Such a distinction, in terms of agency, of course, is easily outlined but less easy, methodologically, to implement. It scarcely needs to be said that both 'state' and 'church' are abstractions. The identities they incorporate, the allegiances they claim, the obligations they entail and the spheres they inhabit, all overlap and are fluid. It is evident that 'the dynamics of religious reform' are to be found in a complicated dialectic. This volumes suggests that there is only a limited sense in which, across the board, we can think of 'church' and 'state' existing in clear compartments.

27

It is only to be expected that this is most apparent in the case of 'the Protestant Church' though no reader of the contributions in this volume will suppose that any such construct existed. Only in Prussia, with an outcome not altogether what the monarch had predicted, did the state attempt to fuse together Lutherans and Reformed in a way that he thought good for them (and for himself). We may be tempted to see in 'Protestant countries' not so much a dichotomy between 'church' and 'state' but rather an untidy quarrelsome wrestling within a Protestantism so enmeshed in the structures of the state that 'separation' or even 'distance' set off tremors which unsettled the very basis of the state itself, or perhaps one should say nation. In all the countries of Protestant majority under review their 'national' or 'established' churches were churches of the Reformation and, as such, integrated into a national-ecclesiastical composite. To ask a Danish Lutheran or an English Anglican to 'divide' his or her personality and allegiance into appropriate manageable compartments was a complex task and one therefore either resisted or ignored. So it was elsewhere. Statesmen might well themselves be Laodicean but the national church was an intrinsic element in what it was, for example, to be Swedish or Scottish. It was not that such a perspective was inherently xenophobic - though in some cases it could be - as that 'the church', as constituted, acknowledged no ecclesiastical authority outside the state. The monarch, as has already been alluded to, brought the two aspects of the nation together. Such a fusion was of particular significance where, as in Denmark in the later 1860s the very survival of the state was in some doubt. It is also to be noted that it was as a once, and then future bishop, that D.G. Monrad was the Danish prime minister in 1863/1864.

Yet, while our contributions, particularly in Scandinavia, stress the scale of this penetration, and its durability, this intimacy was under stress in all the countries under review, to greater or lesser extent. For its part, the state, we generally observe, continued to want to patrol, and in some cases, actually to police the nature and scale of this penetration. It decided the terms. There were instances where the church could be useful for the state - the establishment of a new diocese near the Finnish border is a Swedish case in point. Yet old structures and assumptions could not survive intact. In the Swedish case this becomes clear with the political/constitutional changes from the 1860s onwards. It was a situation which compelled the national church, so long self-evidently such, to begin to think of itself as 'the Church of Sweden'. It was placed in that awkward situation where 'religious reform' from within and without intersected. Leading ecclesiastics were disinclined to abandon such prominent roles in national political life as were still open to them. They did not want to be 'sectarian'. In Sweden, however, as elsewhere in Scandinavia and in Germany, independent congregations or 'extra-mural' religious groups wanted their own kind of renewal and reform. This was a time when 'convinced' believers, whether remaining within the existing churches or detaching themselves from them, sought to challenge a broad, haphazard and rather shapeless communal acknowledgement of 'religion'. Charles Wordsworth encountered this mingling in Sweden on his visit in 1833. It made a very unfavourable impression on him that, at the close of a church service, the minister "gave out a long succession of notices of the most secular kind, relating not only to births, deaths and marriages, but to auctions, markets etc., which occupied not less than a quarter of an hour!". 'Religious reform' from below was a striving for 'religious self-determination' over against the notion that the church was a part of the state's administration and subordinate to it. It expressed a desire to draw a boundary round the sacred - whatever the theology which informed such a desire.

The contributors demonstrate that accommodation within the national church, by some means or other, or detachment, was the issue over many decades. It raised the question of whether suppression or restriction was, or was not, a matter for the state. Here, starkly, was the problem of religious liberty, and whether freedom was defined only in terms of the private as opposed to the public domain. As is clear in Germany, this remained a complex matter of legal regulation until the end of our period (a picture complicated here as elsewhere by the fact that many of the independent or free church congregations had alien, chiefly 'Anglo-Saxon' origins, contacts or support). This was clearly not a situation in which the majority churches pressed the state strongly to concede the principle of full religious equality. On the contrary, clergy, in particular, generally wished to oppose and frustrate any such 'reform'. In this case, debates fused with wider political issues and, in doing so, raised the question, in Protestant churches, of 'ownership' of decision-making. We observe in this context the various moves made, or unsuccessfully attempted, to create national church conferences with some level of authority or at least influence. How synods or comparable bodies should be composed raised controversial questions both for church and state. What was the balance to be between clergy and lay participation? Was there not some sense, varying from country to country, that parliaments not only had the right to legislate in church matters but in doing so expressed the views of 'ordinary' church people more closely than clerical zealots did in bodies which started to claim to be 'representative bodies'. In England, it could still find expression in the view that parliament was the real home of the laity. In all these matters, it is clear that there were still tangled and unresolved issues, even in 1920. It is pointed out that it was only in the context, post-First World War, of devising a new constitution in Germany that anomalies and rough edges were addressed in a comprehensive common framework.

It was inevitable that questions of finance came frequently to the fore. 'Secularisation' left in its wake in the early nineteenth century, with reverberations still to the end of the period, issues of compensation for the appropriation of church property. In itself that act could be taken as the state determining what was or what was not 'useful' about religion. In the Low Countries and in the jungle that was Germany in this regard, questions of value, ownership and financial provision proved both protracted and intractable. The outcomes, in so far as one can speak of arrangements which were settled and mutually acceptable, varied from country to country but constituted a central aspect of religious reform. It involved the attempt to place clerical salaries on a 'proper footing' as an early modern world of provision struggled into the nineteenth century. Depending on the precise arrangements which were put in place, it left uncertainty about the extent to which clergy were to be regarded as civil servants. If they were, could they not to a degree reasonably and properly be instructed by the state? Its support in this way naturally privileged such 'established' churches as against those 'free' congregations who had to rely on their own financial capacity. Whilst such a situation was manifestly 'unequal' such congregations did not seek state funding for themselves but argued that no church should be beholden to the state. It is not surprising, therefore, to find that contributors detect a variety of 'solutions' which left ambivalent how 'state support for the church' was being perceived.

The focus of comment in this Part, until this juncture, has been on a Scandinavia characterised by overwhelming adherence to national churches. Religious pluralism scarcely existed. What was taking place, therefore, was a kind of internal church/state monologue, not a scene in which the state had the task of monitoring and balancing the often competing claims of significant churches. The position was rather different in mixed confessional situations. In this regard, the United Kingdom stands in striking contrast. All the countries under review had tiny minorities from other confessions (Catholics in Sweden or Protestants in Belgium) but only the

United Kingdom and perhaps the Northern Netherlands, had a pluralism which can be described as rampant. As our contributors bring out, this plurality was in part a function of its multi-territoriality and the fact that all the churches had some purchase on national identities. It resulted in diverse 'ecclesiastical families'. All, by mid-century had some weight within the state. The status of the 'national churches' was under threat. The state eventually came to the conclusion that the minority established Protestant church in Ireland could no longer be sustained in the wider context of British-Irish relations. The state might eventually decide that the situation in Wales too might not be sustainable. How and when these steps were taken would of course depend on the policies of Liberal governments. Neither step was welcomed by the Church of England and seen by it as commendable 'reform'. It feared for the future in England. The Anti-State-Church Society, later taking the name Liberation Society, pressed for the disestablishment of the Church of England, but success eluded it. Such a campaign was not, as it was in some other countries, the product of a secularist or anticlerical movement. It came from Free Churches agitating under the banner of 'a Free Church in a Free State'. There was little likelihood that a United Kingdom government would embark on disestablishing the Church of England. It was still integral to a certain sense of the English nation. On the other hand, the United Kingdom state was not the English state. It was best not to probe the meaning of the arrangements too far. The Church of England could have some more freedom to determine its own affairs, but not complete freedom, and nor did it want too much freedom.

As regards Germany, in this matter of reconciling, over time, a sort of parity between churches with some form of continuing establishment, our contributors stress that territorial adjustments after the Congress of Vienna, and later, inevitably affected the pattern so long laid down since the seventeenth century. A Bavaria, perceived to be quintessentially Catholic, with a Catholic monarch, found itself having to fashion a Protestant church. The basis on which it would be done would in turn tell on the loyalty new subjects would display. Protestant rulers, accustomed to intervention, found themselves in trouble when they aspired to the same role, as they sometimes did, in Catholic church affairs. Our contributors trace a path through the complex of 'arrangements' that were reached, here and elsewhere. They note the scope of culture wars, great and small. They emphasise the growth of ultramontane sentiment. The Catholic Church in Germany or Belgium might have its own ethos and its members were not without a sentiment that was national but it was not itself national. If the state wished to deal with the church, it could not do so simply with indigenous bishops, though it might find some more pliable than others, but had to deal with the Vatican. Moreover, it was not a Vatican disposed to bend before the wind of the times. The scope for accommodation appeared to be small. This is not the place to embark on a comprehensive account of its internal development. The stance taken by the Vatican, however, raised issues about the relationship between church, state and society in an apparently ever-widening 'democratic' set of governments which had general significance. It entailed dispute about the meanings of 'liberty' and the rights of 'truth'. If all states were becoming more 'constitutional' and their governments, to one degree

30

or another, now depended upon 'the will of the people', as expressed through parties with 'programmes' and in elections, did they not now have a legitimacy which absolutist rulers had never possessed. But, paradoxically perhaps, might not 'democratic' states be as absolutist in their policies, perhaps even more absolutist, than their predecessors. The tensions generated in mix-confessional states were considerable. The dogmatic trends evident in the First Vatican Council, together with certain devotional tendencies, offended many, if not most Protestants, and some 'liberal' Catholics. It seemed to preclude a Catholic-Protestant 'Christian' alliance. Protestants, however, could not altogether feel comfortable with the rise of what could be perceived or portrayed as anti-Christian forces who might in time 'capture' the state.

So the issue of the nature of the state's authority, the reach and scope of its activities, moved to the centre of public affairs in Germany and the Low Countries. There was one apparent 'solution' available, though it was not without its paradoxical aspects. The Papacy might not like many of the political and social trends of the 'modernity' which it was encountering, and indeed might be suspicious of democracy and the rhetoric of liberty, but Catholics were not some marginal minority in these countries. Catholics could be organised and 'participate' with the best. Much is said, in what follows, about the phenomenon of Catholic mobilisation, not in constant battle against the state's 'improper' intervention in what it regarded as its own affairs, though that could and did happen, but also as a positive assertion of its place as an element among other elements in the composition of society. The state should not arrogate to itself a monopoly of wisdom and truth (and nor should the church). Neither should the state (nor the church) believe that its organs should directly assume responsibility for all aspects of social life. Neither party might find such a maxim altogether congenial. It entailed the acceptance, within the design of a constitutional, plural 'modern' state that a government of Catholic composition had to accept certain constraints, as did liberal parties of an anti-clerical disposition. Such pluralism, regulated from the top, had its counterpart, as our contributors discuss, in that socio-cultural phenomenon described as 'pillarisation'. In relation to the significant areas of education and social welfare in particular, however, more will subsequently be said in other volumes specifically devoted to these issues. The form such debates continue to take in the twenty-first century still rest, in some underlying matters, on decisions and adjustments made between 1780 and 1920. They also remain, as they were then, contentious.

31

Bibliography

Aprille, Sylvie and Fabrice Bensimon, eds. *La France et l'Angleterre au XIXᵉ siècle.* Paris, 2008.

Arnstein, Walter L. "Queen Victoria and Religion" in: Gail Malmgreen, ed. *Religion in the Lives of English Women 1760-1930.* London, 1986, 88-128.

Aronsson, Peter et al. "Nordic National Histories" in: Stefan Berger and Chris Lorenz, eds. *The Contested Nation: Ethnicity, Class, Religion and Gender in National Histories.* Basingstoke, 2008, 256-282.

Bjørn, Claus. "From Danish Patriot to Patriotic Dane: C.D.F. Reventlow and the Development of Danishness in the Early Nineteenth Century" in: Claus Bjørn, Alexander Grant and Keith J. Stringer, eds. *Social and Political Identities in Western History.* Copenhagen, 1994, 179-192.

Black, Judith, ed. *Sweden-Britain: A Thousand Years of Friendship.* Stockholm, 2007.

Borg, D.R. "*Volkskirche*, 'Christian State' and the Weimar Republic". *Church History*, 35 (1961) 2, 186-206.

Burleigh, Michael. *Earthly Powers: The Clash between Religion and Politics in Europe from the French Revolution to the Great War.* London, 2005.

Clark, Christopher and Kaiser, Wolfram, eds. *Culture Wars: Secular-Catholic Conflict in Nineteenth-Century Europe.* Cambridge, 2003.

Coleman, Bruce I., ed. *The Idea of the City in Victorian Britain.* London, 1973.

Davies, Norman. *Europe: A History.* Oxford, 1996.

Davis, John R., ed. *Richard Cobden's German Diaries.* Munich, 2007.

Davis, John R. *The Victorians and Germany.* Bern, 2007.

Drummond, A.L. *The Kirk and the Continent.* Edinburgh, 1956.

Duroselle, Jean-Baptiste. *Europe: A history of its People.* Transl. Richard Mayne. London, 1990.

Dyos, H.J. and Wolff, Michael, eds. *The Victorian City.* London, 1973, 2 vols.

Elliott, Marianne. *When God took Sides: Religion and Identity in Ireland: Unfinished History.* Oxford, 2009.

Ensor, Robert Charles K. *Belgium.* London, 1915.

Fahrmeir, Andreas. *Citizenship: The Rise and Fall of a Modern Concept.* New Haven-London, 2007.

Fjågesund, Peter and Symes, Ruth A. *British Perceptions of Norway in the Nineteenth Century.* Amsterdam-New York, 2003.

Geppert, Dominik and Gerwath, Robert, eds. *Wilhelmine Germany and Edwardian Britain: Essays in Cultural Affinity.* Oxford, 2008.

Griffiths, Tony. *Scandinavia.* Kent Town, 1991.

Grimley, Matthew. "The Religion of Englishness: Puritanism, Providentialism, and 'National Character', 1918-1923". *Journal of British Studies*, 45 (2007), 884-906.

Kaarsted, Tage. *Great Britain and Denmark, 1914-1920.* Odense, 1979.

Kennedy, James. "Religion, Nation and European Representations of the Past" in: Stefan Berger and Chris Lorenz, eds. *The Contested Nation: Ethnicity, Class, Religion and Gender in National Histories.* Basingstoke, 2008, 104-134.

Liedtke, Rainer and Wendehorst, Stephan, eds. *The Emancipation of Catholics, Jews and Protestants: Minorities and the Nation-state in Nineteenth-century Europe.* Manchester, 1999.

McEvedy, Colin and Jones, Richard. *Atlas of World Population History.* London, 1978.

McLean, Roderick R. *Royalty and Diplomacy in Europe, 1890-1914.* Cambridge, 2001.

McLeod, Hugh, ed. *European Religion in the Age of Great Cities.* London, 1995.

Matthew, H.C.G., ed. *The Gladstone Diaries.* 11: *31 July 1883 - December 1886.* Oxford, 1990.

Morgan, Marjorie. *National Identities and Travel in Victorian Britain.* Basingstoke, 2001.

Neisen, Robert. "Das Bild der Französischen Revolution in Grossbritannien - Nationale Alterität im politisch-historischen Diskurs der postnapoleonischen Ära" in: Michael Einfalt et al., eds. *Konstrukte nationaler Identität: Deutschland, Frankreich und Grossbritannien (19. und 20. Jahrhundert)*. Würzburg, 2002, 213-230.

O'Connor, Thomas, ed. *The Irish in Europe 1580-1815*. Dublin, n.d.

Paulmann, Johannes. *Pomp und Politik: Monarchen-begegnungen in Europa zwischen Ancien Regime und Ersten Weltkrieg*. Paderborn, 2000.

Rasmussen, Jens Rahbek. "Patriotic Perceptions: Denmark and Sweden 1450-1850" in: Claus Bjørn, Alexander Grant and Keith J. Stringer, eds. *Nations, Nationalism and Patriotism in the European Past*. Copenhagen, 1994, 161-176.

Renckstorf, Karsten and Lange, Olaf. *Niederländer über Deutsche. Eine empirische Studie zur Exploration des Bildes der Niederländer von den Deutschen*. Nijmegen, 1990.

Robbins, Keith. *Nineteenth-Century Britain: Integration and Diversity*. Oxford, 1988.

Robbins, Keith. *Protestant Germany through British Eyes: A Complex Victorian Encounter*. London, 1993.

Robbins, Keith. *The Eclipse of a Great Power: Modern Britain, 1870-1992*. London-New York, 1994.

Robbins, Keith. *Great Britain: Identities, Institutions and the Idea of Britishness*. London-New York, 1998.

Robbins, Keith. "The Monarch's Concept of Foreign Policy: Victoria and Edward VII" in: Adolf M. Birke, Magnus Brechtgen and Alaric Searle, eds. *An Anglo-German Dialogue: The Munich Lectures on the History of International Relations*. Munich, 2000, 115-130.

Robbins, Keith. "Location and Dislocation: Ireland, Scotland and Wales in their Insular Alignment" in John Morrill, ed. *The Promotion of Knowledge: Lectures to mark the Centenary of the British Academy 1902-2002*. Oxford, 2004, 163-180.

Robbins, Keith. *Britain and Europe, 1789-2005*. London, 2005.

Robbins, Keith. "Ethnicity, Religion, Class and Gender and the 'Island Story/ies': Great Britain and Ireland" in: Stefan Berger and Chris Lorenz, eds. *The Contested Nation: Ethnicity, Class, Religion and Gender in National Histories*. Basingstoke, 2008, 231-255.

Robbins, Keith. "L'histoire britannique et la 'Britishness'". *Revue d'Histoire du XIXe Siècle*, 37 (2008), 111-126.

Robbins, Keith and Fisher, John, eds. *Religion and Diplomacy: Religion and British Foreign Policy, 1815-1941*. Dordrecht, 2010.

Salmon, Patrick. *Scandinavia and the Great Powers, 1890-1940*. Cambridge, 1997.

Schönpflug, Daniel. "One European Family? A Quantitative Approach to Royal Marriage Circles 1700-1918" in: Karina Urbach, ed. *Royal Kinship: Anglo-German Family Networks 1815-1918*. Munich, 2008, 25-34.

Schulze, Hagen. *Staat und Nation in der europäischen Geschichte*. Munich, 1994.

Simon, Aloïs. *Léopold 1er*. Brussels, 1962.

Stibbe, Matthew. *German Anglophobia and the Great War, 1914-1918*. Cambridge, 2001.

Süssmuth, Hans, ed. *Deutschlandbilder in Dänemark und England, in Frankreich und den Niederländen*. Baden-Baden, 1996.

Tamse, Coenraad and Trausch, Gilbert, eds. *Die Beziehungen zwischen den Niederlanden und Luxemburg im 19. und 20. Jahrhundert*. Zoetermeer, 1991.

Thyssen, Anders Pontoppidan and Allchin, A.M. "Grundtvig's Relationship to England" in: A.M. Allchin et al., eds. *Heritage and Prophecy: Grundtvig and the English-Speaking World*. Aarhus, 1993, 19-32.

Urbach, Karina, ed. *Royal Kinship: Anglo-German Family Networks*. Munich, 2008.

Wallace, Stuart. *War and the Image of Germany: British Academics 1914-1918*. Edinburgh, 1988.

Winkler, Heinrich August. *Der Lange Weg nach Westen*. Munich, 2000, 2 vols.

Wolffe, John. *Great Deaths: Grieving, Religion, and Nationhood in Victorian and Edwardian Britain*. Oxford, 2000.

Woolf, Stuart. *Napoleon's Integration of Europe*. London, 1991.

Wordsworth, Charles. *Annals of My Early Life 1806-1846*. London, 1891.

33

THE UNITED KINGDOM OF GREAT BRITAIN & IRELAND

The two chapters in this section cover the United Kingdom of Great Britain and Ireland - the name adopted by the state two decades after the beginning of the period under review and which was about to break up, with the establishment of the Irish Free State, at its conclusion (with Northern Ireland remaining within the United Kingdom). It is not the mid-century but c.1870 which constitutes the point of division between the two chapters. It is arguable that the 'year of revolution' 1848, which even in failure erupts so significantly elsewhere in this volume, does not have quite the same resonance in the United Kingdom. A division in 1870, or thereabouts, can be said to coincide with another significant phase of political and legal reform. There was a new Liberal government, properly so called for the first time, elected after a further extension of the male franchise in 1867. It was a Liberal government which took the United Kingdom to war in 1914. It is in the period 1870-1914 that 'the Irish Question' assumes major significance. The authors attempt to deal with developments in the two islands (conscious, too, that with regard to the relationship between state and church, 'Britain' produced different stories).

The Reform and Extension of Established Churches in the United Kingdom, 1780-1870

Stewart J. Brown

During the latter phase of the Napoleonic Wars, the United Kingdom began directing unprecedented amounts of public money towards improving and extending its established churches. Despite the massive costs of the war, the parliamentary state invested heavily in building new churches, repairing and enlarging existing churches, providing church-based schools, building residence houses for the clergy, and increasing the incomes of poorly paid clergy. Combined with grants of money, the state also enacted measures of church reform, strengthening the powers of bishops, requiring higher standards of pastoral care from the clergy, and improving the incomes and conditions of curates. This movement to reform and extend the established churches was in part a response to the social unrest resulting from early industrialisation and the new democratic movements inspired by the American and French Revolutions. There was a real concern that labouring people, many of them experiencing dire poverty in the rapidly growing industrial districts, were becoming dangerously disaffected from the social and political order. Some were rejecting Christian beliefs altogether; many more were joining dissenting religious bodies that, it was feared, had no loyalty to the monarchical state, proclaimed 'democratic' ideas regarding the equality of all people before God, and dreamed of an approaching millennium that would include the levelling of social ranks.

For the Tory governments of Spencer Perceval (1809-1812) and Lord Liverpool (1812-1827), and their supporters among Britain's governing classes, the best antidote to the spread of such revolutionary ideas was to extend a state-sanctioned Protestant Christianity among the lower social orders. Such a Christianity would promote the virtues of passive obedience and non-resistance to the powers that be, and quiet resignation in the face of worldly adversity and injustice. It would teach the common people to direct their aspirations, not to revolution and a new social order in this world, but to a personal reward in Christ's heavenly kingdom. It would promote loyalty and service to the state, as the expression of God's order and purpose on earth. And so, beginning about 1808, the parliamentary state provided major grants of public money to the established churches; indeed never in its history did the parliamentary state invest so heavily in the established churches as it did between 1808 and 1824.

Some also began to believe that the extension of the established churches could be a means of consolidating the United Kingdom politically. The United Kingdom was a recent creation. It had been formed with the Act of Union of 1801, which had united the exclusively Protestant parliaments of the overwhelmingly Protestant Great Britain and the overwhelmingly Roman Catholic Ireland. The Union had been enacted following a revolutionary uprising in Ireland in 1798, a bloody struggle that had begun as a French-inspired republican rising but that had quickly degenerated into a sectarian civil war, which had cost over 30,000 lives and added to the legacy of hatred between Ireland's Protestants and Catholics. The prime minister, William Pitt, had intended to secure a measure of Catholic emancipation immediately following the Act of Union, but emancipation had been thwarted, largely by the opposition of King George III, and as a result the Irish Catholic population remained largely alienated from the Union state. Of a total population of about 15,846,000 making up the United Kingdom in 1801, approximately 5,216,000 - or nearly a third - were Irish, and of these, about three-quarters were Roman Catholic. Could a state, in which about a quarter of the population were disaffected, have much chance of achieving stability?

For some among Britain's governing classes, the only real hope for securing the Union on a permanent basis was for a large proportion of the Irish Catholic population to convert to Protestantism. And, they believed, the best way to achieve these conversions was through a well-resourced, efficient and effective established Protestant Church in Ireland. Some extended this ideal of enhanced political unity through religious uniformity to the whole of the United Kingdom. They envisaged the different nationalities of the United Kingdom - England, Ireland, Wales and Scotland - all organised under the authority of the established churches into close-knit parish communities of less than 1,000 inhabitants. In these communities, people would come together for Sunday worship within the parish church, educate their children together in parish schools, accept the moral discipline of the church courts, and embrace shared religious and moral values.

In this chapter, I will explore the political and legal reform movements relating to the churches of the United Kingdom between 1780 and 1870, giving particular attention to the church extension movement - that is, the effort to provide new churches and clergymen, and to strengthen pastoral outreach, within the established churches. The first phase of reform, between about 1780 and 1825, was dominated by the emerging movement for church extension, seen both as a means of forming a stable social order and as a form of nation-building, and by significant state funding and support for church extension. The second phase, between about 1825 and 1850, saw a militant response by Protestant Dissenters, Roman Catholics, and political radicals to the church extension movement, and the struggle between the opponents and supporters of church extension. The combined pressure of Dissenters, Catholics and radicals led to concessions, and a liberal political order began to take shape, in which adherents of all Christian denominations gained new political rights. But at the same time, the established churches were reformed and quietly began to gain popular support. The third phase, between about 1850 and 1870, witnessed not only the continued growth of toleration and religious equality, but also a steady growth in the influence of the established churches, at least in England and Scotland. The established churches found that they could no longer look for additional state grants to support church extension, but they developed new means of funding church extension from their own resources. They learned to adapt to the more liberal society of the mid-Victorian years, in which the established churches had to exist alongside other denominations in an increasingly pluralistic environment.

Church Reform and Extension
The First Phase, 1780-1829

The term 'religious establishment' in early modern Britain and Ireland referred to the liturgical practices and set of doctrines that had been legally 'established' by the monarchical state. As the Anglican theologian and political theorist, J. Neville Figgis, observed in 1911, 'establishment' in the British and Irish context did not arise from the state selecting one denomination from among several to be the established church. Rather, it meant that the state had legally authorised certain liturgical practices and doctrinal positions within the historic national church; 'establishment' thus referred "not to the origin of the Church, but to its control".[1] At the Reformation, the Tudor monarchical states in England and Ireland (which shared a common monarch), and the separate Stuart monarchical state in Scotland, had 'established' Protestant liturgies and statements of doctrine, and had required their subjects to worship according to the established forms - with penalties, fines and imprisonment imposed on those who declined to do so. There was one church with one set of established doctrines and formularies in each kingdom. These 'establishments' represented the idea of a confessional state, or the notion that positions of trust in the government of the realm should be restricted to those subjects who demonstrated their loyalty by worshipping in the church as sanctioned by the Crown and Parliament. Until the passing of Toleration Acts in England in 1689, Scotland in 1711, and Ireland in 1719, the monarchical states had not recognised the existence of any religious bodies outside the national church. After the passing of these Toleration Acts, the states allowed Trinitarian Protestant groups to worship outside the establishment, but only under conditions. In Ireland, a degree of legal toleration was also extended to Roman Catholics from the 1770s. With the Toleration Acts, the states in Britain and Ireland became 'semi-confessional' - that is, they enshrined the principle that only those who worshipped within the established

---

[1] Figgis, *Churches in the Modern State*, 9-12.

churches should be trusted with public office, while they provided a degree of tolera-tion and limited political participation to those outside the established churches. Prot-estant Dissenters, it should be added, were never disqualified from sitting in the House of Commons in either Britain or Ireland, and the British Commons normally had a few dissenting MPs on its benches throughout the eighteenth century.

There were three established churches within the British Isles in 1780. The larg-est of these was the Church of England and Wales. It was episcopalian in structure, and was organised into two provinces, the province of Canterbury and the much smaller province of York - each presided over by an archbishop. The two provinces included a total of twenty-four dioceses (including four dioceses in Wales), each governed by its bishop. The dioceses varied greatly in size, from Rochester, with fewer than 100 pa-rishes, to Lincoln, with some 1,250 parishes. There was also considerable variation in the incomes of the bishops. Each diocese had a cathedral, which was the mother church of the diocese; it provided worship on the grand scale and often maintained choir schools and massed choirs. The cathedrals were staffed by a dean and usually twelve canons. There were also a total of some 10,500 parishes. Laid down largely in the later medieval period, the parish system reflected the medieval patterns of population, with a preponderance of parishes in the south-east of the country. Most parishes had a church, often a venerable medieval building, which formed the centre of commu-nity life. Virtually every parish had an incumbent clergyman and two church wardens. Discipline at the parish level was maintained by the church wardens and at the dioc-esan level by the bishops' courts, while each province had its archbishop's court. The church possessed considerable landed properties and also received financial support from the tithe, a notional ten per cent of agricultural produce, and from the church rate, a local parish tax upon property. Many parishes also charged rents for sittings in the church. The church's theological standards were defined by the Thirty-Nine Arti-cles, a compendium of short doctrinal statements that reached its final form between 1563 and 1571. Its worship was determined by the Book of Common Prayer, a set of litur-gies rooted in medieval service books and taking its final shape after the Reformation. Most of the clergy were trained at Oxford or Cambridge Universities, where fellowships and degrees were restricted to members of the established church.

The Church of England and Wales was closely connected to the state at many levels. The supreme governor of the church was the monarch, the Crown's Privy Council was the highest ecclesiastical court of appeal, and Parliament served as the church's lay synod. All the bishops sat in the House of Lords, and many members of the clergy acted as local magistrates, sitting as judges on the magistrates' courts and imposing civil punishments. Perhaps a quarter of the late eighteenth-century magis-trates were clergy.[2] The church played an integral role in state ceremonials. The large majority of the English and Welsh population - probably over 90% - at least nominally

---

[2] Evans, "Some Reasons for the Growth of English Rural Anticlericalism", 101; Gilbert, *Religion and Society*, 80-81.

adhered to the established church in 1780. Most people viewed their parish church as the centre of their community. The parish church was where the community gathered, where royal proclamations were read out and major state events celebrated with the peeling of bells, and the churchyard was where the ancestors rested. The parish church defined the stages of each life with rites of passage - baptism, confirmation, marriage and burial. Many knew by heart the sombre cadences of the Prayer Book, which they heard Sunday after Sunday throughout their lives. Children often gained basic literacy and scriptural knowledge in the parish schools.

And yet, the Church of England also had serious problems, and these were weakening its influence and pastoral effectiveness. Among the most pressing of these problems was a huge disparity in clerical incomes. While some church livings were opulent, allowing their incumbents to live in great luxury, the incomes of many parish livings were far too small to support a clergyman with a family. The system of patronage in the appointment of parish clergy was subject to abuse, and nepotism and simony led to the appointment of some unsuitable ministers who neglected their duties, while devoting themselves to hunting, fishing, port wine, fashionable spas and extramarital affairs. There was widespread pluralism, with single clergymen sometimes holding as many as four livings, often separated by considerable distances. Many clerics did not reside in their parishes, and had little connection with the day-to-day life of the parishioners. When incumbents were non-resident, they were legally required to pay a curate to perform their duties, but this requirement was often ignored, or in many cases curates were paid starvation wages. Further, there were too many parishes in the rural south-east, and too few parishes in London and the north and west of the country. As the north and west began to industrialise after 1780, the populations of these regions increased rapidly, but legal complications made it difficult and expensive to erect new churches where they were needed. The existence of proprietary pews and the practice of charging rents for seating, moreover, effectively excluded many labouring people. All this meant that the Church of England was failing to provide religious instruction, Christian observances and pastoral care to a large and growing portion of the population.

41

The second establishment was the Church of Ireland. This church was also episcopal and Anglican. It was organised into four provinces and a total of twenty-two dioceses, and was governed by four archbishops and eighteen bishops. Most of the dioceses had a cathedral, staffed by a dean and often a dozen or more canons; indeed, it was a church top-heavy with dignitaries. The sizes of the Irish dioceses and the incomes of the Irish bishops varied considerably. The country was organised into some 2,400 legal parishes, but many of these had been united, which meant there were only about 1,200 parish livings. The Irish Church was supported by the tithe and also by the church cess, an Irish version of the English church rate. Most of the clergy were trained at Trinity College, Dublin, Ireland's only university, where fellowships and degrees were restricted to adherents of the established church. The doctrine of the Church of Ireland was defined by the Anglican Thirty-Nine Articles and its worship by the Anglican Book of Common Prayer; it was often referred to as the Church of England in Ireland. The Church of Ireland was closely connected with the monarchical state. The monarch was supreme governor of the Irish Church, Irish bishops sat in the Irish House of Lords, and Irish established clergy served as magistrates.

Unlike the Church of England, however, the Church of Ireland could not claim to be national. Rather, it was a minority establishment. In 1780 only about 15% of the Irish population adhered to the Church of Ireland, while some 75% of the Irish population were Roman Catholic and about 10% were Presbyterian. This raised serious questions about its position as the established church in Ireland. Confronted by these statistics, apologists for the Church of Ireland insisted that a true church was not necessarily a majority church, as religious truth was not dependent on numbers. Theirs, they insisted, was the Irish Church founded by St Patrick, and preserved through the historic episcopate, the guidance of the Holy Spirit, and the blood of the martyrs.[3] But if so, this lofty legacy had not preserved the Irish Church from corruption. It suffered from widespread pluralism, non-residence, nepotism, sinecures and pastoral neglect. In many parishes, the congregation consisted of a single landed family and its servants, and in some parishes not even that. The church and its wealth were greatly resented by much of the Irish peasantry, one of the poorest in Europe. Roman Catholic tenant farmers were forced to pay tithe to support parish churches they did not attend and clergy whose teachings they reviled as heretical. In the North of Ireland, Presbyterians harboured similar resentments concerning the Church of Ireland, despite their shared Protestantism. In 1801, with the Act uniting Great Britain and Ireland, the established Church of England and Wales and the Church of Ireland were united. They were now one body, the United Church of England and Ireland, and for many in the Church of Ireland, this radically changed their status. They were no longer merely a small minority in Ireland; they were now an integral part of the United Church, which was the majority establishment of the United Kingdom.

The third of the established churches was the Church of Scotland. The Scottish religious establishment differed fundamentally from the establishments of England and Ireland. First, the Church of Scotland was Presbyterian in organisation. It was governed, not by bishops, but by a hierarchy of territorial church courts - parish kirk-sessions, district presbyteries, regional synods and a national General Assembly - in which ministers had equal status. Second, the Church of Scotland was Reformed, or Calvinist, in its theology, with its doctrine closely defined by the Westminster Confession of Faith. The monarchical state had established Calvinist Presbyterianism in Scotland, largely because this had become the faith of the large majority of the Scottish people after the Reformation. However, the relations of church and state were different in Scotland from those in England and Wales, or Ireland. Unlike the established churches of England and Ireland, the established church of Scotland did not recognise the Crown as its supreme governor, but insisted on the independence of the church in all 'spiritual' matters. The Church of Scotland did not view the British Parliament as

---

[3] Eccleshall, "Anglican Political Thought", 40-44.

its lay synod, it had no bishops to sit in the House of Lords, and only rarely would a Scottish minister serve as a magistrate.

The late eighteenth-century Church of Scotland held the allegiance of the large majority of the Scottish people. It was organised on a parochial basis. There were in 1780 some 970 parishes in Scotland, each with its church and minister. The parish clergy were supported by the teinds, the Scottish equivalent to the tithe, a notional ten per cent of agricultural produce and fishing. The church possessed some landed property, and some parishes charged rents for sittings, but it was on the whole much poorer than its sister establishments. Only two burghs, Edinburgh and Montrose, had a church rate. The Scottish establishment had a strong commitment to popular education, with a national system of parish schools that was reasonably effective in providing mass literacy. There were five universities (including two in Aberdeen), each with a divinity faculty for training ministers of the established church.

The Scottish Church was not affected by the same abuses as the establishments in England and Ireland. Its church courts were generally effective in disciplining ministers for pastoral neglect, and only one form of pluralism (the union of a parish living and university chair) was permitted. There were, however, serious problems surrounding the institution of lay patronage. Nearly every Scottish parish had a lay patron - usually the Crown or a member of the landed classes - who was empowered to present a qualified minister or probationer minister to the parish living when it became vacant. Patronage was highly contentious in Scotland. While the upper social orders supported lay patronage as a means to ensure the appointment of cultivated ministers, the large majority of the Scottish people strongly opposed the system, which they believed gave certain individuals unwarranted privileges and power within Christ's Church. Patron's candidates for church livings were frequently opposed by parish communities, who believed as a matter of principle that the parishioners (or rather the male heads of family) should be allowed to select their minister. The popular opposition to patronage sometimes turned violent, with ordinations taking place under armed guard in the presence of angry crowds.[4]

43

From about 1780, the authority of the established churches throughout Britain and Ireland was coming under a new threat. This threat was the evangelical movement that was spreading across the North Atlantic world. Evangelicalism placed emphasis on individual conversion, a heart-felt piety, and a strict Bible-based morality. Many evangelicals came to view the established churches as worldly and lax, more concerned with upholding the hierarchical social order than with proclaiming the gospel. Growing numbers deserted their parish churches to join gathered churches of true believers, particularly the churches of what became known as evangelical dissent, including Baptists, Congregationalists, and especially Methodists. Such believers, who came largely from the middle and lower social orders, removed themselves not only from

---

[4] Sher and Murdoch, "Patronage and Party in the Church of Scotland".

T. Rowlandson, Joanna Southcott, the Prophetess
Excommunicating the Bishops, *handcoloured
etching, 1814.*
[London, British Museum]

their parish churches but also from the traditional parish communities; they placed their personal conviction above conformity.

A further challenge to the established churches came from the republican and democratic ideas that were spreading across the North Atlantic world, and that had led to revolution first in Britain's North American colonies from the 1770s and then, after 1789, to revolution in France and across Europe. British and Irish radicals and republicans rejected the established churches as bulwarks of an oppressive regime and unjust social order. The British and Irish democratic and evangelical movements converged in some districts, promoting notions that people of all social orders could be inspired with divine truth and that the world was entering a new dispensation. Amid the massive political and military upheavals of the Revolutionary and Napoleonic era, many discerned the hand of providence. Labouring men and women, who felt a divine calling, began preaching and gathering followers, often holding services in barns, cottages or in the open fields. New prophets emerged - among them Richard Brothers and Joanna Southcott, who proclaimed the return of the miraculous gifts of the Spirit, the imminent return of Christ in glory, the impending conflict of Christ and Satan, and the coming of the millennium (or the thousand-year reign of the saints on earth).[5]

The years of the Revolutionary and Napoleonic Wars witnessed a massive growth in the numbers separating themselves from the established churches. In 1780, probably over 90% of the population in Britain adhered, at least nominally, to the established religion. By 1815, that had fallen to perhaps 70% or less, while dissent grew most rapidly in the industrialising towns and cities. Between 1781 and 1787, 878 new dissenting places of worship in England and Wales had been registered with the civil authorities (as required under the terms of the Toleration Act); this number rose to 1,812 new registrations between 1788 and 1794, and 3,378 new registrations between 1795 and 1801.[6] In Ireland, there was rapid population growth among the Catholic population, and the percentage of adherents of the established church fell to about 10% of the Irish people. Among the governing classes, there was alarm over the situation. They feared that the growing number of evangelical Dissenters, millenarians, Irish Catholics, and democratic reformers had no loyalty to the existing political order. In London, one author calculated in 1815 that of a total population of 1,162,300 residing within an eight-mile radius of St Paul's cathedral, 946,000 did not attend the established church and were being drawn either to sectarian enthusiasm or infidelity. This situation, he insisted, could not "be contemplated without terror by any real and rational Friend of our Established Government in Church and State".[7]

There was a strong belief that the explosive growth of dissent needed to be halted and reversed, if the social and political order were to be preserved. This was particularly the case in Ireland, where the large and disaffected Catholic population was perceived as a threat not only to social peace, but also to the union of Ireland and Britain. For many in the governing orders, the best antidote to all this popular unrest was to revive the influence of established religion; the cure for the revolutionary contagion was to make the parish churches once again the centres of communities. And so, beginning about 1808, the parliamentary state began acting to reform the established churches and extend their influence. In that year, Parliament passed an act on clerical residence in the Church of Ireland, giving the Irish bishops new powers to require clerics either to reside in their parishes and perform their duties, or to pay a curate fairly to act for them. In the same year, Parliament greatly increased the grants of money to the Irish Church and enacted legislation to promote the better use of these funds for church building and repair. Between 1808 and 1822, grants of nearly £1,000,000 were made to the Church of Ireland for church extension.[8] There were also increased annual public grants to educational societies in connection with the established church in Ireland - including £9,000 a year to one society - and these encouraged increased private giving. Parliament also invested heavily in the English establishment. Between 1809 and 1821, Parliament made eleven annual grants of £100,000, or a total of

---

[5] Harrison, *The Second Coming*, 57-134.
[6] Murray, *The Influence of the French Revolution on the Church of England*, 201.

[7] Yates, *The Church in Danger*, 49-52.
[8] Akenson, *The Church of Ireland*, 113-122; Brynn, *The Church of Ireland*, 127-135.

£1,100,000, to increase the incomes of small livings in the Church of England, with the aim of improving the quality of the parish ministry. In 1805, Parliament passed an act requiring Church of England bishops to report annually on the number of non-resident clergy, and in 1813, it passed a Curates Act, empowering bishops to require improved incomes and conditions for this often hard-pressed group of clerics. In 1818, it made a grant of £1,000,000 to promote the building of additional churches in connection with the Church of England. The grant, which was augmented by a further £500,000 in 1824, was distributed by a newly formed church-building commission; the public funds were intended to stimulate local fund-raising efforts. In this, they were success-ful. During the 1820s, a total of some £6,000,000, most of it private donations, was spent in church-building in the Church of England.[9] Hundreds of new churches were built, mainly in the growing towns and cities; they were known as 'Waterloo churches' and were viewed as monuments to the victory over Napoleonic France. The estab-lished Church of Scotland also received additional support. In 1810, Parliament raised the minimum clerical income in the Church of Scotland, providing an annual grant, initially of £10,000, but steadily increasing, to supplement the Scottish teinds. In 1823, it provided a grant to build churches in the Highlands and Islands; by the early 1830s, it had built 43 additional churches and endowed the incomes of 42 additional minis-ters, at a cost of some £180,000.[10] The levels of state grants to the three establishments between 1808 and 1824 were unprecedented.

With the increased funding, a new confidence infused the established churches. More and more students prepared for ordination at the universities. The number of newly ordained Church of England clergymen rose from an average of 277 a year between 1800 and 1809 to an average of 531 a year between 1820 and 1829. New Angli-can colleges were formed - St David's, Lampeter (1822), King's College, London (1831) and Durham University (1833). In Scotland, the number of candidates training for the ministry of the established church also greatly increased, until by the later 1820s the number of candidates was nearly four times the number of vacancies. Romantic poets and authors, including Robert Southey, William Wordsworth, Samuel Taylor Coleridge and John Keble, celebrated the central role of the Church of England in shap-ing English national history and culture. Christian political economists, among them T.R. Malthus, J.B. Sumner and Thomas Chalmers, argued that the established parish churches instilled a Christian communal responsibility - including delayed marriage and sexual abstinence outside marriage - that formed the best safeguard against over-population, social deprivation and rising poor relief costs. The early 1820s saw the beginning of a so-called 'New Reformation' movement in the Church of Ireland, with a major expansion of the work of Protestant educational and evangelical societies and a new zeal for converts among many of the established clergy. This movement, many believed, would soon bring most of the Catholic population into conformity with the

---

[9] Soloway, *Prelates and People*, 298; Ward, *Religion and Society in England*, 110.

[10] MacIver, "Unfinished Business?"; Maclean, *Telford's Highland Churches*.

G. Yates, St Luke's Church, West Norwood,
aquarelle, 1825. This 'Waterloo church' was
designed by F. Bedford.
[London, Lambeth Archives: 703]

established Protestant Church, and thus consolidate the Union of Ireland and Great Britain around a shared religious culture.

Across Britain and Ireland, prominent members of the landed gentry and aristocracy actively promoted the revival of the established churches. They included Lords Farnham, Roden and Powerscourt in Ireland, Lord Harrowby and Sir Thomas Dyke Acland in England, and James Douglas of Cavers in Scotland. Such 'Bible gentry', as they were called, embraced a Christian paternalism, viewing the tenants and labourers on their estates as their extended families, and seeking to ensure that they attended the established church regularly, educated their children in its principles, and embraced a Christian humility and resignation. These landed families, and especially the wives and daughters, taught in Sunday schools, distributed bibles and religious tracts, visited the sick and the poor, provided charity, supported home missionary societies, and sometimes employed evangelists or moral agents on their estates. They formed part of a larger Christian conservative ethos that took hold across much of Europe following the end of the Napoleonic Wars in 1815.

The unprecedented state support for the established churches, not surprisingly, aroused resentment among Protestant Dissenters and Roman Catholics. They objected to the revival of the confessional state ideal and resisted the renewed pressure to conform to the established religion. In Ireland, Roman Catholics responded vigorously to the New Reformation campaign. In what became known from 1824 as the 'Bible war', Catholics disrupted New Reformation meetings and challenged Church of Ireland evangelists to public debates.[11] Under the leadership of the flamboyant Irish Catholic barrister, Daniel O'Connell, a Catholic Association was formed to protect Catholic rights. In 1825, the Association moved to the offensive, organising increased Catholic resistance to the New Reformation, and also launching a popular, national agitation aimed at emancipating Catholics from all civic disabilities. More than that, the Catholic Association called for the separation of church and state, the disestablishment of the church in Ireland, and the equality of all persons under the law, regardless of their religious beliefs. They demanded, in short, a revolution that would bring an end to the semi-confessional state and inaugurate a new, pluralistic religious and political order. O'Connell's movement gained the support of much of Ireland's Roman Catholic clergy - with James Doyle, Catholic bishop of Kildare and Leighlin, rising to prominence with his spirited pamphlets in support of religious liberty and equality. Soon the progress of the New Reformation campaign had stalled. Confrontations between Catholics and Protestants grew more and more heated, until by 1828 sectarian civil war in Ireland seemed imminent.

48

Britain now experienced what some historians have described as a 'constitutional revolution'.[12] In 1828, amid the mounting tensions between Protestants and Catholics in Ireland and the established churches and Dissenters in Britain, the Whigs brought forward a parliamentary motion to repeal the English Test and Corporation Acts. These Acts, which dated from the late seventeenth century, legally excluded Protestant Dissenters from holding a number of civil and military offices. They enshrined the principle that only those who worshipped within the established church could be trusted with positions of responsibility within the state. Dissenters had long sought the repeal of the Acts, though without success. But on this occasion, the Tory government decided not to oppose the Whig repeal motion. Some Tories believed that by repealing the legal disabilities on Protestant Dissenters, they would gain the support of Dissenters in resisting the Catholic claims. But astute observers, such as the Tory jurist, Lord Eldon, recognised that repeal of the Test and Corporation Acts dealt a major, even a fatal blow to the semi-confessional state. "The Church of England combined with the State", Eldon proclaimed in the House of Lords in April 1828, "formed together the Constitution of Great Britain, and [...] the Test and Corporation Acts were necessary to the preservation of that Constitution".[13] Nonetheless, a measure repealing the acts now rapidly passed through both houses of Parliament.

Catholic emancipation soon followed. Early in 1829, to avoid civil war in Ireland, the Tory government of the Duke of Wellington and Sir Robert Peel reluctantly introduced a Catholic emancipation bill, which would remove most remaining civil disabili-

---

[11] Whelan, *The Bible War in Ireland.*
[12] Best, "The Constitutional Revolution"; Clark, *English Society*, 393-408.

[13] Twiss, *Public and Private Life of Lord Chancellor Eldon*, II, 204.

Handkerchief commemorating Daniel O'Connell's
victory in the elections in the Clare District, *1828*.
[Dublin, National Museum of Ireland]

ties from Catholics, including the prohibition from voting in parliamentary elections in Britain. Both popular opinion in Britain and King George IV vehemently opposed emancipation, and large-scale anti-emancipation demonstrations were hastily organised in Britain. But it was difficult to defend the principle of Catholic disabilities once the disabilities had been removed from Protestant Dissenters, and the Tory government managed to get the measure through Parliament. O'Connell and Irish Catholics were ecstatic; it was, O'Connell proclaimed, "one of the greatest triumphs recorded in history - a bloodless revolution" achieved through "moral force".[14] In late 1830, soon after the passing of emancipation, Wellington's Tory government - its ministers viewed as traitors to the Protestant constitution by many former supporters - fell from power. This brought an end to four decades of nearly uninterrupted Tory government. The

---

[14] MacDonagh, *O'Connell*, 268-269.

Whigs came to office, committed to political reform, and the subsequent general election swelled their numbers in the House of Commons. In 1832, the Whig-dominated Parliament passed the Reform Act, providing more equal electoral districts and a modest expansion of the franchise from 3.2% to 4.7% of the population.[15] Although a moderate measure, the Reform Act represented the principle that political authority was rooted in the general will of the people (or rather, of property-holding men); it further demolished the semi-confessional state and further increased the political influence of middle-class Dissenters, Catholics and radicals. Subsequent reforms of municipal government, first in Scotland in 1834 and then in England and Wales in 1835 made local government more representative of popular opinion, and this strengthened the local civic influence of Dissenters and Catholics. There had indeed been a constitutional revolution.

Church Reform and Extension
The Second Phase 1832-1851

50

With the constitutional reforms of 1828 to 1832 came new efforts to bring an end to the established churches. In 1831, Roman Catholic tenants in parts of Ireland began refusing to pay tithe, believing that emancipation must logically be followed by the abolition of the established church in Ireland. Soldiers were sent to collect the tithe. They proved a blunt and brutal instrument, and there were bloody confrontations with the Catholic peasantry (while little tithe was collected). Public opinion was sickened by the reports of people being killed in order to collect money for Christ's Church. The anti-tithe movement spread, and demands for Irish disestablishment grew more strident. By 1833, many Church of Ireland clergy were not receiving any income and some, fearing for their lives, were fleeing the country.[16] The anti-establishment movement, meanwhile, spread to Britain by 1832. The agitation began in Scotland, where Scottish Dissenters called for the end to any connection of church and state. Naming their agitation the 'Voluntary campaign', they insisted that each person's religious adherence should be an entirely voluntary decision, with no element of state coercion. There should, some argued, be a free, competitive marketplace in religion; indeed, the movement became linked to liberal calls for free trade and the removal of state interference from the market-place. The Voluntary agitation quickly spread to England. Voluntaries held public meetings and demonstrations, organised petitions to Parliament, circulated tracts and pamphlets, and founded journals. They received support from philosophical radicals - followers of the rationalist legal reformer Jeremy Bentham and many of them atheists - who portrayed the established churches as relics of a dark age

---

[15] Hilton, *A Mad, Bad & Dangerous People*, 422-424.

[16] O'Donoghue, "Causes of the Opposition to Tithes" and "Opposition to Tithe Payment".

of superstition and priestcraft, and called for the appropriation of their property to support modern education and the promotion of rational culture.

While Voluntaries demanded the entire end to the established churches, more moderate Dissenters, with their leadership based mainly in prosperous London congregations, began campaigning from 1834 for the redress of specific grievances - including the end of the legal requirements that all marriages had to be solemnised in the Church of England, that all births and deaths had to be registered in parish churches, that burials in churchyards had to be conducted according to Anglican rites, and that Dissenters could not take degrees at Oxford and Cambridge universities. These moderate Dissenters did not call for the end of the established churches, and they tended to view the Voluntaries as extremists whose agitation threatened property and political order. Moderate Dissenters had no desire to associate their cause with the violent tithe war in Ireland or with philosophical and atheistic radicalism.

In 1833, in an effort to end the tithe war and related unrest in Ireland, the reformed Parliament passed the Irish Church Temporalities Act. This Act reduced the size of the established church in Ireland, abolishing ten bishoprics and suspending a number of parish churches. It also ended the church cess in Ireland, and imposed an income tax on larger church incomes. Many had called for the appropriation of Irish Church incomes and their use for secular purposes - such as poor relief and education in Ireland. Indeed, an appropriation clause had been included in the original bill, but was later dropped in order to ensure passage of the bill through the House of Lords.[17] Yet, although there was no appropriation of church property, the Irish Church Temporalities Act did effectively recognise that the Church of Ireland would never be more than a minority church. Further, O'Connell and other Irish Catholic leaders continued to press for the appropriation of the church's income. In Britain, meanwhile, Protestant Voluntaries and radicals were greatly encouraged by the Irish Act, seeing the reduction of the church in Ireland as the first step towards general disestablishment across the United Kingdom. The Voluntary agitation grew increasingly heated during 1834, and in some English towns, the church rate was voted down, depriving the Church of England of vital local sources of revenue.

The established churches were under serious threat. During the agitation for parliamentary reform in 1832, popular reformers had denounced the established churches as bulwarks of tyranny and enemies of popular rights, and these attacks continued after the Reform Act was passed. Critics scrutinised and publicised the established churches' failings, including the continuing problems with patronage, pluralism, pastoral neglect, small livings, insufficient supervision of clergy, and clerical scandals. For such critics - among them the radical John Wade in his widely read *Extraordinary Black Book* of 1832 - established churches were bastions of privilege and remnants of a corrupt old order, an order that was destined to be swept away in the

---

[17] Brose, "The Irish Precedent for English Church Reform".

new era of reform. "If such ecclesiastical establishments [...] be much longer tolerated in their existing state", Wade asserted, "the people will evince a patience and fatuity far exceeding any previous estimate".[18]

With their very survival in question, the established churches reluctantly accepted the need for fundamental changes in their structures and government. New leaders emerged within the established churches - among them J.B. Sumner, Thomas Chalmers, and C.J. Blomfield - figures who were prepared to embrace the ethos of popular reform. Such leaders, both clerical and lay, acknowledged that the established churches faced a crisis, and that they had to become more popular, more national, and more efficient in their pastoral work. They needed to become true churches of the people, especially of the poor, and they needed to reach the large numbers, especially in the urban districts, who were outside the influence of Christianity.

The movement for the popular reform of the established churches began in Scotland. There, under the influence of the evangelical Church of Scotland minister, theologian and political economist, Thomas Chalmers, the General Assembly of the Church of Scotland enacted a series of reforms. A fluent author and passionate speaker, Chalmers had long maintained that only the established churches could preserve the social fabric. Only the established churches, he argued, could inculcate a sense of communal responsibility and collective self-help in all the parishes of the land and thus unite and elevate the whole population, including the urban working classes, through shared Christian social values. The established church, he insisted, must become a "poor man's church", offering religious observances and pastoral care to all who needed it, regardless of their ability to contribute financially to the church.[19] Inspired by Chalmers's vision, the General Assembly of 1834 acted to rejuvenate the Church of Scotland. It reformed its patronage system for appointing new ministers to parish churches, placing limits on the powers of private patrons and increasing the popular voice of parishioners in the selection process. The same General Assembly also empowered the church to create new parish churches, each with full representation in the Presbyterian system of church courts.

Most important, the General Assembly of 1834 launched a new church extension campaign, which called for popular effort in raising money for the building of new parish churches. Local committees were to be formed, which would collect statistics on church attendance and decide where new churches were needed. Once need was determined, the local committees would collect money to build the churches. The local initiatives would be supported by a national committee, which would raise additional donations through a national church extension campaign. Although he was seriously ill with a weak heart, Chalmers was appointed as convener of the church extension committee and he threw himself into the fray. He and his supporters sought to involve Scots of all social ranks in church extension. Wealthy landowners and merchants were called upon to subscribe large amounts to the national committee, while the labour-

---

[18] [Wade], *The Extraordinary Black Book*, 182.   [19] Brown, *Thomas Chalmers*, 144-151, 194-203.

ing poor were encouraged to subscribe a penny a week. Hundreds of thousands of such small donations, Chalmers argued, would both maximise the amounts raised (through what he termed the "power of littles") and would give the campaign a broad popular base. Church extension would become a Scottish national cause, and all those subscribing to the campaign would have a stake in the movement to transform Scotland into a godly commonwealth. Church extensionists portrayed their Voluntary opponents as a selfish minority, who put their private interests above the general interest of the nation, and whose ideal of a free marketplace in religion benefited those who could pay for their churches while effectively excluding the poor from Christ's church.

According to Chalmers's plan, once the people of Scotland had begun building new churches through voluntary giving, the church would approach Parliament and request that each new church be given a modest state endowment that would pay part of the minister's stipend. The state endowments were viewed as vital to ensure that the new churches were not dependent on the contributions of well-to-do members, but would be able to conduct a vigorous home mission among the labouring orders and become true churches of the people. The Scottish church extension movement made a fair start, and over the next five years, nearly 200 new churches were built. The achievements in church extension, meanwhile, encouraged other initiatives in the Church of Scotland, including the formation of new schools and the expansion of overseas missions and colonial churches. Popular giving to the established Church of Scotland increased fourteen-fold between 1834 and 1839.

A similar reform movement also emerged in the Church of England, inspired in part by the Scottish example. In 1834, Church of England leaders, most notably the capable and energetic Charles James Blomfield, bishop of London, agreed to co-operate with Parliament in a programme of reforms aimed at strengthening the church's parish work, especially among the labouring orders in the expanding towns and cities. In early 1835, Sir Robert Peel's Tory Government appointed an Ecclesiastical Commission, with representatives from both the church and Parliament, to develop the reform plan. Blomfield soon came to dominate the Commission. "Till Blomfield comes", wrote one member of the meetings of the Commission, "we all sit and mend our pens, and talk about the weather".[20] For Blomfield, the aims of church reform were essentially pragmatic and popular; he was prepared to sacrifice ornamental aspects of the church, such as large cathedral establishments, in order "to enhance and give lustre to the true beauty of the church - the beauty of its holy usefulness" in bringing religious instruction and observances to the masses.[21] The Commission submitted its reform plan in 1836 and the plan was subsequently expressed in three parliamentary acts - passed in 1836, 1838 and 1840. Taken together, these improved episcopal supervision of the clergy, restricted the number of pluralities, reduced the number of sinecure posts and

53

---

[20] Blomfield, *A Memoir of Charles James Blomfield*, 167.

[21] Id., *A Charge delivered to the Clergy of the Diocese of London*, 16-17.

cathedral canons, and directed more of the church's resources to church extension and parish work.

At the same time, the Church of England organised local and diocesan church extension societies, including a Metropolis Churches Fund for London, which raised significant private donations for church building. As with the Scottish church reformers, the Church of England leaders expected that once the established church had done all it could to remove abuses, make more efficient use of its existing resources, and raise donations for church building, it could expect Parliament to provide it with new grants of public money for church extension. During the later 1830s, contributions to the Church of England multiplied, and hundreds of new churches were built. In 1834, for example, the diocese of Chester formed a church building society, and by 1838 it had built or begun building over fifty new churches.[22] Funds were also raised to expand the system of Church of England schools and to support additional clergymen and salaried lay workers in crowded urban parishes.

Parliament, meanwhile, was taking steps at this time to redress some of the grievances of moderate Dissenters. In 1836, Parliament passed an act that legalised the celebration of marriages outside the established churches, and another act that provided for the civil registration of births, marriages and deaths. The intention was to provide full civil equality for Dissenters, and thus end the grievances that fed the Voluntary agitation. That same year, Parliament also reformed the system of tithes in England and Wales, enabling parishes to commute tithe from payments in kind (grain or animals) into regularised money payments. This simplified tithe payment and made it less of a burden.

Many Dissenters, however, were not placated by the redress of grievances. They would be satisfied with nothing less than the complete abolition of the religious establishments, which they viewed as essential for religious equality within a liberal society. Growing numbers of Dissenters embraced the Voluntary cause during the later 1830s, and the disestablishment campaign grew more strident. In Ireland, the tithe war had continued to rage, until in 1838 Parliament abolished the hated Irish tithe and replaced it with a land tax payable by landowners. But the abolition of the Irish tithe did not dampen Irish Catholic demands for disestablishment; for them the Church of Ireland was the symbol of historic oppression and injustice and until it was abolished there could be no peace. In English towns and cities, meanwhile, Protestant Dissenters began refusing to pay their legal church rate for the support of the Church of England; some suffered the seizure of their household goods and even imprisonment, becoming martyrs to the cause of religious equality. In Scotland, the warfare between the Voluntaries and church extensionists grew increasingly heated. It became a struggle over the religious nature of the Scottish nation. Was Scotland to be a godly commonwealth, with education, poor relief and local order controlled mainly by the established church, and

[22] Sumner, *A Charge delivered to the Clergy of the Diocese of Chester*, 21-22.

Brooch on the Disruption of the Church of Scotland, *1843. The dates refer to relevant landmarks in the history of the Church; Chalmers, Dunlop and Candlish were important leaders of the 1843 protest.* [Edinburgh, The University of Edinburgh, Museum]

the large majority of the Scottish people attending their parish church each Sunday and sharing similar beliefs and values? Or was Scotland to become a liberal society, in which the state would leave religion entirely to the efforts of voluntary churches and all denominations would be equal before the law?

In 1838, Parliament came to a decision on the question of new state grants for Scottish church extension. A parliamentary commission of inquiry had determined in early 1838 that Scotland did have a real need for additional churches. However, the Whig government of Viscount Melbourne determined that the British people would not abide new tax-supported grants to the Church of Scotland. In March 1838, Melbourne responded to the parliamentary commission's report by announcing that his government would not support additional parliamentary grants to endow the new churches being built within the Church of Scotland. If the Scottish establishment wanted more parish churches, it would have to find the money itself. It was a momentous decision. Although the Scottish population was growing at a rapid rate, the state would not provide additional public funds to enable the established church to provide church accommodation for this growing population. The leaders of the Church of Scotland, and especially Chalmers, were devastated, but their appeals to both the government and public opinion proved unavailing. As the prospect of state endowments evaporated, voluntary donations for church building also dried up. By 1841 the church extension campaign came to an end.

Two years later, in 1840, the House of Commons narrowly defeated a motion brought forward by the Tory Anglican MP for Oxford University, Sir Robert Harry Inglis, to provide new grants of public money for church extension in the Church of England. Now it was the turn of the English establishment to drink from the cup of bitterness. It had submitted to a rigorous programme of legislative reform and it had raised considerable contributions for church building; it felt it had earned the right to receive additional help from the state. Some Anglicans, meanwhile, did not see the decision of 1840 as final and they looked to the Tory Government of Sir Robert Peel, which came to power in the summer of 1841, to provide new state church extension grants. But they were let down. Peel's Government did introduce a church extension bill that was passed in 1843. It was, however, a very modest measure, which simply enabled the Church of England to make more effective use of its own resources for church building while removing certain legal obstacles to the creation of new parishes.

In Scotland the failure of church extension contributed to a crisis in church-state relations. Only a few years after the collapse of its church extension movement, the established Church of Scotland was split in two by the great Disruption. The cause of the split was a legal conflict arising out of the church's reform efforts. The civil courts in Scotland had ruled that the church's attempt to increase the popular voice in the selection of its ministers was illegal. The church, the civil courts ruled, had no legal authority to interfere with the property rights of private church patrons, and the preferences of congregations could have no legal weight in the selection of ministers. With the state refusing to support church extension and now thwarting the church's reform efforts, a large proportion of the Church of Scotland membership now renounced their connection with the state. At the Disruption in May 1843, over a third of the clergy and nearly half the lay membership left the Church of Scotland. They formed the Free Church, which they proclaimed to be a free national Presbyterian Church, liberated from what its adherents now viewed as the corrupting effects of the state connection. The outgoing ministers included Chalmers and other men of talent, vision and conviction. They received particular support from the urban middle classes and from substantial tenant farmers. Within five years, the Free Church had erected some 730 new churches (organised on a territorial basis, which mirrored the old parish system), some 400 manses for the ministers, over 500 schools (educating some 44,000 pupils) and a college in Edinburgh (New College) for training ministers. The remnant established church, meanwhile, came under the dominance of reactionaries, who rescinded nearly all the reforms of recent years, subordinated the church to the civil authorities, accepted unrestricted patronage and denounced the popular voice in the selection of ministers. As a result, the Church of Scotland suffered years of stagnant membership and waning national influence.

The established Church of England, meanwhile, was also becoming increasingly distracted - in this case by internal conflicts aroused by the High Church Tractarian movement. This movement had commenced in 1833 at Oxford University, in response to the threats to the Anglican establishment, and it was associated particularly with a series of Tracts for the Times, in which various High Church authors, among them John Henry Newman, John Keble, E.B. Pusey and Richard Hurrell Froude, endeavoured to rouse popular support for the church by appealing to its historic continuities with the Ancient Church. Tractarian authors insisted that the Church of England was more than a religious establishment and they refuted the Dissenters' claim that it was a mere creation of the state. Rather, Tractarians insisted, the Church of England was a true branch of the Holy Catholic Church, and its bishops were part of the apostolic succession that began when Christ laid his hands on the first apostles. Tractarians venerated ancient and medieval piety, devotional practices, church architecture and Christian art. Some also openly deprecated the Reformation as a tragic and unnecessary break in the historic continuity of Christ's Church. This resulted in bitter controversy within the church by the early 1840s, with evangelicals and moderates opposing the extreme Tractarians as Romanisers, who, they feared, would bring the Church of England under the authority of Rome. As the conflict intensified, some Tractarians came to view the Church of England as fundamentally corrupted by the state connection. From 1845, moreover, Newman and a number of Tractarians joined the Roman Catholic Church. But the ecclesiastical tensions within the Church of England continued.

In 1842, the established Church of Ireland came under renewed threat when Daniel O'Connell launched a popular Irish campaign for the repeal of the Union with Great Britain, proclaiming that 1843 would be "the year of repeal". Peel's Tory Government responded to the repeal agitation by prohibiting mass repeal meetings and arresting O'Connell for sedition in October 1843. It then sought to placate the Catholic majority, by securing the passage through Parliament of three conciliatory acts in 1844-1845. These included the Charitable Bequests Act, which strengthened the rights of Catholics to leave legacies to the Roman Catholic Church in Ireland, and the Colleges Act, by which the state endowed new colleges in Belfast, Galway and Cork, which were intended primarily for Catholic and Presbyterian youth. Most controversially, there was the Maynooth Act, by which the state provided a permanent state endowment for St Patrick's College, Maynooth, Ireland's seminary for the training of Catholic priests. This last act aroused a clamorous opposition from British Protestants, who were incensed that Parliament should thus endow the Catholic Church in Ireland. But Peel's government was committed to winning Catholics away from the repeal cause and it secured the passage of the Maynooth endowment despite Protestant rage and deep divisions within the Tory ranks.[23] Any good this concessionary legislation might have achieved, however, was soon dissipated by the trauma of the great Irish famine. This began with the failure of the potato crop in the autumn of 1845 and it would claim over a million lives during the next five years, leaving an enduring legacy of Irish grievance towards a Union state that failed to do enough to feed Ireland's people.

In Britain, meanwhile, despite all the disappointments, some continued to call during the 1840s for state-supported church extension. They knew that church accommodation was not keeping pace with Britain's growing population, and that a large proportion of the population was receiving no religious instruction. A revival of working-class unrest in the late 1840s, combined with the spectacle of revolutions across the Continent in 1848, aroused new fears for the social order. In the late 1840s, a series of sensationalist articles by Henry Mayhew in the London *Morning Chronicle*, and a novel, *Alton Locke* by the Christian Socialist parson, Charles Kingsley, provided graphic and distressing revelations of the appalling suffering, immorality and irreligion among London's poor. Such poverty and human degradation were scandalous in what was still viewed as a Christian state.

In response to the allegations of growing irreligion and the continued calls for church extension, Parliament conducted in March 1851 the first census of public worship, aimed at determining whether much of the population did in truth not attend church. The census was restricted to Great Britain, and it endeavoured to gain statistics both of the numbers attending church on a given Sunday, and of the total number of churches and sittings provided by all denominations. The findings of the census, published in 1853, were, for many, deeply disturbing. They revealed that the majority of the British population did not attend church on the census Sunday. This non-attendance, moreover, was evidently not the result of an insufficient number of churches. Rather, many churches were half empty on census Sunday, and many people, especially among the labouring orders, could have gone to a church but chose not to do so. Further, the established churches seemed to be declining in numbers and influence. In England as a whole, a little over half the population who attended public worship on the census Sunday went to an established church. In Scotland, less than a third of church-goers attended the established church, while in Wales, it was less than a quarter of church-goers.[24] The religious census had not included Ireland, but had it done so, it would have shown that little more than 10% of Ireland's people were adherents of the established church.

Thus by mid-century, the established churches seemed to be failing. They were minority churches in Ireland, Scotland and Wales, and the established church, it seemed, would soon be a minority church in England as well. The established

---

[23] Kerr, *Peel, Priests and Politics*.

[24] Inglis, "Patterns of Religious Worship in 1851"; Pickering, "The 1851 Religious Census"; Withrington, "The 1851 Census of Religious Worship".

churches were proving largely ineffective in stemming the alarming spread of poverty, crime, prostitution and alcohol abuse. More and more people questioned the reasons for maintaining established churches, and it now seemed only a matter of time before the connection of church and state was severed. Voluntaries argued that religion in Britain and Ireland would be much healthier if church adherence was based solely on the voluntary decision of individuals. In 1844, Voluntaries had formed the British Anti-State Church Association to co-ordinate the disestablishment campaign. In 1853, this organisation assumed the new, more positive name of Liberation Society, and it was soon gaining broad popular support.

Church Extension
The Third Phase, 1851-1870

After 1851, it was clear that the established churches could look for no further state grants for church extension. The population of the United Kingdom continued to grow rapidly, but the state would not give the established churches additional resources to build more churches and schools, and provide more pastors and teachers for this growing population. If the Voluntary agitation being co-ordinated by the Liberation Society did not bring disestablishment, it seemed that demographics alone would ensure the marginalisation of established religion in the United Kingdom.

59

The mid-Victorian state, meanwhile, was continuing to move towards ever fuller religious toleration. This movement was not always straightforward. Indeed, for a brief time in 1851, Parliament returned to a policy of anti-Catholic penal legislation that was reminiscent of the pre-1829 period. This episode had been sparked by the decision of the Roman Catholic Church to restore its episcopate and diocesan organisation in England and Wales, and by the triumphalist language used on the occasion by the Catholic primate, Cardinal Nicholas Wiseman, who had spoken of England being at long last restored to the "orbit" of the papacy. There was widespread Protestant outrage, including outrage from Queen Victoria, and in July 1851, Parliament passed the Ecclesiastical Titles Act, which declared the Catholic diocesan episcopate illegal and imposed fines and imprisonment on any Catholic prelate who assumed a diocesan episcopal title. But the public soon grew uncomfortable with the prospect of renewed penal legislation. The Roman Catholic Church in England and Wales simply ignored the Act, and the civil authorities made no attempt to enforce its provisions (it was later quietly repealed in 1871). There was thus no return to state-sanctioned anti-Catholic persecution.

Several years later, Jews gained the right to sit in Parliament. Again, the path to Jewish emancipation was by no means straightforward. After the repeal of the Test and Corporation Acts and Catholic emancipation in 1828-1829, many had believed that Jews would be next to receive their political rights through legislation. From 1830, no fewer than thirteen Jewish emancipation bills were introduced in Parliament. But

Parliament was not prepared to relinquish the idea that the state was fundamentally Christian, and the bills all failed. Then in 1847, the campaign for Jewish emancipation took a new direction when a wealthy Jewish banker, Lionel de Rothschild, was elected to the House of Commons by the City of London. He could not take his seat because, as a Jew, he was unable to take the required oath of allegiance "upon the true faith of a Christian"; none the less, his constituency continued to re-elect him to the seat (in 1849, 1852 and 1857), and the whole situation appeared manifestly unjust. Finally, in 1858, the conservative Government of Lord Derby agreed that the two houses of Parliament could each revise the wording of the oath required of their new members. The Commons immediately dropped the phrase "upon the true faith of a Christian" from its oath, and Rothschild was permitted to take his seat. The House of Lords dropped the phrase from its oath in 1866, and the first Jew to be raised to the peerage, Lionel de Rothschild's son, entered the Lords in 1886.[25]

While the larger society, by fits and starts, moved towards ever fuller religious toleration, the mid-nineteenth-century Church of England was distracted by intense warfare between two major ecclesiastical parties, neither of which viewed religious toleration as necessarily a good thing. On the one hand, there was the Evangelical party, with its emphasis on individual conversion, biblical authority, and a strict Bible-based social and personal morality. Evangelicals were active in home and overseas missions, and were prepared to co-operate closely with Protestant Dissenters in spreading the gospel message. Church structures and clerical authority were for them far less important than the religion of the individual heart. On the other hand, there was the High Church party, made up of supporters of the old alliance of church and state, and also advocates of Tractarian teachings and ritualism. For them, Evangelicals were unsound on the fundamental doctrines of apostolic succession, church authority and sacramental grace. The later 1840s and early 1850s witnessed a bitter struggle between the parties that threatened for a time to break up the Church of England.

The conflict focused on the doctrine of baptismal regeneration, or the belief that through the sacrament of baptism the individual was sanctified by the Spirit and cleansed of all sin. This doctrine was expressed in the Prayer Book and was fervently held by High Anglicans and Tractarians. Evangelicals, however, did not accept the doctrine. They placed their emphasis not on the baptismal rite, but on the personal faith of the baptised individual. In 1847, the curmudgeonly, High Church bishop of Exeter, Henry Phillpotts, refused to admit an Evangelical clergyman, George Cornelius Gorham, to a parish church in his diocese because Gorham would not affirm the High Church view of baptismal regeneration. Phillpotts's decision was upheld on appeal to the archbishop of Canterbury's provincial court, and for a time it seemed that all Evangelicals who could not embrace the High Church interpretation of baptismal regeneration might be forced out of the church as heretics. However, the Evangelicals found protection in the 'royal supremacy' (or the queen's role as supreme governor

---

[25] Salbstein, *The Emancipation of the Jews in Britain.*

61

H. Barraud, Lionel Nathan de Rothschild introduced in the House of Commons on 26 July 1858
by Lord John Russell and Mr Abel Smith, *oil on
canvas, 1872*.
[London, The Rothschild Archive]

of the church). Gorham took his case to the Queen's Privy Council, which formed the highest court of appeal in ecclesiastical cases, and in 1850 the judicial committee of the Privy Council found in Gorham's favour. Now it was the High Church party that was in distress, believing that the Privy Council was undermining orthodox doctrine in the established church and that High Anglicans could not in conscience remain in such a heterodox society. Some High Anglicans began calling for disestablishment, as a means of liberating the Church of England from such state inference; indeed, a number of High Church clerics, including the able Henry Manning, archdeacon of Chichester, did now leave the Church of England for the Roman Catholic Church. During the 1850s and 1860s, the battle between the parties continued to rage. Increasingly, it focused on Evangelical opposition to the use of surplices, decorated altars and elaborate ritual by High Church divines.

Amid this bitter warfare between the Evangelical and High Church parties, a third ecclesiastical movement came to prominence. This was the so-called 'Broad Church' movement, which consisted of a disparate group of liberal Christian scholars, theologians and authors, who sought to play down doctrinal disputes, promote further toleration, and define an inclusive, undogmatic Christianity. The Broad Church movement had its origins in the comprehensive theological visions of the seventeenth-century Cambridge Platonists and eighteenth-century latitudinarians, and also in the theological writings of Samuel Taylor Coleridge, Thomas Arnold and Thomas Erskine of Linlathen during the 1820s. Mid-nineteenth-century Anglican Broad Church thinkers included such figures as F.D. Maurice, A.C. Tait, A.P. Stanley, Benjamin Jowett, and Charles Kingsley. There was also a Broad Church movement (sometimes referred to as 'liberal evangelical') in Scotland, which included James Robertson, John Tulloch, John Caird and Norman MacLeod. Broad churchmen, whether English or Scottish, emphasised belief in moral and intellectual progress, in the importance of Christian engagement with advances in science and historical studies, and above all in the need for a national church. "The idea of a National Church", insisted the Broad Church clergyman, John Llewelyn Davies, in 1868, meant "that a Christian nation should publicly confess its Christianity". "A nation which acts publicly in the sphere of religion", he added, "is setting the highest possible estimate on its own functions".[26] In a series of seminal works, including *Culture and Anarchy* (1869) and *St Paul and Protestantism* (1870), the Broad Church poet and essayist, Matthew Arnold, portrayed the established churches as cultivating a unified and harmonious national culture, characterised by "sweetness and light".

62

Both Evangelical and High Church Anglicans denounced the Broad Church thinkers, believing that they would undermine Christian orthodoxy, including such key doctrines as the divine inspiration of Scripture and eternal punishment for the wicked. However, Broad Church thinkers found protection in the 'royal supremacy'. Twice in the early 1860s, conservative Anglicans secured heresy convictions of Broad Church thinkers in the episcopal courts, only to have the convictions overturned by the Privy Council. The first of these cases involved two clerical authors who had contributed essays to a controversial volume, *Essays and Reviews*, in 1860. The two were convicted of heretical teaching on biblical inspiration and eternal punishment in the archbishop of Canterbury's court and suspended from their livings. They appealed, however, to the Privy Council, which in 1864 found in their favour and set aside the suspensions. The second case involved a colonial bishop, John William Colenso, who was deposed as bishop of Natal for heretical writings on the Old Testament by a court convened by the bishop of Cape Town. Colenso appealed to the Privy Council, which in 1865 set aside the deposition and reaffirmed his right to hold the bishopric. Although conservatives, both Evangelical and High Church, organised formal protests against these Privy Council decisions, the Church of England was gradually forced to accept an increased latitude of belief among its clergy and members. This new latitude also found expression in the Clerical Subscription Act of 1865, by which Parliament eased the terms of subscription to the Thirty-Nine Articles and Book of Common Prayer among new clergy - an act welcomed by the Broad Church group.[27] Moreover, leading politicians, and especially Queen Victoria, were attracted to the Broad Church vision of an inclusive national church, and from the mid-1860s, Broad Church thinkers were appointed to a

---

[26] Davies, "The Voluntary Principle", 236.   [27] Chadwick, *The Victorian Church*, II, 132-134.

number of key positions of leadership within the established churches and universities of England and Scotland.

The 1850s and 1860s brought moves to introduce more representative forms of government to the Church of England. The motives behind these moves varied, with some believing that more representative government would make the church more efficient in its ministry, and others hoping to strengthen the independence of the church from the state. The first of these moves involved the revival of the Convocations of Canterbury and York. The Convocations were provincial assemblies of the clergy of the two provinces which had first emerged in the eighth century. For centuries, they had met periodically to hear grievances and approve taxes levied on the clergy.[28] However, the deliberations of Convocation had been suspended by the Crown in 1717, and for over a century, the two provincial Convocations met only at the commencement of Parliament to adopt an address of loyalty to the Crown and then immediately disperse. High Church Anglicans, however, became convinced that the church needed a deliberative body in order to preserve its spiritual independence and defend its doctrines and formularies. They called for the revival of Convocation. Evangelicals and Broad Churchmen were, on the whole, opposed to any such revival, fearing that the High Church party would seek to use Convocation to condemn and excommunicate their opponents as heretics. But the High Church party was persistent, and at the opening of Parliament after the general election of 1852, the archbishop of Canterbury reluctantly allowed Convocation to discuss briefly some clerical grievances. The deliberations were conducted in a spirit of moderation and decorum, and Evangelicals and Broad Churchmen soon came to see the benefits of such a forum - with the result that the experiment was repeated. By 1855, the Convocation of Canterbury was meeting annually for deliberations, and the Convocation of York began regular annual meetings in 1861. Other representative bodies now emerged in the Church of England. In 1861, the church began holding annual church congresses in different cities for the discussion of issues relating to the church's life and mission. In 1867, the Church of England held the first Lambeth Conference, bringing together some seventy-six bishops from the world Anglican communion. Representative diocesan conferences or assemblies were introduced in the dioceses of Ely (1866), Lichfield (1868) and Lincoln (1871), and the movement soon spread, until by 1882 all but three Church of England dioceses had such assemblies.

The three decades that followed the defeat of the parliamentary church-extension grants in 1838-1840, meanwhile, saw significant church building within the established churches of England and Scotland - despite Parliament's refusal to provide additional grants of public money. The reforms of the 1830s had focused the churches' attention on the parish ministry, while the churches learned to make efficient use of their existing resources and to raise substantial contributions for church building.

---

[28] Thirlwall, *Remains Literary and Theological*, I, 198-229.

This was a time of widespread belief in the civilising mission of the Empire and the providential role of the British state; many, especially among the middle and upper classes, were prepared to give generously to the established churches as contributors to the power and influence of imperial Britain. This was demonstrated in 1841, when clerical and lay leaders of the Church of England, including the Tory MP, William Ewart Gladstone, established the Colonial Bishoprics Fund, in order to expand the established church overseas. That same year, Parliament passed the Colonial Bishoprics Act, granting the Church of England the legal authority to create new bishoprics in the colonies as required.[29] During the next fifty years, the Colonial Bishoprics Fund raised collected voluntary contributions to create and endow some seventy-eight bishoprics in the expanding empire.

In the Church of England, money for church building was raised through diocesan church extension societies, of which there were some 24 in existence across England and Wales by 1864. Between 1841 and 1876, the established church added 3,199 new churches or chapels in England and Wales, increasing its total number of churches by 25%.[30] As well as building new churches, diocesan societies also rebuilt and restored churches. For example, in the diocese of Oxford between 1860 and 1863, the diocesan society built 10 new churches, while it rebuilt or restored another 43 churches.[31] Many new churches were built in the expanding suburbs on the peripheries of major cities. The established church showed significant growth in the industrial districts of South Wales, with the Llandaff Diocesan Church Extension Society raising some £359,000 for building and enlarging churches between 1840 and 1877.[32] "We live in an age", proclaimed A.C. Tait, archbishop of Canterbury, in 1876, "of restored churches, of increased services, of vastly increased numbers of communicants".[33]

The Church of Scotland, though its membership had been greatly reduced by the Disruption of 1843, also became active in church extension and began to recover its sense of national mission. The Scottish movement was associated with James Robertson, the Broad Church professor of ecclesiastical history at the University of Edinburgh. In 1846, Robertson launched a Church of Scotland campaign to raise private donations to endow the 222 church extension churches that had been built under Thomas Chalmers's leadership between 1834 and 1841. A one-time protégé of Chalmers, Robertson revived his mentor's arguments concerning the importance of an endowed parish ministry for home mission work, and on the value of organising the Scottish population into close-knit parish communities, with shared religious and moral values. By the time of his death in 1860, Robertson's campaign had raised over £400,000. As well as endowing the 222 churches, it also built and endowed another 60 churches.[34] By

---

[29] Strong, *Anglicanism and the British Empire*, 209-211.
[30] Brooks and Saint, eds., *The Victorian Church*, 9.
[31] Wilberforce, *Charge delivered to the Diocese of Oxford*, 15-17.

[32] Davies, *Religion in the Industrial Revolution in South Wales*, 104.
[33] Tait, *Some Thoughts on the Duties of the Established Church*, 18-19.
[34] Charteris, *The Life of the Rev. James Robertson*, 254-269.

1870, the established Church of Scotland possessed 1,254 churches, and according to marriage and education statistics, its membership represented about 44% of the Scottish population. This was a marked improvement from the religious census of 1851, when its adherents had accounted for a mere 32% of church-goers.[35]

Other Broad Church figures contributed to the recovery of the established Church of Scotland. Norman MacLeod, the popular minister of the Barony church in central Glasgow, pursued an active urban pastorate and edited a successful magazine, *Good Words*. In 1865, he opposed a religiously-inspired campaign to stop the running of Sunday trains between Glasgow and Edinburgh, arguing that Old Testament laws concerning the Sabbath did not apply in a Christian country and calling for the Sunday openings of museums, art galleries and parks. His public stand marked the beginning of an easing of Scotland's strict Sabbath legislation. In Edinburgh, the Broad Church minister of Greyfriars parish church, Robert Lee, introduced innovations in worship, including organ music, read prayers, and congregational responses. His liturgical innovations were denounced as illegal by conservatives in the Church of Scotland and Lee was harried to a stroke in 1866 and premature death.[36] But others took up his innovations, while presbyteries proved reluctant to suppress innovations that had the support of congregations. The result was a renaissance of worship within the established church. By 1869, a newly confident Church of Scotland was petitioning Parliament for the abolition of patronage, and working for reunion with the Free Church.

One part of the United Kingdom, however, did not share in this mid-Victorian revival of established religion. For the Catholic majority (and much of the Presbyterian minority) in Ireland, the established Church of Ireland remained a symbol of oppression and injustice. Popular hostility to the Protestant establishment had been fuelled by the horrors of the great Irish famine of 1846-1851. During the famine, some Church of Ireland Evangelicals had sought to revive the Protestant crusade and by 1851 they had claimed some 35,000 Catholic converts to Protestantism; this had created deep resentments among Catholics, with widespread allegations of 'souperism', or the claim that established church leaders had sought to buy conversions from starving Catholics with offers of soup.[37] The famine also contributed to what the historian Emmet Larkin has termed a "devotional revolution" in Irish Catholicism, sweeping away remnants of Irish folk religion, bringing famine survivors to embrace strict Roman devotional practices, and greatly enhancing the influence and authority of the institutional Roman Catholic Church in post-famine Irish society.[38]

The established Church of Ireland remained the church of a small minority in post-famine Ireland. The reforms of 1833, to be sure, had left the Irish Church leaner and more efficient. After 1850, there was some new church building, and some evangelical and educational effort. The overall proportion of the Irish population adher-

65

---

[35] Wallace, "Church Tendencies in Scotland", 187, 230.
[36] Story, *Life and Remains of Robert Lee*, II, 54-107, 212-294.

[37] Kerr, *"A Nation of Beggars"?*, 210-211; Bowen, *Souperism, Myth or Reality*.
[38] Larkin, "The Devotional Revolution in Ireland".

66

Bridget O'Donnel and her two children during the
Irish Potato Famine, *engraving published in the*
Illustrated London News, *22 December 1849.*
[London, British Library]

ing to the Church of Ireland increased slightly, from 10.7% in 1834 to 11.9% in 1861.[39] However, this increase was negligible, while the hatred of many Irish Catholics for the established church was great. Finally, in 1869, in response to growing social and political unrest in Ireland, the Liberal government of William Gladstone (who had by now abandoned the strong commitment to established religion that he had held in the 1840s) introduced legislation to disestablish and disendow the Church of Ireland. While some viewed this as a further betrayal of the Protestant cause, there was little support for the Irish established church in Britain. The Irish disestablishment act passed quickly through both houses and from 1 January 1871 the Church of Ireland was deprived of its state connection and much of its income.

British Voluntaries were greatly encouraged by Irish disestablishment. They had received still further encouragement from Parliament's decision in 1868 to abolish the church rate in England and Wales, an act which severed an important tie between the parish churches and their local communities. In England and Wales, Voluntaries revived the disestablishment campaign, holding meetings and demonstrations, issuing tracts and bringing motions for the disestablishment of the Church of England before Parliament in 1871, 1872 and 1873.[40] In 1874, the two largest non-established churches in Scotland - the Free Church and the United Presbyterian Church - joined to revive the Scottish disestablishment campaign. Many expected a speedy victory. After all, the religious census of 1851 had shown the establishments to be minority churches in Scotland and Wales, and nearly a minority church in England. For its advocates, disestablishment would be a logical consequence of the 'constitutional revolution' of 1828-1832; it would be a step along the inexorable liberal advance towards greater individual autonomy and less government regulation, whether in the economic marketplace, the marketplace of ideas, or the religious marketplace.

However, Dissenters, or Nonconformists as they were now generally known, soon discovered that the established churches in Britain had experienced a significant recovery in numbers and influence since 1851. In England and Scotland, the established churches were able to call on broad support within the population as a whole for the cause of church defence. (In Wales, the established church was much more vulnerable, but even here there were signs of recovery, especially in industrial South Wales.[41]) The established churches had eliminated most of the abuses of pluralism, non-residence, sinecures, nepotism, and pastoral neglect that had weakened their pastoral work and tarnished their image in the early decades of the nineteenth century. They were now making efficient use of their resources and were proving effective in raising voluntary contributions to build churches and schools, and support their home and overseas missions. Their clergy were increasingly perceived as dedicated pastors who were content with moderate incomes, identified themselves with their parish-

---

[39] Emerson, "The Last Phase of the Establishment", 314-315.
[40] Mackintosh, *Disestablishment and Liberation*, 242-249.

[41] Davies, *Religion in the Industrial Revolution in South Wales*, 97-140.

ioners and served the broader needs of their communities. The established churches were, in many districts, churches for the poor, which provided Christian instruction, pastoral care and religious observances - including the rites of passage of baptism, first communion, marriage and burial - to those who needed, but could not afford to pay for them.

There remained serious problems. The rage of party continued within the Church of England, with bitter confrontations between the High Church and Evangelical parties, especially over ritual in public worship. Some believed that Parliament and the Privy Council continued to exercise too much influence over matters of doctrine and discipline within the English Church. And despite the significant achievements in church extension, large numbers, especially in the industrial cities, were outside all Christian influence. The renewal of the disestablishment agitation in the late 1860s, moreover, indicated that a significant portion of the population remained opposed to the principle of an established church. Nonetheless, the established churches demonstrated energy and commitment in responding to these challenges, and the connection of church and state remained strong in much of Britain. Moreover, the apparatus of an authoritative established church imposing its beliefs with the aid of state power - the old confessional state - had been almost entirely dismantled by liberal legislation since 1828, and few now viewed the established churches as threats to their individual liberties.

Church Establishment, Disestablishment and Democracy in the United Kingdom of Great Britain and Ireland, 1870-1920

Keith Robbins

Prelude

In June 1895, a historian who had once threatened to detonate a mine when he was in Rome observing the Vatican Council in 1870 - where it was decreeing what he thought ought not to have been decreed - delivered his inaugural lecture as Regius Professor of History in the University of Cambridge. His text ran to seventy-four pages, the notes to fifty-seven, but the smaller print of the notes meant that they contained many words more than the lecture. No man in the England of his time had thought more about 'church and state' over the long European past than the lecturer, Lord Acton. No man had brooded more intently on the path to freedom, as he put it, in a country whose present was linked with the distant past to an exceptional degree. No man had felt more strongly within himself the conflict between legitimism and the desire for freedom. He read and read. He took lots of notes. As a boy he had been incarcerated with a private tutor in Edinburgh with a view to going to Cambridge. However, three of its colleges turned him down because he was a Catholic. He became a Cambridge man only on becoming a professor. It was an indication that much, though not all, had changed in the England of his lifetime with regard to diversity of religious belief and practice. This Englishman, however, was not a 'typical Englishman', nor, in the end, a 'typical Catholic'. He was born in Naples and was to die at Tegernsee, Bavaria, in 1902. He was half a Rhinelander and married a Bavarian. He lived, one might say, at cross-roads. The expectations these terms aroused, experience taught him, changed with their environment. He sat in the House of Commons for six years from 1859 representing the Irish constituency of Carlow. He knew 'Europe' (or that part of it which 'mattered') better than his own country. Human society, he supposed, was in progress. Absolutism, he thought, was dead. As a Catholic, he praised English seventeenth-century puritan Dissenters. With the Dutch, they had paved the path towards religious liberty. 'England' was a country which made its adjustments piecemeal rather in the form of declaratory statements of principle. It was often difficult for foreigners to discern the scale of change in a country apparently so adept at investing old forms and institutions with new meanings. No pretence is being made here that Lord Acton is a 'representative figure'. A cosmopolitan aristocrat turned 'professional' historian is too idiosyncratic (and perhaps too attractive) a phenomenon to receive that designation. Yet, for the period under consideration, his experiences and attitudes provide an intriguing way into considering 'reform' as viewed from the perspective of the 'state' in the United Kingdom in the latter decades of the century. His inner conflicts were complex, but the issues with which he was concerned were those debated by the British political, cultural and intellectual elite in a country with a variety of ecclesiastical balances and arrangements in its component parts.

'The state', could not be indifferent to the manifestly shifting patterns of religious allegiance and their significance for national identity and political stability. The United Kingdom, as it had existed since 1801, as Professor Brown has explained in this volume and elsewhere, was a semi-confessional state. Subjects were expected to conform to the worship and discipline of the established church in whichever historic kingdom they resided. His chapter has demonstrated the stresses and strains placed upon this expectation over subsequent decades. Even in 1801, however, expectation and reality were distinct. Dissent, as it were, was firmly 'established' and could not be eradicated. Dissent, however, had endemic dissidence, embracing different organisational structures and theological persuasions: Baptists, Congregationalists (Independents), Presbyterians (in England) and the new and fissiparous phenomenon of Methodism, to which might be added Unitarians and Quakers. Ever since 1732, elected laymen from London congregations of the first three bodies, the 'Protestant Dissenting Deputies', had worked diligently to protect the Civil Rights of Dissenters and to protest against the restrictions and exclusions which still applied to them. Religious Dissent could be equated with political dissent, though not universally. The tide of the time, as the previous chapter has made clear, appeared to be with them. There were still matters - for example, the payment of church rates - which irked, and which were still fought over, but Nonconformity was evidently 'here to stay'.

It is partly for this reason that the term 'semi-confessional' is appropriate (the other being that the state sustained two 'establishments' - the 'United Church of England and Ireland' and the Church of Scotland - which were not 'in communion' with each other. It might be said, therefore, that the state, since 1707, had an inherently split 'personality'. 'The state' *de facto* and, substantially, *de iure* had accepted 'plurality', even if that word was not used. Leaving the case of Scotland aside, however, it had done so in England and Wales on the assumption that Dissent was a 'minority' (gratifyingly 'loyal') and in the hope that it would remain so. It was indeed its 'minority' status, and its social consequences, which could be said to maintain its cohesion. It could be gratifying to be everywhere spoken against. Yet here was a problem. Dissent was evidently growing, indeed, as the decades passed, prominent men in their ranks thought their beliefs and structures were more in tune with the new urban Britain than was a 'rural' church. That might mean that it could become a 'majority', indeed, in certain selected areas of the country might already be so. So did this mean that the historic antithesis between 'National Church' and 'Dissent' was becoming obsolete? Should not 'the state' occupy a neutral 'public space' equidistant from any organised Christian body? It might offer public revenues, perhaps in relation to education and social welfare, and perhaps even for the benefit of religion itself (acknowledged as a 'public good') in some proportional relationship to size and without 'privileging' on any other grounds. Should/could the state have a 'conscience' of its own or was it to acknowledge the church (or the churches) as its conscience? It might, on the other hand, manifest its 'neutrality' by offering no public support to churches in any aspect of their work. Their members must finance their own activities. These questions, of course, were only one aspect of a constant and wide-ranging discussion about 'the state' in general.

The mid-Victorian United Kingdom, as Professor Brown has shown in his chapter, had come near to these issues in the post-1832 political world, but the contours were complicated and no general consensus had been reached, and perhaps could not be reached. If the latter, that was a reflection on the complexity of the United Kingdom itself. The general issue, to one degree or another, as is evident elsewhere in this volume, affected all the countries under consideration. What gave the United Kingdom its particular character was that one size clearly did not fit all its constituent parts yet unity, though not uniformity, was a political necessity, or perceived to be so. Further, as has been noted, there was the paradox that it was 'Anglican Protestant establishmentarians' who most vigorously upheld the principle of the confessional state so beloved by conservative continental Catholics, while British and Irish Catholics frequently appealed to liberal principles of legal equality at the same time as Catholicism was at war with political liberals in most of the rest of Europe.[1] There were certain contexts in which Dissenters, Protestant and Catholic, were on the same side, at least in Britain. In Ireland, however, Protestant Dissent (Presbyterian or Methodist) was generally restrained in its enthusiasm for legal equality by fear that legal equality, at some stage or other, would be abused by Catholics who did not themselves really believe in it.

Whilst Laodiceans were not unknown in the ranks of both major political parties, what is perhaps more striking, however, is the continuing personal 'Church of England' commitment, expressed in different ways, to be found in leading figures of the post-1832 era in United Kingdom politics.[2] 'Religious reform' was not merely a tiresome interruption distracting them from the main business of government. It had

---

[1] Hempton, *Religion and Political Culture in Britain and Ireland*, 148-149.

[2] Lord Derby, the first British statesman to become Prime Minister three times, and the leader of the Conservative Party for twenty-two years from 1846, published books on the Parables and an interpretation of *The Miracles of Our Lord* (1839). He had a firm commitment to the defence of the established church, viewed as legal and civic rather than apostolic. When a young (then) Tory MP, William Gladstone, sent Derby (then Lord Stanley) a complimentary copy of his book *The State in its Relations with the Church* in February 1839, Stanley did not respond. He did not like the insistence on the apostolic authority of the church. Hawkins, *The Forgotten Prime Minister*, 210.

a central significance. It was important that religion should flourish. It was equally important, however, that liberty should flourish. The reconciliation of these desiderata, as events showed, was easily capable of bringing back to life long memories of ecclesiastical conflict in all of the territories of the United Kingdom. Things could not go on as they were in the 'management' of religion, but the options for change were not straightforward. The memories of struggles in previous centuries certainly did not lead to any notion that the state could or should seek to re-impose ecclesiastical uniformity. As 'guardian of the national past', however, governments of the day were entangled with the myths and symbols which expressed who the British (English/Irish/Scottish/Welsh) were and these notions determined their role, not an insignificant one, in Europe, together with their 'imperial mission' in the wider world. A national self-perception as a country revelling in freedom - as English Protestantism had come to understand freedom - was ingrained. In so far as this heritage, implicitly if not explicitly, remained embodied in British minds, it greatly complicated 'religious reform' for United Kingdom governments.

The articulation of the United Kingdom state was a complicated business - even more if we note the waxing responsibilities of 'imperial management': integration and diversity jostled uneasily.[3] It was in the wake of the Indian 'mutiny' of 1857 that the British government took over from the East India Company direct responsibility for the government of India. 'Religious reform' therefore posed implications both far and near, decisions and developments within this global 'British sphere' could have unintended consequences. Unless a 'Protestant Crusade' really did succeed in Ireland - and the likelihood seemed increasingly remote - the reality was that Ireland would continue to be a 'Catholic country', although one in which there were significant Anglican and Presbyterian regional presences. 'Catholic Emancipation' had passed through Parliament in 1829 but arguably too late to ease the prospects of the British-Irish political union of three decades earlier. From that standpoint, it was no longer desirable to trumpet, or at least not excessively, the virtues of 'British Protestantism' - a not insignificant reason being the substantial presence of Irish Catholic soldiers in the British army. Further, in the 1840s, the extent of Irish immigration into Britain - largely but not exclusively Catholic - in the wake of the disaster of the Irish famine, together with some celebrated conversions to Roman Catholicism, made it more difficult to make a simple contrast between 'Protestant Britain' and 'Catholic Ireland'. In a curious way, it has been argued, Irish emigration "made the British Isles more culturally homogeneous by exporting the peculiar sectarian tensions of Ireland to dozens of new frontiers in British towns and cities".[4] However, and in some contradiction, there was no call to soft-pedal those virtues or to retreat from 'religious freedom' as intrinsic to what a 'modern state' should embody. From the perspective of vocal Protestant figures, clerical or lay, it was the Roman Catholic Church itself, in its own ecclesiastical structures, and in the guise of the papal states and the policies of rulers of 'Catholic states', which did

[3] Robbins, "An Imperial and Multinational Polity".

[4] Hempton, *Religion and Political Culture in Britain and Ireland*, 148.

not believe in 'religious freedom'. Lord Ashley, later the Earl of Shaftesbury, wanted to see Britain aligned internationally in 1844 with Sweden, Denmark and Prussia - an alliance which would apparently enable the country "to defy the infidel and political Popery of the Parisian Rabble".[5] For decades, a collection of Protestant societies did battle on behalf of 'Reformation principles', identifying 'Popery' as the antithesis of a true and vital Christianity. The papal restoration of the hierarchy to England and Wales in 1850-1851 was presented as 'Papal Aggression'. The 'anti-Catholic' sentiment which was generated gained strength from the examples - chiefly in Italy - where Protestant evangelists had been imprisoned for their proselytising activities. Nevertheless, it is held that Victorian 'No Popery' agitations were "almost the last expressions of a long tradition".[6]

On the one hand, therefore, 'religious freedom' required that the Roman Catholic Church should be free to organise itself in England and Wales in whatever way it chose. But, on the other hand, was this not a church, where it was in political position to do so, which would restrict the right of Protestants to worship and organise themselves as they saw fit? The outbreak of the Crimean War, a few years later, also saw much predictable emphasis on the virtues being displayed, across class, by Englishmen on the field of battle. Charles Kingsley, a muscular and Protestant Christian, (one of Lord Acton's professorial predecessors in Cambridge), and a man whose thousand word sermons were thought of admirable length by Queen Victoria, believed that England's people had physical strength, animal courage and the self-dependence of freemen. 'Religious reform' should not unsettle this glorious national character.[7]

Turning to Democracy

The years 1867-70, however, constituted some kind of turning point. A number of matters appeared to be coming to a head and were not altogether unrelated in their consequences and implications. Politically, in the United Kingdom, they saw further reform of the franchise and thus a further venturing into the problematic world of 'democracy'. Ecclesiastically, they saw the Vatican Council and the interpretation placed upon its proceedings in the British Isles. Militarily, they saw the Franco-Prussian war, with its implications for the European balance, and for the United Kingdom in particular. Philosophers could and did continue to reflect on the nature of 'the state' along lines which have just been sketched. Whatever ideas might gain ascendancy, a governing elite had to reach a further accommodation with 'the people', an accommodation which would have to have a religious dimension.

73

---

[5] Cited in Wolffe, "British Protestants and Europe", 215.
[6] Norman, *Anti-Catholicism in Victorian England*, 21. Dr. Norman rightly observes, in introducing his collection of pertinent documents, that the agitation became the vehicle for discussing very significant alterations in the religious office of the state itself.
[7] Mandler, *The English National Character*, 68-72.

The 'Liberal Era' had begun. Matters which have been dealt with by Professor Brown in the first half of the nineteenth century, and which have also been alluded to in the foregoing introductory remarks, seemed to be settling into a new context. Reform, considered as the conscious pursuit of renewal, with the aim of adapting organised religion to the changing relations between church, state and society, had reached a significant stage. 'Adapting organised religion' is of course a two-way process. It is necessarily difficult to disentangle internally generated adaptation on the part of religious bodies from change imposed upon them either by specific legislative enactment or by wider patterns of social change. The thrust of this volume remains with the adaptations within the structure of 'church and state' brought about through the political process. In the United Kingdom, 'reform' reached a new juncture. The latter has mulled over the problems posed by the way in which some ecclesiastical historians of nineteenth-century Britain have suggested that by mid-century the 'age of reform' had in fact come to an end. Further, for decades, notwithstanding a frequent identification of a 'long nineteenth century' extending to 1914, general British historians of Britain have made a break at 1870 or thereabouts. For example, an influential volume in the Oxford History of England covering the years 1815-1870, had as title *The Age of Reform*. The author of the successor volume had earlier wisely stuck to dates and refrained from an attempted characterisation. In another widely used more recent series Eric Evans concluded *The Forging of the Modern State* in 1870. This present author followed it with a 'Modern Britain' which began at that date. From the point of view of this chapter, too, it is worth remarking that this transition point is roughly half way in the life of the state 'Great Britain and Ireland', though of course contemporaries could not be aware of that fact. Other well-known historians have concerned themselves with the 'mid-Victorian' generation in a hey-day which they have identified as having come to an end in the late 1860s or early 1870s. Historians with an explicitly political focus have likewise taken comparable dates. This is clearly not the place to embark on a protracted discussion of the merits of one or other attempt at a periodization of insular history. A continuing historical engagement with 'the Victorian Age' (1837-1901) as a totality remains an entirely plausible activity.

That said, however, domestically, in the United Kingdom, the 1832 'reform' settlement, which had supposedly been 'full and final' was under sustained pressure in the late 1860s and with it the *modus vivendi* which had been achieved over those decades in relation to 'church politics'. Individuals whose careers had been forged in the 1840s now found themselves centre-stage. For hundreds of thousands, John Bright became an icon. It might seem an unlikely prominence. Quakers were a very small but distinctive sect. Many of them had frowned on direct political activity, but Bright, a Lancashire cotton mill owner, had begun his career by campaigning against church rates and then, together with the Anglican, Richard Cobden, had campaigned with great vigour against the Corn Laws. He had opposed the Crimean War. His career recovered momentum when he toured the country addressing major meetings in the cause of further parliamentary reform. "Let us try the nation" he cried in Glasgow in October 1866. In addresses to vast audiences in England, Ireland and Scotland, he declared that justice would not be obtained from a class but only from the whole nation, the whole people.[8] The British Constitution should be 'restored' to them and government would no longer be conducted by a privileged class in a sham parliament. Freedom's battle had been joined. The Church of England, conceived as a part of this privileged order, had long been in his sights. He had been disgusted by the Protestant/National 'outrage' at the restoration of the Catholic hierarchy, considering that the Prime Minister, Lord John Russell was sinking into 'hopeless imbecility'. The agitation, he thought, was not intended to discredit Popery because it was Popery but because it threatened the English and Irish Establishments. To talk of the nation, its Crown and independence being menaced by a petty sovereign at Rome was 'too ludicrous'. Fellow MPs would know that, as a Quaker, he was no friend to any bishops but if the Anglican Church needed them he saw no reason why the Roman Church should not have them also.[9] The 'moral revolution' of which Bright was the symbol would not distinguish between political and ecclesiastical reform. They were one and the same. That a Quaker could appear to lead this campaign was itself significant. He was an 'outsider' pitched against that nexus of the Church of England, the public (i.e. private) schools (which had been mushrooming in number and with only a few exceptions were Anglican in ethos), and Oxford and Cambridge universities, whose products dominated the political system at its highest levels.

75

It was, however, a Conservative government, with Derby and Disraeli at the helm, which in 1867 had taken a 'leap in the dark' and passed a new parliamentary Reform Act. A flamboyant novelist had risen to the top of the greasy pole of politics. Disraeli, too, was an 'outsider' in a different sense from Bright. He had been baptised into the Church of England but, in his imagination, as has been much emphasised recently, he identified himself as a Jew. He was scarcely a 'typical Church of England man'. It was unusual, in European terms, to find a Jew, even a baptised Jew, at the helm of a Conservative party. After a decade of controversy, which broadly but not entirely followed party lines, with Whigs in favour and Tories against, the question of the admission of practising Jews to parliament had been settled in their favour in 1858. Twenty years later, a Jew received a peerage and entered the House of Lords. When she entertained her new baron at Windsor Castle the queen ordered the kitchens to prepare a special harmless pie for dinner. On her accession, she had thought it 'quite right' that she should be the first British monarch to confer a knighthood on a Jew. In itself, these steps were a fundamental breach in the notion of parliament as a Christian assembly. It has been suggested that by this juncture Jews were increasingly portrayed as Englishmen rather than foreigners - in the cartons of the magazine *Punch* for example. There was no reason why they could not be perceived as 'model citizens'.[10] This cautious accommodation - not without some reservations amongst Jews themselves who were apprehensive that in 'conforming' the distinctiveness of Jewish belief and

---

[8] Joyce, "The Narrative Structure of Victorian Politics".
[9] Robbins, *John Bright*, 87-88.

[10] Gibson, *Church, State and Society*, 164-167; Morris, "1798-1992: Les Juifs de Grande-Bretagne", 236-238.

J. Tenniel, Disraeli and Queen Victoria Exchanging Gifts, *cartoon published in* Punch, *15 April 1876.*
[Leuven, K.U.Leuven, Centrale bibliotheek: Z2065]

practice might be obscured. It has been noted that the Chief Rabbi wore not merely the gaiters associated with an Anglican bishop but imitation went so far as to sport a quasi-episcopal shovel hat.[11] The immediate post-emancipation generation, it is suggested, feeling itself to be 'on trial', considered itself under an obligation to conform to Gentile expectations of acceptable Jewish behaviour.[12] Tensions were further exacerbated by the arrival of Jews from Russia later in the century, leading by 1914 to a Jewish population of over 300,000 compared with 60,000 in 1880. The scale of this immigration, too, led directly into the Aliens Act (1905) aimed at curbing this inflow, though a door was still open for those who were fleeing persecution. It was, of course, the 'Jewish Question', if it was a religious question, which brought into sharp focus the extent to which state allegiance, national or ethnic identity and religious affiliation formed a seamless web. That question appeared to have been answered. No such commonality could be required by the state in the matter of 'membership'. It was 'toleration' applied to a 'minority'. Christians, if they were so minded, could continue to seek to convert Jews, though the state gave no explicit encouragement to such an objective. It seemed reasonable to suppose that 'alien' minorities as a whole would remain very small (between 1841 and 1871, the number of aliens had only increased from 0.25% of the population to 0.44% of the population of England and Wales).[13] Islam and South Asian religions also made their small appearance, though naturally it was 'back home' in the British Empire that the United Kingdom government encountered such adherents. Supporters of missionary societies in the United Kingdom, and missionaries 'in the field' by no means invariably saw themselves in accord with government, either at home or also 'in the field', anxious about the extent to which Christian activity would threaten stability and order.

77

The question of 'citizenship' - what it entailed, who possessed it and who did not - was a common issue in all Western European societies at this juncture. The inhabitants of the United Kingdom, however, were 'subjects' rather than 'citizens'. Their allegiance was to the Crown, and in this case to the queen whose very long reign gave the 'age' a symbolic coherence. She was a queen who became an empress, though only of India. Earlier, when Britain took formal control over India she had proclaimed herself to be firmly relying on the truth of Christianity but she had informed her Indian subjects that she disclaimed both the right and desire to impose her convictions on them. Moreover, a woman was playing the 'male' role of sovereign. She exercised it in a society in which women had no formal place in the political process. It was indubitable that the monarchy was 'constitutional' and 'limited' but the queen by no means saw herself without 'influence', and perhaps more. The monarchy was 'popular', though not invariably so.

The Crown embodied the unity of the United Kingdom. Royal deaths, it is argued, in particular the funerals of 1884 and 1892, complemented the jubilees of 1887 and 1897. Civil religion blended almost seamlessly into that of orthodox Chris-

---

[11] Newman, "The Jewish Presence in Britain and France", 262.

[12] Alderman, *Modern British Jewry*, 71.
[13] Fahrmeir, *Citizenship*, 79.

tianity.[14] Archbishops, some with some reluctance, were inevitably drawn into jubilee celebrations. Archbishop Temple, in 1897, showed more awareness than most of the problems posed for the service in St Paul's cathedral by the fact of Her Majesty's latter-day incontinence.[15] Royal visits sought to cement the unity of the kingdom. In Scotland, the castle at Balmoral gave the queen and her family a regular base and a 'Scottish face'. No royal home existed in Wales.[16] Visits to Ireland, at different times, evoked varied responses. The monarch could not but be the emblem of power.[17] She could not be the embodiment of her state's ecclesiastical unity, for there was no ecclesiastical unity. In 1867 she was still the Supreme Governor of the Church of England with its Welsh dioceses and supposedly 'united' with the Church of Ireland. It was a church in which, outside England, English bishops were not uncommon.[18] Bishops were appointed by the Crown on the advice of the Prime Minister. As a breed, she did not apparently greatly care for bishops. The advice which she received in relation to particular appointments was not invariably what she wanted to hear or in which she lamely acquiesced.[19] In her ecclesiastical role she was again a woman in a man's world. Prime Ministers, some of whom might not be thought to be especially 'religious' were prepared to give a good deal of attention to this aspect of their duties.[20] She appointed a 'Lord High Commissioner', on an annual basis, to the General Assembly of the Church of Scotland but she had no authority over the Kirk. It was, however, in an Anglo-Scottish context, that in 1873 she took what might be thought her most symbolically significant ecclesiastical step. When at Balmoral, she worshipped in Crathie parish church (Church of Scotland), contrary to the view that the leading Anglican lay person should only worship in the Scottish Episcopal Church. She found the service at Crathie congenial. In that year, however, she decided to go further. She would receive the sacrament. 'Her' two churches were not in communion with each other. She boldly went where churchmen feared to tread and there was at least one public claim that the church was in great peril from a Kirk-going queen.[21] What message did that send out in a democratising age, not only about the relationship between the two 'national' and 'established' churches, but also, at least by implication, on how the Crown had to position itself in relation to a religious Nonconformity? In 1867 the queen had told her eldest daughter that in religion she was "very nearly a Dissenter", though she qualified that by saying "rather more a Presbyterian". For their part, at the successive jubilees of her reign, English Dissenters were very ready to present loyal addresses. To one in 1887 she replied repeating her conviction, confirmed by experience, of the beneficial results which flowed from "a large and generous toleration extended to every form

[14] So argues Wolffe in *Great Deaths*, 218-219.
[15] Hinchliff, *Frederick Temple*, 271.
[16] But see Davies, "Victoria and Victorian Wales".
[17] Paseta, "Nationalist Responses to Two Royal Visits to Ireland".
[18] Robbins, "England, Englishmen and the Church of England".
[19] Bahlman, "The Queen, Mr Gladstone and Church Patronage".
[20] Wolffe, "Lord Palmerston and Religion".
[21] Chadwick, "The Sacrament at Crathie, 1873".

W. Monk, The Royal Jubilee Celebrations at
St Paul's Cathedral, *etching, 1897.*
[Private collection]

of earnest religious belief". [22] Notwithstanding such acknowledgement, however, the occasions on which the queen came into direct contact with English/Welsh Dissent were few. The ambience of the Court was Anglican. Even so, as Dr Parker, celebrated Congregationalist minister of the London City Temple remarked on Victoria's death in 1901 that from their heart of hearts Nonconformists were intensely loyal: "We all loved the Queen. Everybody wanted to start the National Anthem whenever it was hinted at in any public Nonconformist assembly".[23]

'Toleration', however, was what an 'Establishment' conceded. The queen had her own likes and dislikes about the Church of England - and her vast network of European connections also gave her a range of familiarity with Lutheranism and Orthodoxy beyond the knowledge of her subjects - but she was firm that it should be established. England would not be England without that nexus of church and state which stemmed, ultimately, from the Henrician Reformation and the Elizabethan Settlement. She was instrumental in ending the annual Anglican commemoration of the foiling of the

---

[22] Cited in Arnstein, "Queen Victoria and Religion", 114. Various other observations made in this section are also indebted to this article.

[23] Adamson, *The Life of the Rev. Joseph Parker*, 328.

Gunpowder Plot of 1603, but she could not think of a monarchy which could be divorced from the Church of England. The one buttressed the other. Pope Pius IX's actions in restoring the Roman Catholic 'Hierarchy' seemed to her "in the highest degree wrong" and a direct infringement of her prerogative. She had not opposed the Ecclesiastical Titles Act, though she thought public abuse of the Roman Catholic religion "unchristian and unwise". She was proud of her generous pan-Protestantism. What upset her was the evident lack, as she perceived it, of any disposition on the part of the Papacy to show tolerance. Papal Infallibility upset her as much as it did Lord Acton, though there is no record of the queen contemplating setting off a mine. It followed, she thought, taking a not unsympathetic interpretation of Bismarck's *Kulturkampf*, that all over Europe, notably in Prussia and Ireland, there was "an attempt made to resist authority and to defy it, by the Priesthood". She told her daughter in Potsdam that "we should all try and unite the Protestant Churches as much as possible together in order to make a strong front and protest against sacerdotal tyranny". But who were the 'all' who should do this? What did 'the democracy' think?

The Reform Acts of 1867-1868 applying in England and Wales and different in detail in Ireland and Scotland, meant that one in three of the adult male population was given the vote in parliamentary elections. The 'secret ballot' came in 1872. Further reforms in 1884-1885 extended the UK electorate so that, roughly speaking, in 1886 two in three males in England and Wales, three in five in Scotland and one in two in Ireland were enfranchised. There was no further change in the parliamentary franchise until the end of the First World War when the Representation of the People Act (1918), by abolishing the property qualification for voting, enfranchised virtually the entire adult male population and for the first time enfranchised women - over the age of 30. 'Votes for women' had been acutely controversial in the pre-war decade. Enfranchisement, of course, was only one aspect of the story. It does not tell us how registration was carried out, who actually voted, what type of constituency existed, what kind of plural voting still survived and so on. There was room for controversy on all these matters. These reform measures were generally taken to be steps along the road to 'democracy' but it was never clear quite what democracy was. 'People power' - the power of 'the masses' might be a brutish thing unless it could be 'educated' (1870 saw the passage of a significant Education Act in England and Wales).[24] These changes were presented and celebrated as part of a glorious nineteenth-century constitutional evolution: one measure at a time. Change took place within continuity. That was the country's particular genius. It was not accompanied by formal declarations which purported to set out rights and embody them in legal codes. The queen sat firmly on the throne and seemed likely, as British queens regnant tend to do, to sit for ever. Trying to find out how this great imperial power worked politically, therefore, was a puzzling business. Various

---

[24] Education forms an obvious element, into the twentieth century, in church/state relations but, since it is being given explicit treatment in another volume, it is merely alluded to here. Its modest mention, however, should not be taken as suggesting that it was not important, perhaps central.

constitutional writers tried to disentangle ceremony and reality, without invariable success.

Continuity seemed further evident in the maintenance, substantially, of a 'two-party system': Tories/Conservatives and Whig/Liberals. Such labels, as in all political parties, were stuck over coalitions of interest and ideology of fluctuating influence. As a generalisation, though in particulars not much more than one, the commonplace assumption was that Tories were for 'Church' and Liberals were for 'Dissent'. The underlying reality, however, was that neither political party, in search of an electoral majority sought too explicit an identification, even if elements in each wished to do so. Notwithstanding the expansion of the franchise, the two great parties oscillated in office. The 'Liberal Era' may have begun in 1868 but it did not last. Gladstonian Liberals (1868-1874) were followed by Disraelian Conservatives (1874-1880) and then, after further oscillation, a decade of Conservative government (1895-1905) and Liberal government (1905-1915) followed by wartime and immediate post-war Coalition. Even so, both parties had sustained major and damaging splits - the Liberals over Irish Home Rule and the Conservatives, in the Edwardian period, over Free Trade. They both presented themselves to the electorate as 'national' bodies whose platforms and programmes were not to be identified with any particular 'class' interest (supposing it was known what a 'class interest' might be). This might or might not be rhetoric. It certainly meant that this same period did not witness the rapid growth of a socialist party. The Labour Party that did emerge was nervous about the word socialist and its modest representation in the House of Commons seemed sometimes part of a 'Lib-Lab' family. That a further extension of the franchise might change this position was probably one reason for delaying it.

81

Such a degree of apparent political/constitutional consensus does not of course imply the absence of partisan politics in relation to particular issues and the inevitable personal rivalries. But it does mean that there was no fundamental divide which split the country between, on the one hand, what we may lump together as a 'Christian-Conservative' segment and on the other a 'Secular-Liberal-Socialist'. Acton was an English Liberal who was very fearful of what he saw as the anticlerical, nationalist and state-centred disposition of 'continental' liberalism. That is not to say that there was no 'secularism'. The atheist Bradlaugh was elected to the Commons in 1880 and claimed the right to affirm his allegiance instead of taking the oath. He was thrice re-elected before he was finally allowed to take his seat in 1886. Bradlaugh, of course, was not only an atheist but had led the republican campaign.[25] It is little surprise that the queen found his "horrible principles" a disgrace to an assembly like the House of Commons. The admission of avowed and campaigning secularists naturally raised questions about parliament and 'the church'. They were, of course, not new ones but the context was shifting. What is important, however, is to remember that the issues cannot be considered in terms of a contest, collision or conflict (whichever word we

---

[25] D'Arcy, "Charles Bradlaugh".

prefer) between 'the United Kingdom State' on the one hand and 'the United Kingdom Church' on the other for, as has earlier been stressed, although there was a *state* there was no *church*. Whether there was a *nation* or rather a plurality of *nations* was something the democratising of politics was perhaps bringing to the fore. In all these matters, the long arm of history remained potent. It was this complex reality which made 'reform' so difficult.

The figure of William Gladstone dominates the late-Victorian stage. In 1894, at the age of 84, he resigned for the fourth (and last) time as Prime Minister. It almost seemed as though all contemporary currents - national and ecclesiastical - swelled about his person. 'Events' had caused him, over time, to have abandoned notions about the church in its relationship with the state which he had expressed as a young man. A Tory had become a Liberal. The government which he formed in 1868 marked a further stage in the dismantling of ecclesiastical privilege. It had as one of its major objectives the removal of practices which had come to be the preserve of a particular social group or category. It included a Quaker, John Bright, who found himself surprised but not displeased, to be driven to Windsor Castle. It could look, publicly, as though Dissent had arrived. The reality was that he was ill, probably idle and certainly ineffective as an administrator, but he had a symbolic function.[26] Despite occasional public rhetoric on the matter he had not in fact taken a lead in the matter of disestablishment - perhaps a Quaker was too far on the periphery of Nonconformity to do so.[27] If he did show signs of Dissenting vigour it did not prove difficult for the Prime Minister to slap him down, as one historian has gently put it.[28] Where England was concerned, Gladstone would not countenance disestablishment. In writing to a friend in 1874 he showed consummate obscurity: "I do not feel the dread of disestablishment which you probably entertain: but I desire and seek, so long as standing ground remains, to avert, not to precipitate it". However, he took pains to establish working relationships with prominent Nonconformists and a good deal of mutual admiration took place founded, so it seemed, on a common moral vision. Dr Newman Hall, prominent Congregationalist, went so far in 1897 as to wait for two hours, solitarily, on the platform at Willesden Junction in expectation that he would be able to shake hands with the Grand Old Man as the train taking him from Euston to Hawarden briefly stopped. He was not disappointed. Mrs Gladstone waved her handkerchief as the train moved off. Hall was inevitably among the reverent multitudes around the object of a nation's honour in Westminster Hall the following year.[29]

Despite this adulation, however, it would be misleading to suppose that there was no concerted campaign against the 'state church', but it could never come to a satisfactory peak. There was no lack of effort on the part of the Society for the Liberation of Religion from State Patronage and Control as the Anti-State Church Society had

82

---

[26] Matthew, *Gladstone 1809-1874*, 179-180.
[27] Parry, *Democracy and religion*, 227.

[28] Bentley, *Climax of Liberal Politics*, 58; Robbins, "John Bright and William Gladstone".
[29] Hall, *An Autobiography*, 289-291.

William Gladstone as a battering ram, calling for
disestablishment, *cartoon published in* Judy, *1874.*
[Brussels, Royal Library: E. Fuchs, Die Karikatur
der europäischen Völker vom Jahre 1848 bis zum
Gegenwart *(Berlin, 1903), 277]*

become. Its campaigning could point to some weakening of the outer ramparts but
the bastion remained. It seemed that it remained because in England, given what has
been said about the structure of party politics, there was insufficient appetite. In 1885,
in a treatise, Henry Richard and J. Carvell Williams suggested that the "practical and
persistent character of the English intellect" would prove equal to the challenge.[30] They
were disappointed. Clear expositions of the view that just as a national church was one
of the great impediments to missionary success, so "an Established Church, uttering
as it does law rather than grace or Gospel is *qua* established, in standing contradiction
to the first principle of the religion for which it exists" were listened to, but could not
carry the day.[31] The practical and persistent character of the English intellect, even as it
manifested itself in English Dissent, seemed not to be so moved by these cogent views
from Welshmen and a Scot, respectively.

The universities of Oxford, Cambridge and Durham could no longer impose religious 'Tests' which had been used either to exclude those who would not subscribe
or to withhold their degrees. This again marked a further removal, or at least erosion,
of Anglican privilege. The application of the legislation was monitored closely by

---

[30] Richard and Williams, *Disestablishment*, 142.   [31] Forsyth, *The Charter of the Church*, vi.

Dissenters, who failed in their aspiration to remove the Oxford Chair of Ecclesiastical History, for example, from clerical restriction. They also failed - in a *cause célèbre* - to persuade Oxford's Convocation that R.F. Horton, a Congregational Fellow of New College, was a suitable person to examine in the Rudiments of Faith and Religion.[32] The trend, however, was clear. A college founded by Congregationalists, Mansfield, came to Oxford and, over time, mitigated the university's Anglican character somewhat. All the principal Nonconformist groups were a little later to have colleges in one or other of the ancient universities. One the one hand, such moves showed that the ecclesiastical playing field, if not level, had lost the steepness of its slope. On the other, however, such assimilation might well weaken the distinctiveness of Nonconformity. The editor of the Nonconformist *British Weekly* was not alone in forecasting that in a short time Mansfield would become "a pillar of the Church of England".[33] What might be true of Mansfield and Oxford University might apply in time, and perhaps not a distant time, when the coherence of Dissent/Nonconformity could not be sustained. What was there left to dissent from? If so, it had not arrived. The Liberal Cabinets of 1905-1915 contained a higher proportion of Nonconformists, at least by some measures, than any of their predecessors. The number of Nonconformist MPs, very largely Liberal, looked impressive. Here was 'the Nonconformist Conscience' in action, or at least on the back-benches of the House of Commons. But in England and Scotland the churches were still 'established'. Parity, it seemed, had dribbled down over the final decades of the nineteenth century. It had not been accompanied by or been part of a concerted programme of 'disestablishment'. "We are finding ourselves disestablished almost everywhere", the Bishop of Oxford told the House of Lords in 1913, "except in the lunatic asylums". He was speaking in the matter of the provision of chaplaincies. 'Almost everywhere', of course, did not extend to membership of the House which he was addressing.[34]

Nonconformists struggled to see themselves, and to get others to see them, in a positive light. To describe themselves as being Free Churches was to be positive rather than negative. The Church of England, as such, had no separate legislative or even deliberative body of its own. It was subordinated to parliament. Such a condition, of course, as it is considered in depth by authors in the companion volume, had become increasingly uncomfortable to certain 'parties' within the church. Such Erastianism, if that was the right term, no longer satisfied those in its ranks who wished to assert its 'apostolic' authenticity. The Body of Christ should not be restricted and subordinated. Let the church be the church. If this waxing view should triumph, it would, ultimately, demolish the English national church on the basis on which it had existed. That might turn out to be the case, but as things stood Acts of parliament, in relation to ecclesiastical matters, were supreme. 'Royal supremacy', of course, had a long history. It had become deeply engrained in constitutional and legal formularies. It was part of the

---

[32] Manning, *Protestant Dissenting Deputies*, 379.   [34] Cited in Nicholls, ed., *Church and State*, 5.
[33] Johnson, *The Dissolution of Dissent*, 233.

landscape. Some thought that the pattern that had evolved made England what it was. You could not start tampering with one bit of this structure without endangering the whole edifice that was England. Parliament was properly 'the voice of the church'. It was, or was supposed to be, full of laymen who understood and truly 'represented' at least the men if not the women in the pew. 'Ritualism' for example was not something which the Church of England could simply 'decide for itself'. It was quite proper for parliament to legislate in relation to it, as, successively, it attempted to do.[35] The queen did not like ritualism. Early in the twentieth century, it still seemed proper for a Prime Minister to appoint a Royal Commission to consider the problem and to come to some kind of conclusion (though whether that conclusion could work was another matter). It happened to be the case that the Prime Minister concerned, A.J. Balfour had a deep interest in religion and had done something which no other Prime Minister had done, that is publish a philosophical defence of Theism, but that was accidental.[36] His uncle, and predecessor, Lord Salisbury, had also been a committed churchman but one who felt that religion was in danger of losing its proper and beneficial place in national life because of the clergy who threatened to hi-jack it and turn it into a club which they controlled. Parliament should remain in charge.

Yet all of this was, or was rapidly becoming, a fiction, for a variety of reasons. It was not that the political elite (if we can use such a loose term here) had been entranced by anti-clericalism or secularism and that there was therefore a great gap between what MPs were supposed to do constitutionally in relation to the church and what they themselves actually believed. What remains striking is the reality of the Christian faith and practice to be found amongst the political elite - not that such commitments necessarily had the same theological or political consequences. There was no lack of laymen in the House of Commons, across the parties, whose interest in ecclesiastical matters was serious and sustained. The fiction lay in the notion that they were all Church of England men and thus that the House was really equipped to govern the church. The examples already quoted make it clear that non-Christians were present and their number seemed probably likely to grow. It might be that Jews or adherents of other religions, should there be any, might not be averse to 'establishment' (of the Church of England) as a recognition of the value of 'religion' and perhaps, therefore, some form of protection for themselves as religious minorities - but that was not clear. Strong secularists and atheists, however, would clearly wish to confine religion to the private sphere.

The more significant reality, however, touched on the fictions which underpinned the United Kingdom and which bound it together in a pre-democratic age. The widening of the electorate exposed in all its 'territories', to one degree or another, a 'national' sentiment of uncertain political import. The relationship between ecclesiastical politics and 'ordinary' politics was problematic. It might be that an adjustment

---

[35] See the discussion of the Public Worship Regulation Act in Yates, *Anglican Ritualism*, 235-276.

[36] Adams, *Balfour: The Last Grandee*, 126-129.

of 'establishment', most specifically in Ireland and Wales, would be not only an act of 'justice' but would form part of a mollifying process of political adjustment. It might help to keep the state together, albeit on a different basis, one in which any pretence at the hegemony of a particular church would be abandoned. It might, on the other hand have no such benefit. It might be interpreted as an acknowledgement of Westminster weakness. Far from strengthening the United Kingdom, it would only encourage further political fissiparousness. Further, if the logic of 'disestablishment' was that the state should give no special pre-eminence to any church (that is to say it would not be something which disestablished one church in order to establish another more 'popular' one) then there might well be a 'knock-on' consequence for the Church of England in England. If a state were to 'disestablish' in one part of its territories would it want to, would it be able to, maintain 'establishment' in its most populous and powerful part, namely England. And by 'the state' one means here a government/parliament drawn from across the United Kingdom. The presence of non-Anglican and non-English MPs in the Westminster parliament inevitably meant that, if they chose to use them, they could influence the policy and stance of the Church of England. Put another way, however, was it the case that ecclesiastical policy in Ireland or Wales could, or should, be determined by a parliament in which English MPs were in the majority?

86

The Church of England continued, nonetheless, to behave as though it were the state-church of the United Kingdom. A royal coronation took place within a service of the Church of England. There was no place for any other church. Ex-Presbyterian Scots who became archbishops of Canterbury wanted to keep it that way. Spectacularly 'disrupted' in 1843, the Church of Scotland was in no position to show political muscle within 'Great Britain'. In any case, a disproportionate number of Scottish MPs were Scottish Episcopalians and, while this might make them sensitive to its particular ethos - its ethos was not 'just like the Church of England' - they were not likely to clamour for increased public recognition of the 'two church' character of the British state. Scotland now manifested three main Presbyterian bodies - the Church of Scotland, the Free Church of Scotland and the United Presbyterian Church. The precise nature of the theological and ecclesiological differences between these bodies largely escaped English opinion. These were Scottish matters, it was supposed, to be legally resolved in Scotland, even though the nature (if any) of 'establishment' in Scotland was one of the elements in the divisions that existed and whose resolution might in turn have implications, or at least repercussions, in the United Kingdom as a whole.

'Church and state in Scotland' and 'church and state in England' manifested untidy differences and upset those who looked for uniformity in the British state. On the whole, however, divergence was seen as simply one element in that deal which, for better or for worse, had been struck in 1707. It was not, of course, a deal which had been struck 'democratically'. The advent of democracy might cause it to unravel, at least to the extent of a 'Home Rule' for Scotland. In the absence of such political change, however, the notion of a 'Christian Commonwealth' suffused with Presbyterianism made Scotland 'different'.

R.C. Woodville, The Archbishop of Canterbury crowning Edward VII in Westminster Abbey, *plate published in* The Illustrated London News Record of the Coronation Service and Ceremony. King Edward VII and Queen Alexandra *(June 26, 1902) (London, 1902).*
[Leuven, K.U.Leuven, Centrale bibliotheek: BRES 5C485]

Scotland had an ecclesiastical constitution. Wales had not. There was no Church of Wales, just as there was no different legal or educational system. The Wales of the 1530s was not the Scotland of 1707. Its dioceses were part of the Church of England, and most of its diocesans had been Englishmen. By 1870, however, the situation was not comfortable. On the one hand, there was an agitation within the church in Wales that it should have 'Welsh bishops' and thus demonstrate that it was not 'the English Church' in Wales. A campaign was firmly on foot to disestablish the Church of England in Wales. Census figures, two decades earlier, had revealed that in aggregate, religious Dissenters outnumbered adherents of the church, though like any figures there could be much argument about what that actually meant. The argument was simple. The church was not that of the majority. It should therefore not be treated by the state as though it was. To see substance in this argument, however, was to accept that 'Wales' was an entity capable of being defined and be accorded ecclesiastical arrangements which were not those of England. Campaigners, heavily conscious of Welsh linguistic and cultural distinctiveness and capable of portraying the established church as 'English', had no doubt that Wales needed separate recognition. The struggle carried on throughout the decades under review, achieving parliamentary success on the eve of the First World War. The church in Wales came into its existence as an Anglican province at its conclusion with its own hierarchy. It believed that the terms of its disestablishment and disendowment were unduly harsh. Most of its leading figures had opposed the creation with which they had now been saddled and had to make the best of a bad job. A Liberal government, with non-English MPs disproportionately present at Cabinet level and with Wales massively Liberal in its political representation had agreed to this step. Unless Wales had threatened to become ungovernable, as was sometimes supposed might happen, a Conservative government would not have done so. The Church of England hierarchy in England, with only a few exceptions, had campaigned against disestablishment in Wales. The majority of bishops saw Welsh developments as a precedent for England itself. Yet, if a majority of the people worshipped outside the established church how, in a democratising age, could establishment be justified? The ballot box should be where these matters were settled. The result, by 1920, was that Great Britain consisted of three territories with different church-state relationships.[37]

Wales was not the first territory within the then United Kingdom in which disestablishment had taken place. In 1869 the incoming Gladstonian Liberal government, which had gained its majority the previous year in the first general election under the new franchise, had disestablished the Church of Ireland. It had been, in theory at least, 'united' with the Church of England but its reality was as a separate entity. That it was a minority church was not contestable. If numbers were what counted in a democratic age, its 'established' existence could not be justified. Of course, notwithstanding the Irish-British Union of 1800, for a Westminster government to take such a step was

88

---

[37] Robbins, "Establishing Disestablishment".

to recognise that Ireland was different. From a general political standpoint that logic had become inescapable. A part of the United Kingdom, the only part with a substantial Roman Catholic majority, had to be treated differently. The Presbyterian presence in large numbers in Ulster meant that the Church of Ireland was not even the 'voice of Protestantism'. Ecclesiastical reform in Ireland, therefore, from the standpoint of the London government was necessary in the interests of the political stability of the United Kingdom. It might not in itself be sufficient to achieve this end. Queen Victoria, for one, thought that Irish Church disestablishment was an ill-advised appeasement. She wrote to her Prime Minister that to give way to the Catholics in the hope of conciliating them would not do. They would take everything and not be grateful for it. The history of other countries taught that it was an impossibility to treat them with perfect equality. However, she could not stop her new 'Liberal' government having its way. A Church of Ireland had to endure, as it saw it, the agony of disendowment and its disengagement from its hegemonic status within Ireland. It had to frame a new constitution for itself. It had to work out a way of appointing its own bishops, now that the Crown no longer exercised this right. It scarcely needs to be said that the Irish Church Act was not merely a 'church' matter. The Church of Ireland resisted Catholic complaints that it had no business to call itself the Church of Ireland. It continued to assert that it was 'national', though the nationalism of its members was predominantly a 'unionist nationalism' which had no wish to end the political union. But, of course, a settlement of the church question was only one facet of the British-Irish question. Gladstone was himself, subsequently and unavailingly, and at the cost of splitting his party, to seek to bring 'Home Rule' to Ireland. Queen Victoria's anxieties about Catholicism of thirty years earlier were modified. On her Dublin visit in 1900 she made a point of visiting Roman Catholic institutions. But it was all too late.

In combination, therefore, on the eve of the First World War the United Kingdom was a state in which no 'recognition' was accorded to any church in two of its territories (Ireland and, but lately and still somewhat problematically, Wales) and in which, in its other two, 'establishments' of different kinds prevailed. Differences, however, went even deeper. The disestablishment in Ireland took place against the reality of another church which commanded the allegiance of the majority of the population. It was a church deeply if problematically enmeshed in a national movement. The Irish Home Rule party at Westminster constituted a unique solid bloc. Elsewhere party politics was 'British' if with some individual flavours. The United Kingdom state had no option, in the end, in educational and other spheres, but to come to an accommodation with the Catholic hierarchy. Disestablishment in Wales, however, was different. There was no other single church which commanded the allegiance of the majority of the population. A 'Nonconformist' majority had carried the day but Nonconformity, putting it crudely, was only united in its combined opposition to the established church. Baptists, Congregationalists/Independents and Methodists (Calvinistic and Wesleyan) all had their distinctive tenets. They were not disposed to come together. Post-disestablishment, they continued most frequently to be referred to as 'Nonconformists' but there was now nothing to 'conform' to, though the reality was that the aura of establishment continued to exist in the Church of Wales, not least because its cathedrals continued to seem in some sense 'civic spheres'.

It is this complexity which makes it impossible to suppose that 'church reform' followed one simple line in the United Kingdom between 1870 and 1920. It could, of course, be argued that the most significant change took place on the 'periphery'. The politico-religious pressure from Dissenters (in Ireland, Roman Catholic (and, to a degree, Presbyterians) and in Wales, Protestant), had compelled UK/London governments to abandon that English-style intermingling of church and state which had hitherto done duty. The social and cultural hierarchies which had sustained these structures were left to fend for themselves in the new situation. This 'withdrawal' had not been easy or painless. It did entail a recognition of diversity and, to a very large extent, of parity of esteem, at least formally. The heritage of a Protestant state and a Protestant monarchy could not be abandoned overnight. The fact that these 'withdrawals' took place in stages, however, perhaps testifies to the notion that the state (in the form of the governments of the day) was not implementing some grand strategy of 'secularisation', determined to oust the churches from 'the public sphere'. Disestablishment had arisen from Christian pressure, as churches sought to achieve a 'level playing field' as between themselves. The vigour of their campaigns was sustained by the extent to which they also tapped into the political, economic and cultural grievances of the communities in which they existed. In Ireland, in 1920, the extent of that *conjoncture* became apparent. 'Catholic' and 'Protestant' states were imminent.

Yet it could still be thought that England was 'sound'. There were secularist voices calling for disestablishment but again the pressure, such as it was, came from Protestant Dissenters who had been active, in campaigning mode, from the 1840s onwards. From time to time, particularly in periods of Liberal political ascendancy, they appeared to make some progress but the reality was that the Dissenting element was only one within the coalition that was the Liberal Party. The other reality was that there was no Dissenting majority (be it Catholic or Protestant) in England. There was, however, a steady growth of Nonconformist representation - usually Liberal - in the House of Commons culminating in a sense of triumph in the parliament elected in 1906. Yet even this representation was not a sufficient base from which to mount an assault on the position of the Church of England. The 'democratic' card could not be played. Governments were not under sufficient pressure to cause them to wish to unpick 'church and state' as it existed in England. They might find it irritating, amidst all the other pressing concerns of a global power, to have to have some concern with its problems, but the mood of Liberal England was not that of France. From 1870 onwards, governments had continued to legislate away exclusions which had applied to Dissenters, Protestant or Catholic, as incompatible with a 'liberal state', though that is not to say that there were not still some symbolic restrictions (not least the monarchy itself). In turn, the social solidarities which had been cemented by common exclusions began to lose their potency - particularly amongst Protestant Nonconformists. It looked as though England was muddling through again. The UK as a whole had not become a 'laicised state'.

But what was it? Dissenters had never counted themselves to be 'an ecclesiastical part of the state'. Baptists, Congregationalists and Methodists had, as we have noted, great respect for the queen - though less for her son and his lifestyle - but they did not believe that any church needed a 'Supreme Governor'. It was the business of the church to be the church. Individual Christians could and should be involved in party politics, but no party should have a confessional label. Dissenters were not hostile to the idea of the state as such, but it was not the business of the state to regulate or finance churches. They could and should be left to look after themselves in their own way. Such a stance left the Church of England in a quandary. Of course to speak thus makes one at once aware of the impossibility of making a blanket statement about what *the Church of England* thought. That it was a kind of 'ecclesiastical department' of state was undeniable, but amongst all its various 'parties' there were anxieties, deep or limited, about what such a characterisation had to say about the nature of the church. To think about it as a 'department' in this way might be to compromise its very essence. It was a divine society. How could the Church of England be left in the hands, ultimately at least, of what was becoming an ever more multi-confessional, multi-ethnic, latitudinarian body? But if it was not, where did ultimate authority lie? How could the church 'reform' itself if it did not possess the necessary instruments or institutions to do so? To these questions, of course, various answers were to be contentiously offered. It could still be argued, on the contrary, that MPs still stood for the 'great body of average Church of England people', who could withstand the onslaughts of a clericalism which sought to ringfence 'the church' and detach it from where they still thought it should be, namely at the heart of what was still, if in its own way, a Christian nation of a generalised Protestant disposition. The cry for 'Life and Liberty' went up from some sections of the church. In 1919 an Enabling Act was passed through parliament to create a 'National Assembly of the Church of England'. This did not mean, however, that the church was entirely free to do whatever it wanted in respect of its life and worship. Its wishes were still subordinated to parliament - as it was to discover within a decade when the House of Commons declined to accept its Revised Prayer Book.[38]

Conclusion

It must be apparent from the foregoing discussion that no simple statement, applying equally validly to all its component parts, can summarise the stance of the United Kingdom state in relation to the churches. In 1920, in any event, that state, as it had existed since 1801 was on the brink of dissolution. In a sense, with the creation of the Irish Free State, it became again, numerically, more Protestant in general ethos. The state, however, had no wish to resume a promotional role in the matter of religion. Nevertheless, as the late war had amply demonstrated, 'church and state' had stood

---

[38] Robbins, "Political Anglicanism", 89-104.

'shoulder to shoulder', as the Archbishop of Canterbury put it. Some, either at the time or subsequently, supposed that this solidarity had gone too far.[39] A kind of Christian society still existed and the 'establishments' that still remain in England and Scotland constituted a recognition of this fact. It was not an issue, in the context of other post-war political and social problems, which generated significant controversy. The Church of England might be said to have had a 'good war'. Protestant Dissent, it subsequently became apparent, had peaked in its numerical strength and political influence. Yet, although this may serve as a generalisation, the 'untidiness' or blurring of boundaries which it exemplified was a matter of concern, for a variety of reasons.

The nature of the twentieth-century state came to the fore. The reforms of the Liberal governments after 1906 can only loosely be thought to lay the foundations of 'the welfare state' but certainly 'positive Liberalism' envisaged the enhancement of the role of government. Further, it looked as though the Liberal Party was in serious disarray. At long last, the Labour Party might make rapid progress and Socialism would arrive. The war itself left ambivalent messages in its wake. British propaganda had contrasted 'British freedom' with the all-embracing ambitions of 'Prussianism'. Yet, in the very act of fighting the war, the British state had expanded its controls and functions. There might subsequently be a bonfire of such measures, but perhaps not. Perhaps Leviathan had arrived. In due course, 'religious reform', as interpreted by British governments, might well mean the elimination of the churches from those parts of the public sphere which they still, in their different ways, significantly occupied.

The separation of church and state in France had been watched with concern across the Channel, though reactions naturally differed. There the church had lost its status as a national institution and undergone what might be described as a decisive political defeat. One prominent English Anglican theologian and political theorist, J.N. Figgis, seized on the view of M. Combes that there were no rights but the rights of the state, and no authority but the authority of the republic, to suggest that the struggle to secure the liberty and power of self-development of *Societies* other than the state was going to be the issue which would engage the next two generations. The church was such a society. Before 1914 he had already been convinced that the splendid spires of the western world were crumbling. Victorian complacency, he supposed, was tottering to a fall. Yet, however perspicacious Figgis's observations were, and however cogent his advocacy of a kind of pluralism, they seemed overstated to those who still thought there was acceptable life in the imprecise but not unsatisfactory arrangements of the United Kingdom state in 1920. They should be adapted, if need be, pragmatically and not on the basis of dogma, whether of church or state. It is an argument which has not gone away, and, in a new century, has been returned to with fresh vigour.

---

[39] Robbins, "Onward Christian Soldiers?", 177-198;
Id., "Reconciliation?".

Bibliography

Adams, Ralph James Q. *Balfour: The Last Grandee*. London, 2007.

Adamson, William. *The Life of the Rev. Joseph Parker*. London, 1902.

Akenson, Donald H. *The Church of Ireland: Ecclesiastical Reform and Revolution, 1800-1885*. New Haven, 1971.

Alderman, Geoffrey. *Modern British Jewry*. Oxford, 1992.

Arnstein, Walter L. "Queen Victoria and Religion" in: Gail Malmgreen, ed. *Religion in the Lives of English Women, 1760-1930*. Bloomington, 1986, 88-128.

Bahlman, Dudley W.R. "The Queen, Mr. Gladstone, and Church Patronage". Victorian Studies, 3 (1960), 349-380.

Bentley, Michael. *The Climax of Liberal Politics: British Liberalism in Theory and Practice 1868-1918*. London-Baltimore, 1987.

Best, Geoffrey F.A. "The Constitutional Revolution, 1828-32, and its Consequences for the Established Church". *Theology*, 52 (1959), 226-234.

Blomfield, Alfred. *A Memoir of Charles James Blomfield*. London, 1864².

Blomfield, Charles James. *A Charge delivered to the Clergy of the Diocese of London*. London, 1834.

Bowen, Desmond. *Souperism, Myth or Reality*. Cork, 1970.

Brooks, Chris and Saint, Andrew, eds. *The Victorian Church: Architecture and Society*. Manchester, 1995.

Brose, Olive J. "The Irish Precedent for English Church Reform: The Irish Church Temporalities Act of 1833". *Journal of Ecclesiastical History*, 7 (1956), 204-225.

Brown, Stewart J. *Thomas Chalmers and the Godly Commonwealth in Scotland*. Oxford, 1982.

Brynn, Edward. *The Church of Ireland in the Age of Catholic Emancipation*. New York, 1982.

Chadwick, Owen. *The Victorian Church. 2: 1860-1901*. London, 1972.

Chadwick, Owen. "The Sacrament at Crathie, 1873" in: Stewart J. Brown and George Newlands, eds. *Scottish Christianity in the Modern World: In Honour of A. C. Cheyne*. Edinburgh, 2000, 177-196.

Charteris, Archibald Hamilton. *The Life of the Rev. James Robertson*. Edinburgh, 1863.

Clark, Jonathan C.D. *English Society 1688-1832*. Cambridge, 1985.

D'Arcy, Fergus A. "Charles Bradlaugh and the English Republican Movement, 1868-1878". *The Historical Journal*, 25 (1982), 367-383.

Davies, Ebenezer Thomas. *Religion in the Industrial Revolution in South Wales*. Cardiff, 1965.

Davies, J.L. "The Voluntary Principle" in: Walter Lowe Clay, ed. *Essays on Church Policy*. London, 1868.

Davies, John. "Victoria and Victorian Wales" in: Geraint H. Jenkins and J. Beverley Smith, eds. *Politics and Society in Wales, 1840-1922*. Cardiff, 1988, 7-28.

Eccleshall, Robert. "Anglican Political Thought in the Century after the Revolution of 1688" in: D. George Boyce, Robert Eccleshall and Vincent Geoghegan, eds. *Political Thought in Ireland since the Seventeenth Century*. London, 1993, 36-72.

Emerson, N.D. "The Last Phase of the Establishment" in: Walter Alison Phillips, ed. *History of the Church of Ireland*. Vol. 3. Oxford, 1933, 287 ff.

Evans, Eric. "Some Reasons for the Growth of English Rural Anticlericalism, c.1750-c.1830". *Past and Present*, 66 (1975), 84-109.

Fahrmeir, Andreas. *Citizenship: The Rise and Fall of a Modern Concept*. New Haven-London, 2007.

Figgis, John Neville. *Churches in the Modern State*. London, 1914.

Forsyth, Peter T. *The Charter of the Church: Six Lectures on the Spiritual Principle of Nonconformity*. London, 1896.

Gibson, William. *Church, State and Society, 1760-1850*. Basingstoke-New York, 1994.

Gilbert, Alan D. *Religion and Society in Industrial England*. London, 1978.

Hall, Christopher Newman. *An Autobiography*. London, 1898.

Harrison, John F.C. *The Second Coming: Popular Millenarianism 1780-1850*. London, 1979.

Hawkins, Angus. *The Forgotten Prime Minister: The 14th Earl of Derby*. Oxford, 2007-2008, 2 vols.

Hempton, David. *Religion and Political Culture in Britain and Ireland: From the Glorious Revolution to the Decline of Empire*. Cambridge, 1996.

Hilton, Boyd. *A Mad, Bad & Dangerous People? England 1783-1846*. Oxford, 2006.

Hinchliff, Peter. *Frederick Temple, Archbishop of Canterbury: A Life*. Oxford, 1998.

Inglis, Kenneth. S. "Patterns of Religious Worship in 1851". *Journal of Ecclesiastical History*, 11 (1960), 74-86.

Johnson, Mark D. *The Dissolution of Dissent 1850-1918*. New York-London, 1987.

Joyce, Patrick. "The Constitution and the Narrative Structure of Victorian Politics" in: James Vernon, ed. *Re-reading the Constitution: New Narratives in the Political History of England's long Nineteenth Century*. Cambridge, 1996, 191-196.

Kerr, Donal A. *Peel, Priests and Politics: Sir Robert Peel's Administration and the Roman Catholic Church in Ireland, 1841-1846*. Oxford, 1982.

Kerr, Donal A. *"A Nation of Beggars"? Priests, People, and Politics in Famine Ireland, 1846-1852*. Oxford, 1994.

Larkin, Emmet. "The Devotional Revolution in Ireland, 1850-1875". *American Historical Review*, 77 (1972), 625-652.

Mandler, Peter. *The English National Character: The History of an Idea from Edmund Burke to Tony Blair*. New Haven-London, 2006.

MacDonagh, Oliver. *O'Connell: The Life of Daniel O'Connell 1775-1847*. London, 1991.

MacIver, I.F. "Unfinished Business? The Highland Churches Scheme and the Government of Scotland, 1818-1835". *Records of the Scottish Church History Society*, 25 (1995), 376-399.

Mackintosh, William H. *Disestablishment and Liberation: The Movement for the Separation of the Anglican Church from State Control*. London, 1972.

Maclean, Allan. *Telford's Highland Churches*. Inverness, 1989.

Manning, Bernard Lord. *Protestant Dissenting Deputies*. Ed. Ormerod Greenwood. Cambridge, 1952.

Matthew, Colin G. *Gladstone 1809-1874*. Oxford-New York, 1986.

Morris, Paul. "1798-1992: Les Juifs de Grande-Bretagne à la lisière de l'Europe" in: Hugh McLeod, Stuart Mews and Christiane d'Haussy, eds. *Histoire religieuse des Pays européens*. Paris, 1994, 229-250.

Murray, N.U. *The Influence of the French Revolution on the Church of England and its Revivals*. D. Phil thesis University of Oxford, 1975.

Newman, Aubrey. "The Jewish Presence in Britain and France, 1650-1914" in: Richard Bonney and D.J.B. Trim, eds. *The Development of Pluralism in Modern Britain and France*. Oxford et al., 2007.

Nicholls, David, ed. *Church and State in Britain since 1820*. London, 1967.

Norman, Edward R. *Anti-Catholicism in Victorian England*. London, 1968.

O'Donoghue, Patrick. "Causes of the Opposition to Tithes, 1830-38". *Studia Hibernica*, 5 (1965), 7-28.

O'Donoghue, Patrick. "Opposition to Tithe Payment in 1830-31". *Studia Hibernica*, 6 (1966), 69-98.

Parry, Jonathan. *Democracy and Religion: Gladstone and the Liberal Party, 1867-1875*. Cambridge, 1986.

Paseta, Senia. "Nationalist Responses to Two Royal Visits to Ireland". *Irish Historical Studies*, 31 (1999) 124, 488-504.

Pickering, W.S.F. "The 1851 Religious Census". *British Journal of Sociology*, 18 (1967), 382-407.

Richard, Henry and Williams, J. Carvell. *Disestablishment*. London, 1885.

Robbins, Keith. *John Bright*. London, 1979.

Robbins, Keith. "John Bright and William Gladstone" in: Chris Wrigley, ed. *Warfare, Diplomacy and Politics: Essays in Honour of A.J.P. Taylor*. London, 1986, 29-41.

Robbins, Keith. "An Imperial and Multinational Polity, 1832-1922" in: Alexander Grant and Keith Stringer. *Uniting the Kingdom? The Making of British History*. London, 1995, 244-254.

Robbins, Keith. "Establishing Disestablishment" in: Stewart J. Brown and George Newlands, eds. *Scottish Christianity in the Modern World*. Edinburgh, 2000, 231-254.

Robbins, Keith. "England, Englishmen and the Church of England in the Nineteenth-Century United Kingdom of Great Britain and Ireland: Nation, Church and State" in: Nigel Yates, ed. *Bishop Burgess and his World: Culture, Religion and Society in Britain, Europe and North America in the Eighteenth and Nineteenth Centuries*. Cardiff, 2007, 198-232.

Robbins, Keith. "Reconciliation? Democracy, Peacemaking and the Churches in Britain 1918/19" in: Katarzyna Stoklosa and Andrea Strübind, eds. *Glaube - Freiheit - Diktatur in Europa und den USA. Festschrift für Gerhard Besier zum 60. Geburtstag*. Göttingen, 2007, 321-336.

Robbins, Keith. "Political Anglicanism", in: Nigel Yates, ed. *Anglicanism: Essays in History, Belief and Practice*. Lampeter, 2008, 89-104.

Robbins, Keith. "Onward Christian Soldiers? British Churches and War in the Nineteenth and Twentieth Centuries", in: Gilles Teulié, ed. *Religious Writings & War. Les discours religieux et la guerre*. Montpellier, 2007, 177-198.

Salbstein, Michael C.N. *The Emancipation of the Jews in Britain: The Question of the Admission of the Jews to Parliament 1828-1860*. London, 1982.

Sher, Richard B. and Murdoch, Alexander. "Patronage and Party in the Church of Scotland, 1750-1800" in: Norman McDougall, ed. *Church, Politics and Society: Scotland 1408-1929*. Edinburgh, 1983, 197-220.

Soloway, Richard Allen. *Prelates and People: Ecclesiastical Social Thought in England 1783-1852*. London, 1969.

Story, Robert Herbert. *Life and Remains of Robert Lee*. London, 1870, 2 vols.

Strong, Rowan. *Anglicanism and the British Empire c.1700-1850*. Oxford, 2007.

Sumner, John Bird. *A Charge Delivered to the Clergy of the Diocese of Chester*. London, 1838.

Tait, Archibald Campbell. *Some Thoughts on the Duties of the Established Church of England as a National Church*. London, 1876.

Thirlwall, Connop. *Remains Literary and Theological*. Ed. J.J. Stewart Perowne. London, 1877, 2 vols.

Twiss, Horace. *The Public and Private Life of Lord Chancellor Eldon*. London, 1846, 2 vols.

[Wade, John.] *The Extraordinary Black Book: An Exposition of Abuses in Church and State*. New ed. London, 1832.

Wallace, Robert. "Church Tendencies in Scotland" in: Alexander Grant, ed. *Recess Studies*. Edinburgh, 1870, 187-239.

Ward, William Reginald. *Religion and Society in England 1790-1850*. London, 1972.

Whelan, Irene. *The Bible War in Ireland*. Madison (WI), 2005.

Wilberforce, Samuel. *Charge delivered to the Diocese of Oxford, at his Sixth Visitation*. Oxford, 1863.

Withrington, Donald J. "The 1851 Census of Religious Worship and Education: With a Note on Church Accommodation in Mid-19th-Century Scotland". *Records of the Scottish Church History Society*, 18 (1974), 133-148.

Wolffe, John. "British Protestants and Europe, 1820-60: Some Perceptions and Influences" in: Richard Bonney and D.J.B. Trim, eds. *The Development of Pluralism in Modern Britain and France*. Oxford et al., 2007.

Wolffe, John. *Great Deaths: Grieving, Religion, and Nationhood in Victorian and Edwardian Britain*. Oxford, 2000.

Wolffe, John. "Lord Palmerston and Religion: A Reappraisal". *English Historical Review*, 120 (2005), 907-936.

Yates, Nigel. *Anglican Ritualism in Victorian Britain, 1830-1910*. Oxford, 1999.

Yates, Richard. *The Church in Danger*. London, 1815.

THE LOW COUNTRIES

The Northern and Southern Netherlands formed two different states from the sixteenth century onwards. When, at the end of the eighteenth century, both came under the sphere of influence of revolutionary France, a process of modernisation was initiated. During the Restoration period (1815-1830) they were reunited and constituted the United Kingdom of the Netherlands. However, the contrasts that had developed in the previous centuries and decades turned out to be irreconcilable. The North was a trading nation which, in the cultural field, underwent not only the influence of France but also, and even to a greater extent, of England and Germany. The South was on its way to becoming an industrial region, which led to a new kind of urbanisation, and it was particularly receptive to French cultural influences. Also the religious factor caused dissension. The Northern Netherlands were shaped by religious pluralism - a Calvinist society with a large Catholic minority - whereas the Southern Netherlands were predominantly Catholic. The Catholic Church in the South tried for a long time to defend its privileged position against a mainly hostile government, but eventually chose to safeguard its influence in the context of a general climate of liberty. Thus a coalition was formed with liberal groups that led to a revolution and put an end to the United Kingdom of the Netherlands.

After 1830, Belgium and the Netherlands were again two separate states, yet in the course of the nineteenth century the two countries experienced many of the same social changes, though at a different pace. Both countries went through a similar process of modernisation - the transition to an industrial, urban society, the creation of a liberal, parliamentary state, the advent of large socio-political movements and the shift toward full democracy at the beginning of the twentieth century - but the Netherlands experienced those changes at a somewhat slower pace than Belgium. Also the religious developments ran along very parallel lines, even though the Netherlands predominantly remained a Calvinist state and Belgium to an even greater extent a Catholic state. In both countries, constitutional disestablishment was introduced, yet in Belgium the state still tended to privilege the Catholic Church for a long while, whereas in the Netherlands the Reformed Church received special consideration and attention from the Dutch government. When at the end of the nineteenth century the churches were forced by the liberals to pay more respect to the neutrality of the state, they deliberately opted for the development of a state-free space in which they managed to perpetuate their social influence thanks to an extensive network of organisations.

This process was channelled, to a significant extent, by religious parties which effectively marginalised conservative parties and which contributed to the creation of a 'pillarised', neocorporatist social model. The outcome of all this was that religion for a very long time, up to the second half of the twentieth century, was able to exercise great influence on the social and cultural life of these 'modern' Western European countries.

Liberal State and Confessional Accommodation

The Southern Netherlands / Belgium

Emiel Lamberts

Resistance to Regalism (1780-1830)

In the Southern Netherlands, under Spanish rule in the sixteenth and seventeenth centuries and under Austrian rule in the eighteenth century, the Catholic Church had the position of a state religion, recognised and protected by civil authority. In the first half of the sixteenth century Calvinist influence in these regions had been considerable, but the Catholic Counter Reformation had put an end to that. The Catholic Church had a wide range of activities: it served the pastoral needs of the faithful and also played a dominant role in education and in the care of the poor and sick. The higher clergy was present in political life, mainly via the provincial States in which they participated as an interest group together with the nobility and the urban elite. Still it cannot be said that the church had a great impact on politics in the Southern Netherlands, because political authorities were very keen on their autonomy. Inspired by regalism they were even increasingly inclined to put church organisation and activities under their supervision. The state had more control over the church than vice versa. The Catholic Church offered little resistance to this situation as long as the political authorities did not rein back the sphere of its activities and remained church friendly.

Ultramontanist Resistance to Josephinism (1780-1790)

The situation changed in the second half of the eighteenth century under Austrian rule. In the political sphere, the trend toward centralisation and rationalisation grew stronger. At the same time the principle of legislative sovereignty became generally accepted: not a single area, not a single citizen henceforth escaped from the legislative, ruling authority of the state. More than before, the state also concerned itself with the welfare of its subjects and began to expand its scope of action at the expense of the church. This trend gradually became apparent under the rule of Empress Maria-Theresia (1740-1780) and even more under Joseph II (1780-1790). Church resistance to this was predictable, even more so because ultramontanist trends had gained the upper hand in church circles as a result of the showdown with Jansenism. Characteristic for this ultramontanist stance was its commitment to the supremacy of the church in society, its fidelity to the Papacy, and an emphasis on the independence of the church vis-à-vis the state, which however did not exclude cooperation between both powers (union of Throne and Altar).

Emperor Joseph II decided to subject the Austrian Netherlands to a rigorous programme of reform.[1] A Declaration of Toleration (12 November 1781) gave first Protestants and then Jews the full rights of citizenship and limited freedom of worship. The significance of this measure was largely symbolic, since hardly any Protestants lived in the Austrian Netherlands. But many people felt the decree was a great change, in which the centuries-old alliance between church and state had been sundered. For them, the whole Catholic nature of the country now seemed threatened. In 1783 the emperor began to bring about the end of 'useless' (that is, contemplative) monasteries and developed plans for the abolition of 'superfluous' monastic institutions. In raising revenues through these measures, he hoped to finance reforms in parish life. The dominant position of the church was further affected when marriage legislation became a matter for the state. The Edict of 28 September 1784 essentially made marriage a civil instead of a religious function, thereby robbing the church of a segment of life over which it had enjoyed nearly exclusive jurisdiction. Joseph II also replaced all charitable brotherhoods and foundations with a single Brotherhood of Active Charity (8 April 1786). A real storm broke loose after the government established a General Seminary in Louvain (16 October 1786), with a branch in Luxembourg. All seminarians were to be sent there, where they would be schooled according to the Josephist ideal of a true shepherd: free of ultramontanist thinking, tolerant, the very model of active charity, and full of commitment to the common good. The bishops steadfastly maintained that the formation of the clergy was their task, not the state's. Ecclesiastical resistance gained the support of prominent interest groups in early 1778, when two decrees introduced sweeping administrative and judicial reforms. A first, 'small revolution', was defeated; yet by 1789 the government was losing its control over the situation. On 26 June Cardinal Franckenberg formally condemned the General Seminary. Consequently, the emperor was now regarded by his Catholic opponents as a perjured and condemned heretic. At the same time, the urban bourgeoisie and professional classes were alienated by the government's 'tyrannical' policy. All this led to the so-called 'Brabantine Revolution' at the end of 1789, and to the proclamation of the United Belgian States, by the Act of Union (11 January 1790).[2]

---

[1] Hasquin, *Joseph II.*

[2] Polasky, "The Success of a Counter-Revolution"; Pirenne and Vercruysse, *Les États Belgiques Unis.*

D.G. Guttenberg, Glorification of the religious politics of Joseph II, *engraving, 1786. This print refers to
the abolition of 'useless' monasteries.*
[Leuven, KADOC]

"It seemed that political self-consciousness was too great in the Southern Netherlands for its citizens simply to roll over and accept Joseph's policy of uniformity. The
wealth and power of important social groups were simply too considerable to tolerate the danger that Joseph's reforms presented them. The highly ultramontanist clergy
were far too entrenched in society for Joseph to dismiss them so lightly. Moreover, a
wide segment of the population was not so backward as to be unfamiliar with the new
language of freedom coming out of France in those days. In the Brabantine Revolution
the clergy and the traditional provincial power brokers enjoyed the greatest say."[3] In
the new short-lived state (1790) they pursued a repressive policy against the supporters
of Joseph II and against liberal-minded elements among the urban bourgeoisie who
adhered to the ideals of the French Revolution.

In essence a symbiosis between conservatism and confessionalism was established which later came to characterise political life in the Southern Netherlands.
Moreover, the importance of religious issues and the role played by the clergy in the
1780s would have a lasting effect on the nation's political composition, as the opposi-

---

[3] Roegiers and Van Sas, "Revolution", 295.

tion between clericals and anticlericals was to become the deepest divide in national politics.

The Struggle for Survival under French Rule (1795-1815)

The Brabantine Revolution was crushed after the death of Joseph II (1790) and Austrian rule was restored for a brief period. The new emperor Leopold II scaled down his predecessor's reforms, which led to a reconciliation between the conservative interest groups and the regime. Soon, however, revolutionary France posed a threat. Between November 1792 and June 1794 the Austrian and French armies fought each other with varying success. The French Republic was finally victorious and managed to realise what Louis XIV had attempted in vain: the French annexation of the Southern Netherlands (1 October 1795).[4]

Slowly, the French Republic's laws went into effect, including the Civil Constitution of the Clergy, which provoked a schism and opposed a Constituent to a Refractory clergy, as it did in France. The introduction of freedom of conscience and freedom of religion deprived the church forever of its religious monopoly. At the same time its economic and political power status was dismantled. In the fall of 1796 all monasteries and abbeys were closed, their property assessed, and for the greater part sold to the public. The church lost its voice in the representative bodies. The state took over several of its traditional tasks. The civic registry, designed to replace the church's parochial records, was implemented on 17 June 1796. Around the same time, the French revolutionary calendar was imposed, replacing the Christian one and featuring new republican holidays largely devoted to the 'cult of the law'. The state also to a great extent took over public education and public charities.

All these measures provoked heavy resistance from the Catholic clergy. Most clergymen refused to swear loyalty to the laws of the French Republic, issued under the Directoire. The repression against them increased after the coup of 18 Fructidor, year V (4 September 1797). The law of 19 Fructidor required all clergymen to swear an oath of hatred against the monarchy and an oath of loyalty to the constitution. Some 585 priests were deported for their refusal to do so, and hundreds more were imprisoned. On 25 October 1797 the medieval University of Louvain was abolished as, shortly afterwards, were the seminaries, the cathedral chapters and the last monasteries. Catholics were moreover deeply shocked by the French imprisonment of Pope Pius VI in January 1798.[5] Public discontent swelled to its highest point when the law of 5 September 1798 introduced conscription for young men between the ages of 20 and 25. A revolt, the so-called Peasants' War, broke out and was brutally suppressed.[6] Once again the clergy were the ones who paid most dearly for the uprising. More than 7,500 priests were

---

[4] Hasquin, ed., *La Belgique française*; De Vleeschouwer, "Le cas de la Belgique".
[5] Claeys Bouuaert, *Les déclarations et serments*.
[6] Dhondt, "La guerre des paysans"; Hemblinne, *Chouannerie et contrerévolution*.

sentenced to deportation, yet only 500 were arrested, while the others were hidden by the faithful. A real persecution was thus going on against the ultramontanist church in the newly conquered territories and this would have a lasting impact. The vast majority of the clergy would through word, writing and action oppose the ideology and policy of the French Revolution, thus adding a counter-revolutionary stance to the ultramontanist ideas. This far-reaching event also greatly strengthened the spirit of liberty and the anti-statism of the church in the Southern Netherlands, the only church studied in this volume that was confronted with such an existential experience.

The coup of 18 Brumaire, year VII (9 November 1799) brought the Consulate to power in France. The restoration of law, order, and unity were its chief priorities. The church won a reprieve under the Consulate, but it was not until Bonaparte signed a concordat with the Holy See on 15 July 1801 that people fully saw the government's shift in church policy. The text of the Concordat was preceded by a preamble in which the Catholic religion was acknowledged as 'the religion of a large majority of Frenchmen'. The church was allowed to reorganise. It was no longer excluded from public life and it was given enough space to fulfil its mission, yet the government continued to exercise much influence in ecclesiastical affairs. The reorganisation of dioceses and parishes, as well as the appointment of bishops and parish priests, required the prior agreement of the government. The Organic Articles, added unilaterally to the Concordat by the government, subordinated even more the church to the state in the old royal fashion. They imposed upon the church an organisation corresponding to that of other state agencies. The bishops were virtually given the rights of prefects in their dioceses, with discretionary power over their parish priests, exceeding that of the Old Regime. This strengthening of episcopal authority was to have lasting consequences.

In general, the influence of the Concordat, which established a position of equilibrium between the church and the new society, was enduring. As part of the agreement the church accepted the sale of nationalised church lands. In compensation, the state committed itself to the payment of appropriate salaries to bishops and parish priests and to the maintenance of church buildings. This settlement has been upheld in the Southern Netherlands (present-day Belgium) to this day.

Very quickly, Napoleon's meddlesome ecclesiastical policies ended the public euphoria that had followed the Concordat of 1801. Around 1810, the French regime became more repressive again, generating new resentment. The insistence on a single Catholic catechism for the whole empire found widespread resistance among the clergy. Also the French detention of Pius VII in 1809 caused unrest in many places. The new discontent was expressed in a National Council, which Napoleon convoked in 1811 as a way for the French Catholic Church to organise itself without interference from the pope. Influenced by their ultramontanist clergy the newly appointed bishops of Ghent and Tournai opposed Napoleon's strategy. They were imprisoned and were forced to resign. The local clergy did not recognise their successors, who did not receive the canonical investiture by the pope. Recalcitrant priests were submitted to very repressive measures by the ever-present police. In the diocese of Ghent, seminarians were conscripted into the army, and many of them lost their lives in this adventure. Several

103

dioceses were managed by vicars-general who had gone underground. So it was with great relief that the Catholic hierarchy welcomed the armies of the allied powers, which put an end to Napoleon's regime.

The Decline of Regalism under the United Kingdom (1815-1830)

After the defeat of Napoleon, the Southern Netherlands were reunited with Holland at the instigation of Great Britain. Together, they formed the United Kingdom of the Netherlands, under King Willem I of the House of Orange. The new state was conceived as a constitutional monarchy but not as a parliamentary regime. The new monarch was very much influenced by the German Enlightenment. His rather authoritarian policy was based on the belief that society could be reshaped, with the state playing a guiding and omnipresent role in its transformation. His religious policy reached back to the '*Staatskirchentum*' and continued the line of Josephinism. So, conflicts with the ultramontanist church in the South could be expected.

Already in the starting phase of the new state, Willem I was confronted with reactionary claims of the ultramontanist clergy in the South. Having gained the crowns of martyrdom under Joseph II and especially under the Directoire and Napoleon, they demanded that the Catholic character of the South be constitutionally guaranteed. They rejected the new constitution which promised equal legal status for all churches. Even after passage of this constitution, several bishops and vicars-general continued their resistance and declared that the oath of loyalty to the fundamental law was unacceptable to all Catholics. However, the new archbishop of Malines, François de Méan, proved more flexible and finally the resistance faded away.[7] In 1821 it appeared that the Catholic Church hierarchy in the South had accepted once and for all the right of everyone to religious freedom. Clergymen of the North, where Catholics were a minority and enjoyed the advantages of religious freedom since the 1790s, had contributed significantly to this acceptance of the idea of civil tolerance. So, the church finally accepted that it no longer could enjoy a religious monopoly in the Southern Netherlands.

On the other hand, the Catholic Church was all the more intent on developing in complete freedom and asserting its independence vis-à-vis the state. The Concordat of 1801 was provisionally upheld in the South, thus putting the Catholic Church under the custody of a Calvinist ruler.[8] King Willem I regarded the churches, Catholic and Protestant, as *public* institutions, which were to instruct the people in the right way of living and thinking. Already in 1816, he gave the Dutch Reformed Church a new centralised organisation and effectively turned it into an arm of the state. The king

[7] Chappin, "Entre dogme et diplomatie".   [8] Wagnon, "La reconduction du concordat".

wanted to rearrange the Catholic Church along the same lines, but ran into resistance from Rome and even more from the local clergy.

The church felt shackled by state supervision. The government refused to restore the monasteries and only those congregations which were committed to primary education and charitable works received permission to take on new members. The church was particularly restricted in its educational task. Willem I, as an enlightened king, considered education his proper domain and in a systematic manner he began to develop a public education network, at the primary, secondary and higher levels, at the expense of the Catholic clergy and their schools. The government also attempted to put the bishop's own educational institutions under its control. Royal resolutions of 14 June 1825 demanded that all secondary education be approved by the state, and resulted in the closing of the minor seminaries and several Catholic high schools. The government however overplayed its hand by interfering with the formation of future priests. It decided to establish a 'Collegium Philosophicum' in Louvain. All candidates for the Catholic priesthood would be obliged to attend this institution for a couple of years before they could start their theological studies in the diocesan seminaries. Through this measure the government wanted to further the formation of a tolerant, enlightened clergy, which would be more inclined to see their interests as running parallel with those of the state. With this initiative, all too reminiscent of the Seminary General under Joseph II, the government however ventured too far into the territory of ecclesiastical prerogatives and ran completely counter to the ultramontanist tendency of the church in the Southern Netherlands, which forcefully defended its autonomy towards the state. Discontent about the educational policy became a catalyst for widespread dissatisfaction among Catholics about government policy.[9]

105

The government tried to calm down feelings by signing a concordat with the Holy See in 1827. In broad lines it was in keeping with the Concordat of 1801, which henceforth was declared to be also applicable to the Catholic Church in the Northern regions. In essence it thus confirmed a form of state supervision of the church. The government at the same time allowed concessions to the ecclesiastical opposition: the Philosophical College would become optional and the preparatory seminaries could be organised once more. Anticlerical protest against these decisions led to imposition of the Concordat being postponed, with the result that the Catholics lost all confidence in the king. The increasing opposition would eventually, in 1830, lead to a suspension of all June 1825 decisions, including the Philosophical College. These measures however came too late to contain the opposition movement and stop the disintegration of the United Kingdom of the Netherlands.

On the Catholic side a remarkable process indeed took place from 1825 onwards. Catholic publicists and members of parliament from then on used the constitution in their resistance against the king's church policy. They argued that complete freedom - of religion, education, the press and association - followed from the constitutionally

---

[9] Terlinden, *Guillaume Ier*, 183-204.

Allegoric representation of article 14 in the Belgian
constitution: the Freedom of Religion, *lithograph
published in* Grondwet van België *(Brussels, 1852).*
[Leuven, KADOC: KD10]

guaranteed right to freedom of expression. Henceforth they wanted to realise church
liberties in the context of a general climate of freedom. Their motto became: "la liberté
en tout et pour tous" (freedom in all things and for everyone), a slogan which they
borrowed from the French apologist Félicité de Lamennais, who for many of them
became an idol. This new generation of liberal Catholics, who emphasised individual
liberties, now replaced the old-style ultramontanists in leading the Catholic opposition against royal policy. Even the Catholic hierarchy was to some extent influenced
by this liberal Catholic tendency, which was trying to accomplish the autonomy of the

church, in defence against interventionist tendencies of state authorities, with the help of political liberalism. In this respect, the Southern Netherlands were functioning as a laboratory for a phenomenon which could be observed later on in other continental European countries.[10]

Liberal Catholicism was supported in particular by the younger clergy and by prominent laymen belonging to the rising middle class in the Southern Netherlands, a region that was rapidly industrialising its economy and undergoing a remarkable urbanisation process.[11] A new entrepreneurial middle class became very wealthy and self-confident and was claiming more liberties and even political rights, under the influence of French liberal theorists. This development sustained a growing liberal opposition against the rather authoritarian government of Willem I.

Also on the liberal side a new generation emerged in the Southern regions. It was influenced by French spirituality and readjusted its hostile image of the church. That facilitated an alliance with the Catholic opposition. In 1827 this led to a 'union' between Catholic and liberal opponents, portrayed by the loyalists as a 'monstrous alliance'. The unionists wanted to change the authoritarian government of Willem I into a liberal, parliamentary government. In September 1830, in the wake of the French July revolution, a revolution broke out in Brussels, which eventually led to the formation of an independent Belgian state.

A Privileged Freedom (1830-1847)

After the September Revolution, the Belgians elected their own constituent assembly, the National Congress, which very quickly elaborated a liberal constitution. The 'unionists', who had fiercely opposed the policies of Willem I, had developed a clear political programme which they were now free to implement in the wake of independence. To ensure the primacy of parliament they reduced the royal power, from July 1831 on represented by Leopold I of the house of Saxe-Coburg. They gave greater autonomy to local government, and granted the citizenry and opinion groups more civil and political rights. The new climate of freedom had important consequences for the Catholic Church, which was now freed from all state supervision by a constitution which implicitly separated church and state. The Belgian constitution (7 February 1831) indeed introduced a moderate separation of church and state, in a climate of reciprocal goodwill.[12] The state granted complete religious liberty to its citizens (art. 14,

107

---

[10] Haag, *Les origines du catholicisme libéral.*
[11] Lamberts, *Kerk en liberalisme*, 32-35.

[12] Aubert, "Kirche und Staat in Belgien"; Wagnon, "Le congrès national belge"; Shelley, "Mutual Independence"; Miroir, "L'État et les cultes".

now 19).[13] The churches were freed from all supervision of the state (art. 16, now 21)[14], which for its part abandoned preferential ties with any religion. Churches no longer had a public status.

Nevertheless, they still could count on some state support for their material needs, on the basis of legal regulations that were elaborated as an implementation of the Napoleonic Concordat of 1801. This Concordat was suspended as an international legal instrument. It was tacitly no longer extended by the Belgian government and Rome, yet the concordatarian legislation was at least partially maintained.[15] To be sure, all laws contrary to the stipulations of the new constitution were to be suspended (art. 138, now 188). That applied to the larger part of the Organic Articles of the Concordat of 1801, but not to the regulations about the material aspects of church structuring. Regulations providing state funds for the pay of parish priests and vicars of the recognised denominations (thus not only Catholicism) (art. 117, now 181, § 1)[16] were retained, as well as those for the construction and upkeep of their church buildings. The same was true for stipulations which gave a public status to the administrative bodies of parish churches, cathedral chapters and seminaries. Especially on a municipal and provincial level, public authorities and church institutions were still closely linked.[17]

The constitutional arrangement contained a certain contradiction. On one side, an equal treatment was introduced for all existing religions; on the other side some privileges were still granted to 'recognised' religions, and especially to the dominant Catholic Church.[18] In the first place, the financial support for the recognised denomina-

108

---

[13] "Freedom of worship, public practice of the latter, as well as freedom to demonstrate one's opinions on all matters, are guaranteed, except for the repression of offences committed when using this freedom". Article 15, now 20: "No one can be obliged to contribute in any way whatsoever to the acts and ceremonies of a religion, nor to observe the days of rest".

[14] "The state does not have the right to intervene either in the nomination or in the installation of ministers of any religion whatsoever, nor to forbid these ministers from corresponding with their superiors, from publishing their acts, except, in the latter case, taking into consideration normal responsibilities in matters of press and publication". This article implies that freedom of religion also includes a recognition of the communitarian aspects of a religious persuasion. In Belgium, also the religious communities possess fundamental rights.

[15] Wagnon, "Le concordat de 1801-1827".

[16] "The state awards remuneration and pensions to religious leaders; those amounts required are included in the budget on an annual basis".

[17] The ministers of these religions (parish priests, vicars) receive a salary and later a pension; more-over, the public institutions in charge of the management of properties intended for the religious service are granted legal personality. Also municipalities and provinces are put under certain obligations towards recognised religions, respectively in the Municipal Law and the Provincial Law. Thus financial deficits are covered and financial support is given for restoration works or the construction of buildings destined for religious service.

[18] In order to be recognised by the Belgian state, a religious community has to comply with a few criteria: 1° it must have a great number of followers; 2° it must be organised in such a way that a representative body can deal with civil authorities; 3° it must have been active in the country for a very long time (several decades); 4° its activities must have social benefits. The dominance of the Catholic Church is very evident when one looks at its numerical superiority. In 1835 there were only about 5,000 Protestants and 1,200 Jews in Belgium out of a total of 4,100,000 inhabitants; in 1905 there were 30,000 Protestants and 3,500 Jews out of 7,160,547 in habitants. Non-religious people only formed a tiny minority.

tions was - as in the Concordat of 1801 - justified as a compensation for the nationalisation of church properties in revolutionary France. In the second place it was justified by the social benefits of religious denominations. At that time, even liberals recognised the beneficial effects of religion on society. The combination of both considerations explains the endurance of this settlement up to now. The Catholic religion was, together with Protestantism, already recognised by a French law of 8 April 1802. Jewish religion was recognised by a decree of 17 March 1808. In 1835 Anglicanism received the same status. Much later, on 19 July 1974 Islam was recognised and on 17 April 1985 the Greek and Russian Orthodox Churches.[19]

In 1831, the Belgian bishops were able to convince the very anti-liberal Pope Gregory XVI to tacitly accept the new Belgian constitution. In the 1840s Giacchino Pecci, then nuncio in Belgium, and later on Leo XIII, even took the view, based on personal experience, that the Belgian system combined the advantages of a pragmatic cooperation between church and state with the benefits of real autonomy.

The constitutional settlement was realised in a rather harmonious atmosphere, yet its interpretation later on led to a fierce controversy between clericals and anticlericals in Belgian politics. Nevertheless, this confrontation never provoked a revision of the constitution. Let it be noted in passing that the Belgian constitution was amended in a more democratic sense only at the end of the nineteenth century and in a more federalist direction since the 1970s.

In a first phase, under 'unionist' governments, the position of the Catholic Church became even more promising by a benevolent interpretation of the constitution and by a series of laws and administrative measures. The legislation on the organisational framework of municipalities and provinces referred to their obligations towards church councils, episcopal sees and seminaries (1833 and 1836). By a decree of 3 April 1839 seminarians were exempted from military service.[20] Very important was the education act of 23 September 1842: religious education became compulsory in public elementary schools and the clergy acquired significant supervisory power in those schools. So, public education and in an analogous way public charity came to a large extent under the influence and supervision of the church.[21]

The church could, moreover, freely develop its own institutions. From the beginning, it took advantage of the extended freedom of association and meeting that was granted by the constitution. The conference of bishops met on a regular basis, at least once a year, under the leadership of the archbishop of Malines. From 1834 on, the bishops coordinated their pastoral and political strategies under the supervision of a papal nuncio. They immediately reorganised the ecclesiastical structures,

109

---

[19] De Pooter, *De rechtspositie*. In 2003 the state was paying the salaries of 6,929 Catholic priests, 123 Protestant-evangelical ministers, 14 Anglican ministers, 41 Jewish rabbi's and 53 Orthodox priests. From 2005 on, 6,5% of the budget went to the Islam. A striking point is that, from 1985 on,

also the organised free-thought movement became a 'recognised denomination' and henceforth received 10% of the budget.
[20] Simon, *Le cardinal Sterckx*, I, 209-335.
[21] Lory, *Libéralisme et instruction primaire*.

improved the formation of the seminarians, and developed new pastoral initiatives.[22] The clergy intensified its activities in the educational sector, very often in cooperation with municipal authorities. In 1834 the bishops re-established the Catholic University of Louvain. In the welfare sector (the care of orphans and of sick and elderly people) the clergy obtained a quasi-monopoly. Also here it often cooperated with local authorities. The reconstruction and quick expansion of many religious congregations and orders sustained to a high extent the religious, educational and charitable activities of the church. Male congregations helped out the parish clergy in the pastoral service, especially through a large-scale organisation of popular 'missions' and the foundation and the guidance of devotional groups and fraternities. They also rendered services in the educational and welfare sectors. In the charity sector the help contributed by congregations of nuns was even more essential.[23]

It is conspicuous that the initiative of this first organisational wave after 1830 came mainly from the clergy and that the focus was on religious organisations. This was not merely a question of priorities. The unionist climate in Belgium did not immediately require a political mobilisation of the clergy and the faithful. That does not mean that they were not active in political life. They supported the unionist governments but some cooperated with progressive liberals, others with conservative liberals. The lack of political consensus, even among the clergy, and especially the unionist climate that was favourable for the church, tempered the confessional factor in political life.

The strengthening of the conservative Catholic faction during the 1840s brought about a change. The conservative Catholics not only wanted to confirm the principle of authority in society and curb popular involvement. They also wanted as much as possible to uphold a form of cooperation between church and state. They were strongly guided in their views by the anti-liberal stand of Pope Gregory XVI. Because of their rigid orientation toward Rome, also in political matters, they gradually obtained the exclusive right to the name 'ultramontanists'. Much more than the liberal Catholics, they sought to maintain a permanent link between power and ideology. Their views were a threat to the ideological neutrality and hence the liberal character of the state.

The ultramontanist group among the clergy received support from powerful allies. The monarchy and the nobility wanted to contain the progressive trends within the Belgian church for their own specific interests. They managed to involve the Holy See for this purpose. Rome strengthened the ultramontanist presence within the episcopate, put pressure on the liberal Catholic clergy and led them to a more conservative attitude. The link between the church and the conservative interest groups was strengthened again. The symbiosis between conservatism and confessionalism established during the Brabantine Revolution of 1789 was renewed.

---

[22] Simon, Le *cardinal Sterckx*, II, 11-274.
[23] Tihon, "Les religieuses en Belgique", 31-46. In 1830 there were about 3,000 female religious in Belgium. In 1846 their number had already increased to 8,368; 46% of the latter were active in the educational sector, 28% in the health sector, and 17% in both sectors simultaneously. The number of male religious increased during this same period from about 260 to 2,051.

More resolutely than before, the church hierarchy in the 1840s strove for a form of collaboration with the unionist governments, which increasingly became more conservative. As compensation for its support of the central authority - e.g. during the elections - the church received a number of additional benefits. The liberal bourgeoisie perceived with discontent this growing cooperation between church and state as a return to conditions of the Old Regime. It saw this evolution as a betrayal of the spirit of the constitution of 1831 and reacted against the growing power of the church in public life. 'Clericalism' provoked an anticlerical reaction and this irrevocably led to a political struggle based on religious issues.[24]

The Struggle for Religious Neutrality of the State (1847-1884)

The liberals increasingly departed from the unionist consensus, which they now regarded as a cover for the virtual power exercised by the nobility and the clergy. They staunchly defended urban interests and the civil authority's independence from church influence. They reverted to their initial secularising tendencies and contested the socio-political influence of the church. For them, religion had to be a private issue without any impact on public life. They came into power in 1847 and almost continuously dominated political life in Belgium up to 1884.

111

For several decades, the antagonism between Catholics and anticlericals became the dominant fault line in Belgian politics and an increasing polarisation took place in both camps. In reaction to the formation of a liberal party a Catholic party gradually emerged, affected however by internal tensions. Ultramontanists and liberal Catholics had different views on the ideological orientation of this party. The liberal Catholics, who remained particularly numerous in urban circles and among political dignitaries, had somewhat moderated their views since the 1830s, but they continued to put their trust in the Belgian liberal institutions. They saw the Catholic party more as a constitutional, moderate centre party, which to a large extent had to respect the ideological neutrality of the state yet had to guarantee the free activity of the church. The ultramontanists on the other hand expected the Catholic party to be in the first place a confessional party and to give priority to the defence of ecclesiastical interests. They also remained advocates of a form of state support for the church. The position of the ultramontanists, staunchly supported by the Vatican, gradually gained strength under the pontificate of Pius IX (1846-1878).

This process led to a growing entanglement of religion and politics, of the profane and the religious domains, and thus also had repercussions on the further development of Catholic organisational life. Profane and political organisations gained

---

[24] Witte, *La construction de la Belgique*, 157-164.

a religious justification and religious organisations acquired a political purport. If we observe the development of Catholic organisational life between 1850 and 1880, we notice a widening in concentric circles from specifically religious to more profane spheres. The organisations and initiatives in the outer, more profane spheres were mainly oriented toward the bourgeoisie, which had the right to vote. The popular organisations on the other hand still had a preponderant moral-religious slant. That indicates that the electoral-political factor played an important role in the 'profanisation' of Catholic organisational life.

After 1847, successive liberal governments imposed restrictive measures on the Catholic Church, limiting its property rights, secularising cemeteries and reducing the church's role in public charities and public education. The liberal confrontation with the Catholics was particularly sharp in these last two areas, since charities and schools were vital components in society. In the 1850s, liberals initiated a heated debate over the character of public charity, and finally succeeded in wresting public poor relief away from the influence of the church.

The struggle for the future of the public schools was even more important, and no issue polarised liberals and Catholics more than the fate of the country's schools. Through several successive laws the Catholic Church lost much of its influence over all levels of public education. In 1879, when the liberals wanted to end clerical control over primary education once and for all, and struck religious instruction from the curriculum of the elementary schools, they provoked the most fiercely fought 'school war' in Belgian history, which finally resulted in Catholic triumph. In 1884 the Catholic party came into power and from then on ruled the country, alone or in coalition governments, for more than one century (up to 1999).[25] Nevertheless, as a matter of fact, liberal school policy had undermined the church's influence in public education. Gradually, Catholics themselves recognised that public schools should be religiously neutral, but they compensated for this by establishing their own comprehensive school network.

In the heat of the battle, radical liberals aimed for a complete separation of church and state, abolishing all privileges of the Catholic Church. Others were influenced by the *Kulturkampf* in Germany and wanted to establish once more a form of state supervision of the church. In liberal government circles around 1880 one thus thought of assigning church properties to the state or the municipalities and putting the church councils under stronger supervision of the municipalities. This, however, was a minority trend. The moderate liberals were satisfied with a confirmation of the independence and ideological neutrality of the state. When it eventually turned out that a majority of Catholics were largely willing to respect that independence and neutrality, many liberals joined the ranks of the Catholic party out of fear of the emerging socialism. That too contributed to the basis of a prolonged Catholic government.

---

[25] Lamberts and Lory, *1884*.

Anticlerical cartoon on the impact of the Church
on the elections, *lithograph, 1854. Priests are
driving the 'electoral cattle' to the polling-station.*
[Leuven, KADOC]

The Option for a State-Free Space

Henceforth, Catholics respected more than before the autonomy of state institutions, but through their struggle against the liberal and secularising policies, they had become strongly anti-statist. They now consistently favoured a minimal state which would leave room for free Catholic initiatives. They developed the 'principle of subsidiarity', according to which the state should leave as many tasks as possible to local government and private institutions. They wanted to give their own Catholic organisations, which reached a large segment of the population, every opportunity to develop and pursue their own goals. After 1884, Catholic governments put out a lot of tasks to private (confessional) organisations or institutions. This was the case in the field of education, welfare, social services, housing, etc., and later on also in the cultural sector.

Policies of liberal governments after 1847 had been an important incentive for the development of Catholic initiatives and organisations, not only in the fields of education and health care. The founding of new organisations and associations became a strategy to secure the political as well as the religious influence of the church in society. Those organisations and associations provided an important basis of support for the Conservative party, which turned more and more into a confessional party, especially as a result of the 'school war' (1879-1884). Gradually this Catholic party broadened its electoral basis, especially from the 1890s on, when socio-economic issues became dominant in political life and a democratisation process was taking place. Thanks in particular to the commitment of ultramontanist *'hommes d'œuvres'* and social-minded clergymen, a vigorous Catholic social movement was taking off and Christian popular movements developed, respectively for artisans and workers (Belgian People's League), farmers (Belgian Farmers League), and the lower middle class. They all supported the Catholic party, which became a class-ridden party, with a guaranteed representation of farmers, workers and petty bourgeois. Corporatist ideas, which were very influential in Catholic circles, had a great effect on this development.

It is striking that in time the clergy began to play a more important role in Catholic organisational life. In the older organisations and associations they mostly had been involved in an indirect way. There the initiative mostly lay in the hands of well-to-do laymen who acted fairly autonomously, in part because they financially supported these organisations. In the school war however the bishops had, more than before, taken charge of the Catholic mobilisation and afterwards did not seem inclined to give away that position. This enhanced clerical influence was furthered by the growing number of priests and religious and by their improved formation. The clergy had more competence and manpower than before - the period saw a growing number of vocations with a total in 1900 of 6,237 male religious and 7,660 diocesan priests - to provide Catholic organisational life with the necessary staff. This development even increased after 1900. A new generation of priests then emerged, who had been instructed in the social doctrine of the church (*Rerum Novarum*, 1891) and were keen on playing a social role. These priests had an increasing impact on social study centres and in social organisations. They propagated a complete educational project for the working class and impressed on a wide group of lay people the concept of social harmony.

The increasing clerical influence, especially of the bishops, was also noticeable in political life. In the past there had been regular consultations between the bishops and the Right wing in parliament, but only when the political agenda dealt with matters directly related to the church (education, charity, material goods, cemeteries, etc.). Henceforth the bishops were also consulted on questions such as military service, colonial expansion, suffrage, language laws and social laws.[26] Because the government party had pre-eminently turned into a confessional party, it was not unusual for profane questions to acquire a religious dimension. Moreover, the bishops regularly had to mediate to settle internal tensions within the Catholic party. They wanted indeed in the first place to preserve unity within the party in order to successfully resist the anticlerical forces.

Also liberal organisations and networks were expanding, but especially the socialists were, from the 1880s on, establishing impressive social organisations: trade unions, mutual-aid societies, and cooperatives. As a result of these developments, not only Belgian political life but much of society became segmented, that is, divided into distinct subcultures with religion or (in the case of the liberals) political ideology serving as the basis for these subcultures. Later, social scientists characterised this process as 'pillarisation', in reference to the multiple religious or ideological 'pillars' that buttressed the political system.[27] A similar development took place in the Netherlands at about the same time.

From the 1890s on, 'pillarised' institutions and organisations received substantial state subsidies (the so-called system of 'subsidised freedom'). Public authorities started granting subsidies, first at the local and soon at the national level, to private saving banks, mutual-aid and unemployment societies and to popular housing initiatives. When the democratisation of the educational system, at first of the elementary schools, became a political priority, state subsidies were granted to Catholic elementary schools.

In fact, this mechanism amounted to a form of indirect state support for religious, or at least ideological, organisations and it had in this way an anti-liberal orientation. It should be pointed out, however, that state subsidies were not only given to Catholic initiatives, but also to liberal and socialist activities. Needless to say, state funding of these 'intermediate' institutions, standing between state and individual, only strengthened their social importance. They in turn had a direct impact on state policy through their links with the political parties. So, by the early twentieth century the liberal Belgian state had been given an anti-liberal, semi-corporatist content.

One can conclude that, as a result of a lengthy exercise of power by the Catholic party, the Catholic Church was in an advantageous position in the beginning of the twentieth century. It no longer had to fear hostile state legislation. It could moreover freely develop its own institutions and organisations. The law of 27 June 1921 gave those associations the opportunity to acquire legal personality. The church not only had obtained an extended sphere of action, it also received substantial state funding for its schools and welfare institutions. More than before, the church respected the autonomy of the state, yet the state system was in fact outclassed by a 'societal midfield' of private organisations, in which the Catholic Church had been able to acquire a very strong position.

115

---

[26] Gérin, "La démocratie chrétienne".　　　　[27] Lamberts, "Les sociétés pilarisées".

At the end of the nineteenth century, the Catholic Church gained an even stronger position in the Congo Free State, a colony established in Central Africa in 1884 under the sovereignty of the Belgian king Leopold II and transferred to the Belgian state in October 1908. The Berlin Act guaranteed all inhabitants, natives as well as foreigners, complete freedom of conscience and religion. Article 6 stipulated that the sovereign rulers should protect and stimulate all religious and charitable institutions without distinction of nationality or cult. The public exercise of any cult and the erection of religious buildings must not be subjected to any limitation. Leopold II, however, took care that Catholic evangelisation of the territory was reserved to Belgian missionaries. He promised them special protection and all kinds of material and financial advantages, such as landownership for the establishment of mission posts. Besides them there were many foreign Protestant missionaries but they received fewer advantages and prerogatives. In 1906 a concordat was concluded between Leopold II and the Holy See. The Catholic Church was to apply itself to civilising tasks such as education, charity and health care, whereas the state was to guarantee its security and financially support its economic infrastructure. After 1908, the Belgian state took over the obligations of the Congo Free State. In practice Belgian and especially Catholic missions were given preferential treatment. For a very long time, the missions had a monopoly in the field of education. Only after 1946 were public schools established.[28]

After the First World War, when universal suffrage (for men) was introduced and socialism made great progress in the elections, the Catholic party lost its absolute majority in parliament. Henceforth it was obliged to form coalition governments, mostly with the liberal party and sometimes also with the socialist party. That mitigated the confessional character of the policies pursued. Also, in this period socio-economic questions came to the fore, and ethnic-cultural contrasts between the Dutch-speaking and French-speaking communities began to determine the political agenda more than before. Catholic organisational life however kept its full power and significance. In competition with the socialist workers' movement a strong Christian workers' movement developed, free from the middle-class paternalism which once had dominated it. Also the Farmers' League witnessed a substantial expansion. Moreover, numerous youth movements were incorporated in the Catholic Action. So, the Catholic pillar emerged even stronger and was able to safeguard as yet for a very long time the influence of the church in the Belgian state. Only in the last quarter of the twentieth century a process of secularisation and 'depillarisation' cut back its dominant position in social and political life.

---

[28] Vanthemsche, *La Belgique et le Congo*; Markowitz, *Cross and Sword*.

Dutch Political Developments and Religious Reform

James C. Kennedy

The relation between church and state has seldom commanded much political interest in the Netherlands. One might argue that the Netherlands, arguably the least
'confessionalised' state of continental Europe in the early modern period, had the
least distance to go towards a church-state relationship most people would regard
as 'modern', that is, an arrangement in which there is no privileged or established
church. Already a relatively religiously plural country in 1780, it is not surprising that
the Netherlands had developed a system of 'principled pluralism' by 1920, in which
religious and non-religious organisations alike enjoyed equal access both to the public
sphere and to public goods.[1] Moreover, the transition may be characterised as at once
far-reaching and at the same time relatively free of violence and conflict. The Netherlands knew no religious civil war as Belgium or France experienced in the 1790s and
avoided the hard confrontations of the Wilhelmine *Kulturkampf*, however much some
Dutch liberals appreciated Bismarck's hard-line stance toward the Catholic Church.[2]
Disestablishment did not come in the wake of either a violent revolution or a lost war,
but in the bloodless liberal revolution of 1848, and in the gradual implementation of
church-state separation in ensuing decades. More generally, the country knew little
of the explosive confrontation between anticlericalism and clericalism that wracked
Catholic Europe, where the contests were typically more fierce than the Catholic-Protestant altercations evident in the confessionally mixed countries of Western Europe.[3]
Historically lacking a powerful state and confessionally divided from the outset, Dutch
political and religious actors were compelled by the limits of their own power to seek
a moderate, pragmatic religious settlement that best suited the religious pluriformity
of the nation.

---

[1] Carlson-Thiess, *Democracy in the Netherlands*, 109-132.

[2] Dorsman, "C.W. Opzoomer", 227.
[3] Beyen and Majerus, "Weak and Strong Nations".

There was in fact much on which the Dutch were agreed. Throughout much of the late nineteenth century, most Dutch political and religious leaders continued to be informed by the dualism of Western Christendom, which saw church and state as connected and complementary.[4] Even the most important proponent of the free church, Abraham Kuyper, thought that the church ought to be recognised as a public body and enjoy structured contact with the state. And many liberals (and not a few socialists) maintained a respect for churches as necessary moral arbiters in the public sphere, and were not eager to eliminate the ecclesiastical presence in society. In general religious outlook, the Netherlands more closely resembled Britain and the Scandinavian states than Catholic-dominant countries or Germany.

None of these considerations, however, should obscure the fact that the political path toward greater religious pluralism was a history of sometimes tortuous twists and turns. There was no linear path of religious reform that led to the pluralist religious arrangements the Dutch had made by 1920. In the first half of the nineteenth century, for instance, the Dutch state, in following other continental examples, was hardly interested in freeing religious denominations entirely from state control. Even after 1848, disestablishment reforms took many years to implement, and there were important actors, from conservatives in the Dutch Reformed Church to (in a different way) Catholic ultramontanists, who did not see an unregulated religious sphere as necessarily in the best interests of either church or state. Indeed, one might argue that the reform of 1848 did not 'solve' the church-state issue but broke open existing arrangements, thus intensifying disagreements about the religious settlement, and raising new and difficult issues of how the public sphere should be ordered. Whatever the case, the conflicts between Protestants and Catholics, and later between religious and secular parties, were serious, and they would determine, right up to the present day, the contours of Dutch politics and the organisation of Dutch society.

In looking at Dutch political developments in the long nineteenth century, it might be most helpful to think of two arenas of conflict in which opposing reforming forces came to confront each other. The first contested field of reform, evident in public debate from the 1780s until the 1850s or 1860s - focused on the task of establishing the proper relationship between the institutional church(es) and a state that, after 1795 at least, had foresworn its confessional identity. Efforts to recalibrate the church-state relationship in the wake of Enlightenment and Revolution precipitated at least two, largely opposing reform movements: the first aiming at loosening the bonds between church and state, the other seeking more effective state control over the nation's churches, and the tightening of administrative control over ecclesiastical bodies. After 1850, those who favoured reducing ties between church and state were clearly in the ascendant, but the relation of church to state remained an issue, both for the disestablished Reformed Church (whose claims on the purse of the state continued to serve as

---

[4] Van den Berg, *In vrijheid gebonden*, 7-23, 502.

a political irritant) and for the newly established Dutch Catholic episcopate, whose menacing presence many Protestant regarded with the deepest distrust.

The second arena of religious conflict, evident already in the 1850s but crucial in the development of Dutch politics from the 1870s on, was broader and more diffuse. With the church issue largely settled, this area of conflict was concerned not with the institutional church's ties to the state but on the place that religion, or variations of Christianity more particularly, should play in public life. After 1850, the tension on the place of religion in the public order would not focus on the formal place of the institutional church, but on the place of religion in areas that were increasingly coming under the purview of an increasingly powerful state. As the Dutch Catholic historian J.A. Bornewasser has summarised, the areas that now came into conflict were those issues traditionally defined as the *res mixtae* (that is, those areas traditionally thought to be the concern of both church and state): education, care of the poor, taxes on ecclesiastical incomes and possessions, Sunday rest, and public morals.[5] Of these, education was by far the most important source of conflict, and the focus of opposing reform efforts. The conflict would lead to far-reaching changes in Dutch society. It was the debate over the public financing of schools, of liberal reform to improve public education efforts over and against confessional reform efforts to include state financing for religious schools, that defined the discussion over the place of religion in Dutch public life. More than anything else, the conflict helped create the long-standing political divide in Dutch politics between confessional and non-confessional parties.

This chapter looks at these two arenas of conflict in which the Dutch attempted to achieve their contrasting visions of religious reform. On the second arena of conflict, this contribution will be relatively short, given that issues pertaining to philanthropy and education will be dealt with in subsequent volumes of this series. The starting point is, as the case with other chapters in this volume, in 1780, when the first systematic efforts at political and religious reform began in the Dutch Republic, and 1920, when the Dutch pluralistic arrangement we have come to know as 'pillarisation' (*verzuiling*) was more or less in place. It does so by way of an overview that is both roughly chronological and thematic.

In such a brief overview, there are many themes that can *not* be included here, including a foray into the West and East Indies and the extent of religious reform there. State policies toward the public role of religion in the Dutch colonies, while clearly influenced by religious reforms introduced by the Dutch government in The Hague, often diverged sharply from reform within the Netherlands proper. Though West Indian policies differed from those in the East, and though policies in both colonies were often tailor-made to fit local situations, it is clear that Dutch colonial authorities applied the principle of the state's neutrality toward religion less rigorously than authorities were increasingly obliged to do in the Netherlands. In the East Indies, the presence of tens of millions of Muslims inhibited Dutch colonial authorities from working out

119

---

[5] Bornewasser, "Twee eeuwen kerk en staat".

with any consistency the notion of a religiously neutral state. Not legal prescriptions but a deep sense of probity, the Indonesia-born legal scholar W.H. Alting van Geusau argued in 1917, was the highest aim at which the colonial government could aspire in its treatment of the different religions. In practice, colonial religious policy meant a closer working relationship with leading Christian churches (the Protestant church was disestablished from the colonial government only in 1935), and, after an initially reserved stance, an increasingly extensive partnership with Christian missions.[6] It meant, moreover, a recognition of Islam that left worship unimpeded and made provision for Islamic law in local judicial bodies, but which at the same time included efforts to suppress any 'political' expression of Islam, a danger regarded as subversive both to social progress and to Dutch rule.[7] It meant, finally, a hostile stance toward 'pagan' religion, as evident in the prohibition of *Winti* in Surinam in the 1870s on the basis of its 'idolatry'. It is true that in a few key developments - a greater measure of religious freedom and the state's increasing reliance of religious groups to organise important endeavours like education - reforms in the colonies parallel the reforms in the Netherlands outlined in this chapter. But the asymmetries and inequalities in colonial relations, and the greater use of religious organisations as the extension of state policy also underscore important differences, differences that make the inclusion of the colonies difficult in this short overview.

120

Deconfessionalisation and the Disestablishment of the Public Church (1780-1801)

In most parts of the Dutch Republic (1588-1795), the Dutch Reformed Church was the only 'public church', that is, the only church protected by the state and whose members were permitted to hold public office. That does not mean that all Dutch were obliged to be members of the church, and many in fact were not. The first hard figures on church membership stem from the first census of 1809, in which 55.5% of the population claimed membership in the Reformed Church, with 38.1% claiming to be Roman Catholic and 6.4% were designated as 'other' - Jews, Mennonites, Remonstrants, and Lutherans among them. Moreover, the Republic's decentralised character - a patchwork of autonomous republics and localities - meant that there was no centralised church and state, which in turn made it much more difficult to impose religious uniformity in ways possible elsewhere in Europe. Indeed, the Reformed Church itself did not function as a national body after the important synod of 1618-1619, but was organised according to the seven constituent republics, with regional church bodies (the classis) playing the most important role in regulating church life. Furthermore, the very nature of the

---

[6] Steenbrink, "Staat en religies", 180-181.

[7] Ibid., 193; Snouck Hurgronje, *Nederland en de Islam*; Alting van Geusau, *Neutraliteit der overheid in de Nederlandsche kolonien*, 19-20, 77, 95.

Reformed Church, with its traditional emphasis on internal ecclesiastical discipline, often made it a less than optimal instrument for confessionalisation, however much many of its pastors might have wished otherwise.

Some parts of the Republic consisted of villages and towns barely touched by the Reformation, most clearly the case in those strongly Catholic areas in the east and south of the Netherlands (Twente, Brabant, small parts of Limburg and Zeeland) that fell under Dutch rule only after the Catholic Reformation, chiefly in the early seventeenth century. But it was nearly as true in the heartlands of the Republic, in Holland and Utrecht, where religious minorities, to a large degree Catholics, constituted perhaps a third of the population. Friesland in the north, moreover, initially harboured large numbers of Anabaptists. Furthermore, the religious diversity of its highly urbanised society - furthered by extensive migration and trade - and the pragmatic concessions necessary to maintain order also gravitated against full-scale confessionalisation. In the context of these conditions, the dissenting Protestants, the Catholics and, on the different terms, the Jews (as foreign 'nation') could develop religious organisations and networks that, in many places, were free of significant hinder. In Holland, Protestant minorities were given a certain latitude in public worship in the late seventeenth and eighteenth centuries; for Catholics, the situation improved after about 1730. For these reasons, confessionalisation was all in all less thoroughgoing in the Dutch Republic than in most parts of continental Europe, and helps account for the high numbers of Protestant dissenters and much greater numbers of Roman Catholics who would in 1795 demand an end to the privileges of the public church.

121

The abundance of non-Reformed groups was not the only pressure on the religious monopoly of the 'public church'. After 1750, however, Reformed confessionalism itself was seriously challenged within the Reformed Church by processes occurring elsewhere in Protestant Europe: pietism, rationalism and a stress on virtue all challenged the emphases of confessional orthodoxy.[8] These newer religious sensibilities helped shape an orientation that increasingly set its sights not only on serving the confessional community but a national community.[9] By the 1770s and especially 1780s, the new desire to cultivate a nation of virtuous citizens was accompanied by a measure of political radicalisation, between those loyal to the House of Orange on the one hand (often from inside the Reformed Church, including many of its leading clerics but also many leading Jews), and 'Patriots', critics of ancient regimes oligarchic practices and also critical, to varying degrees, of the legal monopoly of the public church (Catholics, Protestant dissenters, and progressive Reformed clergy and laity). By the mid-1780s, this conflict generated near civil war; Patriot seizure of power was pre-empted only by a Prussian army, which in 1787 scattered the Patriot militias. Orangist triumph was short-lived, however; in 1795 a French revolutionary army, moving north from Belgium, occupied the entire country and ensured the establishment of a Sister Republic and the

---

[8] Van Eijnatten, *Preaching, Sermon and Cultural Change.*

[9] Van Rooden, "Long-term Religious Developments".

success of the Batavian Revolution, so named after reputed freedom-loving ancestors of the Dutch.

As in France, and as in most areas captured by French armies in the 1790s, the revolutionary rule of the new Batavian Republic signalled the formal end to the established church. Already in 1794, when French soldiers had invaded the southern parts of the Republic, Catholics began to claim the old parish churches as their own, and this trend now continued on a very modest scale, in those areas where the Protestant presence was weak. In August of 1796, the Reformed Church was formally disestablished. All churches were put on the same legal footing, and all citizens - including Catholics and Jews - were granted full rights in theory, if not yet in practice, as will be shown. A relatively large number of Catholics and dissenting Protestants were in charge of the reforms, but Reformed Church clergy were among those ushering them in. The changes implemented in 1796 placed only mild restrictions on church life - forbidding the ringing of church bells and the wearing of clerical vestments in public, and the country saw almost none of the violent conflict where French rule was direct, as in Catholic Belgium, or what would become part of Dutch Limburg after 1815. Houses of worship were expected to be supportive of the republic, not least in the cultivation of virtue and patriotism among its members.

122

The high water mark in the process of disestablishment came in 1798, when legislation was passed in which the Reformed Church was, in the course of several years, to be deprived of state financial support. No new Reformed clergy would be financed by the state. All of the properties that had been in the Reformed Church's possession before 1581 were to be considered the collective property of all members of the municipality, with local authorities determining which religious body should make future use of the buildings in question. Under this arrangement, some of the country's landmark churches were to change hands, and be used for Catholic worship in those areas where they formed a substantial majority.[10] All churches, moreover, were to raise their own finances and regulate their own affairs.

The first years of the Batavian Republic can be characterised, in hindsight, as a short-lived and not very thoroughgoing effort to achieve a reasonably amicable separation of church and state. Initially, the state made little systematic effort to control religious bodies for its own political purposes. But the reforms of the late 1790s were certainly serious enough to generate considerable opposition, and radical enough to prevent their effective implementation. The disestablishment of the Reformed Church turned out to be an administrative nightmare, since the ownership of church properties had not been centrally controlled but divided up among hundreds of local landowners, with varying kinds of claims to the properties they managed, with the degree of wealth - or debt - varying vastly from one locale to another. The financing of the church had in part been paid by the various Dutch governments on the basis of their trusteeship over church properties, but local authorities had not always been clear, when financ-

---

[10] Joor, *De Adelaar en het Lam*, 175.

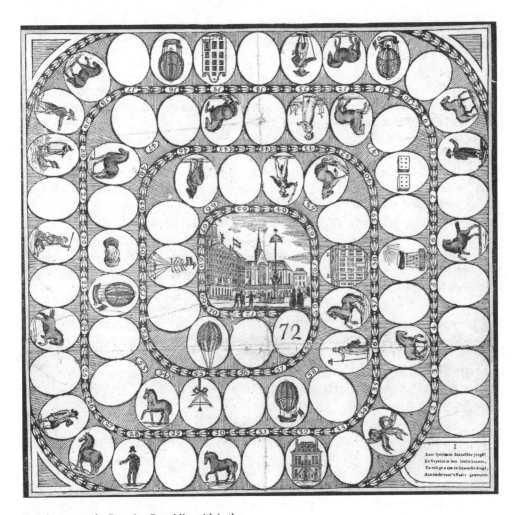

Board game on the Batavian Republic, *with in the centre the tree of liberty in front of the 'Nieuwe Kerk' in Amsterdam, woodcut, 1795-1798.*
[Rotterdam, Atlas Van Stolk: 234]

ing a church, from which of its properties, secular or religious, it had drawn the funds. This was made all the more complicated by the fact that the Reformation, in closing not only the monasteries but many now redundant chapels and churches, had created a property pool that had been used, in countless local arrangements, to finance both church and state institutions in the seventeenth and eighteenth centuries. There was thus a good case to be made that the Reformed Church (and arguably all churches) was entitled to a portion of the realty held by the state. How far the church could stretch its financial claims on the now-secular state proved impossible to calculate, and more to the point at hand, it provided no clear guidance for how the wealth of these properties should be divided among churches.[11]

Moreover, many Reformed had begun to oppose these reforms, as disadvantageous as they were in respect to the previous arrangements. The strong representation of Catholics in government had also triggered a reaction by many Protestants (not, then, only the Reformed) who disliked the Catholic upstarts with whom they were now compelled to share power. They furthermore resented Catholic claims to equality because they suggested, to the irritation of many Reformed, that Catholics had been badly treated during the Dutch Republic. In 1808, Jacobus Didericus Janssen, son of a Reformed minister who would for subsequent decades dominate state religious policy, expressed his contempt for 'Catholic shouting' over past persecution, while the historical record so clearly demonstrated that the Dutch Republic had been uniquely exemplary in its tolerance.[12] Protestants like Janssen, moreover, believed that enlightened Protestant virtues, rather than revolutionary slogans, were the best moral basis for society. It was a sentiment that closely reflected the way many Reformed elites had felt already before the revolutionary changes of the 1790s.

Protestant elite resistance to the reforms of the 1790s were aided by developments in France where the anticlerical Directory had been swept from power by Napoleon Bonaparte, who believed that the state had more to gain from co-opting religious bodies than from repressing them, or casting them off. Napoleon's new religious policies would find Dutch parallels in the last years of the Batavian Republic (1801-1806) and under the direct rule of the Bonapartes (1806-1813).

Enlightened State Oversight over the Churches (1801-1853)

The Batavian Republic, lacking effective leadership and vulnerable to French political and military pressure, witnessed several military overthrows in its short history. The coup of 1801 clearly precipitated a set of reforms that largely reversed many of the disestablishmentarian impulses of the 1790s. Orangists, including recalcitrant Reformed clergy who had resisted the demands of the new republic, regained their positions, and the participation of Catholics in state affairs was now effectively discouraged and blocked. Restorative impulses became stronger, and features of the *ancien régime* began to reappear, including pealing of the church bells, the proclamation of days of prayer and the renewed presence of political commissioners in the provincial synods of the Reformed Church. The new government put a stop to the transfer of church buildings and guaranteed the salaries of Reformed clergy, which effectively protected

---

[11] den Ouden, *De ontknoping van de zilveren koorde*, 22-38; de Jong, "Uitkeringen aan kerken".

[12] Cited in Noordeloos, *De restitutie der kerken*, 256.

the status quo of the pre-revolutionary period. The motivation, however, was not to restore the Reformed Church (or other bodies) to a position of independence vis-à-vis the state. If religion were to be harnessed for the general interest, it must be put under effective government constraint; the government declared in 1803 that religion was too important for the maintenance of civil society for it to be ignored by government. But as noted above, it was now the enlightened Protestant state, not the confessional Reformed Church, that took the lead in determining the place of religion in public life.

This ideal went hand in hand with the transformation of the Dutch state. Under French influence, the Dutch government, historically quite decentralised, was changed into an organ of centralised authority, evidenced most clearly in the Rutger Schimmelpenninck government of 1805-1806 - the last of the Batavian Republic. Next to the thorough reorganisation of state finances, Schimmelpenninck's most important achievement was a far-reaching school law that attempted to standardise primary education. It required all schools to instruct children in the 'Christian and social virtues', thus supplanting confessional models that hitherto had been in place, and removing the role that the churches, in particular the Reformed, had played in education.[13] This important shift in the creation of non-sectarian (if still broadly Christian) public education would generate tensions later on, as we shall see.

Centralisation of the state - not least in respect to religion - continued apace after 1806, when the Kingdom of Holland was created by Napoleon, with his brother Louis serving as King of Holland (1806-1810). In 1808, Louis created in French style the Ministry of Public Worship (*Ministerie van den Openbaren Eeredienst*), charged with regulating and coordinating religious life in the Netherlands, subdivided into two sections, one devoted to the regulation of Roman Catholic worship and one for the remaining denominations. Through these ministries, the state became active in ensuring the proper functioning of church bodies. This included the rationalisation of salaries in the Reformed Church, which the national and local governments continued to finance to an important extent - well over one million guilders per annum. In contrast, government promised 100,000 guilders for Catholic clergy, and another 20,000 per annum for other clergy, but in financially hard times even these small amounts were not paid out. Thus the Catholics, often without suitable buildings, were left to fend for themselves, though local parishes might with success plead for government aid.[14] It should be remembered that throughout this period, the Dutch Catholic Church functioned without a national episcopal hierarchy, this having been abolished by the Reformation.

But the royal decree of 1808 did again make possible the reallocation of church buildings or financial restitution of lost revenues. Louis did restore, for example, to a number of Roman Catholic parishes church buildings held by the Reformed, mostly in peripheral parts of the country, and in places where tiny Reformed minorities held title to the local church, as in overwhelmingly Catholic Brabant but especially in rural

125

---

[13] Kloek and Mijnhardt, *Dutch Culture in a European Perspective*, 167-184.

[14] Noordeloos, *De restitutie der kerken*, 251-252; den Ouden, *De ontknoping van de zilveren koorde*, 68.

Twente, on the German frontier. In practice, Louis' reallocation reform, if adjusting some of the most egregious inequalities, remained very limited in effect, foundering on the same disagreement and resistance that the more ambitious policies of the 1790s had faced. But the point of these exercises, of course, was not to restore church privileges but to expand the role of the state in regulating religious life. The government also saw as its task to ensure that religious expression would not disrupt the public order, and in 1807 the government issued a prohibition on processions in the wake of a Catholic pilgrimage to the North Holland town of Heiloo.[15] This was evident in other terrains as well. In 1811, after the Netherlands had been formally incorporated into the French Empire, the civil code was implemented - for good, as it turned out - requiring the registry of all births, marriages and deaths by secular municipal officials. Churches sustained the old rituals, but it was now the state that registered the most important moments of a person's life.

The defeat of Napoleon and the return to power of the House of Orange late in 1813 in no way reversed this trend. Willem, the son of the last stadtholder, had discreetly let himself be crowned king, and the constitutions of 1814 and 1815 gave him relatively wide latitude to rule according to his own lights. The centralisation of ecclesiastical life was one of Willem I's priorities. That did not mean a return to an establishment of one single, public church, though Willem, shaped by German church-state arrangements, with which he had intimate experience through his many years in exile, preferred such an arrangement. Indeed, the constitution of 1814 had stipulated that the 'Christian Reformed faith is that of the sovereign'. But when the great powers determined in the secret Treaty of London to make Belgium part of the Kingdom of the Netherlands on condition that freedom of worship be guaranteed there Willem had this provision scrapped from the constitution. Had his preference prevailed, Catholics and Protestants would have been united in a single national church. This not being possible, Willem, in forging a single state of Belgium and Holland, sought the next best thing: preventing confessional differences from disrupting the order of his new kingdom. This also meant facilitating, where possible, the formation of key religious elements into a hierarchical organisation with direct ties to the organs of government. After the short-lived re-establishment in 1814-1815, then, there was no single established church in the early-nineteenth-century Netherlands, but rather a set of state-regulated ecclesiastical bodies, with some more clearly tied to the state than others.[16]

Willem's reforms are most classically evident in administrative organisation of the Reformed, the Jews and the Lutherans, which aimed at turning church bodies into the efficient agents of material and spiritual assistance to its members and into teachers of virtue. In 1816 Willem I, informed by Janssen, established a *reglement* for the Reformed Church, which consisted of a top-down organisation with a nineteen-member 'synod' at its top. Unlike past synods, the new synod was not given any author-

---

[15] Joor, *De Adelaar en het Lam*, 172-173.

[16] For a general view of church history in the Netherlands during the nineteenth century, see Wintle, *Pillars of Piety*.

ity to decide theological disputes but was to be solely administrative in purpose. In this way, the Reformed Church could become the national church that it never fully had been, a smoothly-functioning organisation that oversaw a non-dogmatic community chiefly engaged in teaching Christian morality and love of king and fatherland.[17] Under no circumstances was religion to serve as the basis for unrest, but it was to contribute to social harmony, with the state maintaining ties to the churches to ensure that the former be prevented, and the latter encouraged. The state, following the course to which it had recommitted itself since 1801, continued to pay the salaries of Reformed and other Protestant clergy. Similar *reglementen* were drawn up for the Jewish and Lutheran communities. The Jews were in fact the first to undergo this process; already in 1810, the Jewish community had been placed under French statute when the Netherlands was annexed to France, the only religious group for which this was the case. In 1814 Willem I's government went further, compelling by statute that the Sephardic and Ashkenazi Jews merge their bodies into one, so that poor and rich congregations might together fall under a single effective administration of charity. Portuguese and Yiddish were furthermore prohibited as languages of worship.[18] A *reglement* for the Lutherans followed in 1818.[19] Although prejudice and discrimination affected the Jews much more than they did the Lutherans, both religious minorities thought to benefit from the legal status and access to government that the statutory relationship with the state yielded them. The Anabaptists, on the other hand, much less centrally organised than the Lutherans and historically distrustful of the state, evaded a similar relationship.

Willem, in pursuing his religious reforms, could afford to overlook the small General Anabaptist Society. But his ambitions to unite his kingdom through active state policy did not permit such an attitude toward the Roman Catholic Church, whose adherents, with the inclusion of Belgium, now constituted over 70% of the population in the United Kingdom of the Netherlands. The Catholic episcopate in Belgium had been anything but enthusiastic about the imposition of a Protestant prince in 1815, and Willem did little to allay their distrust, developing his own rather aggressive Catholic policy. It is true that the king restored 15 village churches to Catholics in Brabant, belatedly implementing a decision already made by Louis Bonaparte[20], and that he continued to make it possible, through the Ministry of Worship that specialised in Catholic affairs, for local Catholic parishes to apply for local or national government funds to establish, for instance, new churches. But the king's efforts to punish the recalcitrant Belgian bishop De Broglie, restrict correspondence with the Holy See, monitor monastic life, and above all to regulate Catholic theological education by closing smaller schools and requiring that seminarians attend the government-controlled school in Louvain, fomented deep unhappiness among his Catholic subjects. Attempts to further restrict

127

---

[17] Rasker, *De Nederlandse Hervormde Kerk*, 24-31.
[18] Wallet, *Nieuwe Nederlanders*.
[19] Diepenhorst, *De verhouding tusschen kerk en staat*, 74-78.
[20] Noordeloos, *De restitutie der kerken*, 428-431.

128

D. Sluyter, Allegorical picture of the Concordat of
1827 between 'Rome' and the Kingdom of the Netherlands, *engraving. The Dutch delegate presents
the Concordat to the Pope; the three women in the
foreground are personifications of Faith, Firmness
and Purity.*
[Amsterdam, Rijksprentenkabinet]

religious processions also caused tensions.[21] This was probably true of the Belgians in particular, who had hoped the end of French rule would bring about a restoration of the church's rights under the *ancien régime*. Although Willem had initially sought to create a national Catholicism independent of the Holy See, the government was obliged in 1827 to conclude a concordat with the papacy that sought to regulate and improve the relationship between church and state.[22] The Concordat allowed, for instance, the king to veto episcopal candidates on lists drawn up the church. It also provided the framework for the return of Dutch bishops to the Northern Netherlands. But this agreement did not essentially change the antagonistic relationship between Willem and Belgian Catholics, and their unhappiness with Willem's religious policy was one source of the successful Belgian revolt of 1830. In the wake of Belgian independence, the Concordat of 1827 became a dead letter on both sides of the new frontier, and it signalled the failure of Willem's reforming efforts to assert a measure of state control over the Catholic Church. After the successful secession of Belgium, the Dutch government enacted no important new initiatives to reassert a greater measure of control over the Catholic Church.

Protestants were much more quiescent in respect to Willem's reforms; few initially protested against his *reglement* for the Reformed Church, which, if it did not bring about re-establishment of the 'public church', gave the church a central institutional role in the kingdom. Indeed, the Reformed Church had become, for the first time, a national body, with close contacts with national government, and this arrangement, many Reformed felt, enhanced, not diminished, the status and authority of the church. By the 1830s, however, a small number of orthodox Protestants challenged the authority of the church hierarchy, whose theological and liturgical innovations, as well as their sometimes barely-disguised contempt for the old confessional creeds, they regarded as un-Reformed and heretical. Some of these separatists refused to apply for government recognition, and for a few years they were accordingly persecuted by the authorities by quartering soldiers in their houses, or fining and imprisoning them for meeting together. The fate of these seceders generated debate in the 1830s over both the limits of religious freedom and the spiritual state of the Reformed Church. In different ways, then, the conflict with Catholics and seceders revealed the limits of Willem I's reforms aimed at coordinating and directing Dutch religious life under a centralised royal government.

After Willem I's abdication as king in 1840 the religious status quo, as it had developed since the beginning of the nineteenth century, remained intact: state-financed, state-regulated churches, with the Catholic Church operating legally, if still far from the centre of power in a rather assertively Protestant state, and with the Dutch Reformed Church enjoying the status of a *primus inter pares*. Well-to-do and enlightened Protestants of all stripes could participate in public life without any real restrictions, but the Reformed remained dominant: the church's leadership enjoyed

---

[21] Margry, *Teedere Quaesties*, 218-261.   [22] Houkes, "Het succes van 1848", 90.

the access to government made possible by the fact that most government officials (as well as the country's cultural elite) were members of the same church. Through the 1840s, Dutch Reformed ministers plausibly could claim that their church was the spiritual centre of the nation, cherished and protected by a monarch and a ministry that sought to give the church a prominent role in Dutch society.

In the 1840s, however, a new attitude toward religion in the public sphere had become evident. To begin with, Willem II (1840-1849) soon demonstrated a different religious sensibility from his father. He possessed little of the same drive to centralise and manage ecclesiastical life that his father had possessed, perhaps due in part, it is often speculated, to his sustained friendship with a leading Catholic cleric, the later Archbishop of Utrecht, Joannes Zwijsen. In 1841 the prosecutions of Reformed seceders stopped, and in 1842 the government claimed that it was not 'authorised' (*bevoegd*) to interfere in the affairs of the Dutch Reformed Church, unless required by the good order and the security of the state to do so. The 1840s saw the advent of a new genera-tion of liberals who argued that church and state ought not to be so closely associated, an idea articulated by parliamentarian and jurist J.R. Thorbecke, a Lutheran shaped by the German idealism of the 1820s. Disestablishment thus became one of the aims of a relatively small group of liberal parliamentarians in the 1840s, and even within the Synod there were private discussions about whether a change in the church-state relationship was necessary or desirable.[23]

The decisive move toward political reforms that signalled a retreat from state trusteeship of the church occurred only in the early spring of 1848, when, in the wake of revolutions elsewhere, Willem II charged the liberal Thorbecke with the writing of a new constitution. Thorbecke himself subscribed to a Christianity that transcended confessional divisions, and he insisted that he wanted churches, even as private bodies, to exercise public authority and thus constitute an important component in the life of the nation. But churches - and of course everyone thought first and foremost of the still-privileged Reformed Church - would now have to carry out their work in society under their own steam. In concrete terms, it meant that local congregations would have to become far more important in generating the resources and strategies necessary if they were to conduct their own affairs. Changes in 1852 to the *reglement* 'congregationalised' the church by placing more in the hands of these local bodies, a process that would be further worked out in subsequent years.[24]

Thorbecke's disestablishmentarian reforms were not popular, as one might expect, among the leadership of the Reformed synod, who not only bemoaned the church's loss of status but became fearful that the church might thus be delivered over to the whims of its members. And many liberals - including Thorbecke's first minister responsible for worship of the Reformed and other non-Catholic communions from 1848 to 1849 - came to see disestablishment as a potential disaster. In their view it

---

[23] Vree, "De herziening van het hervormde Alge-meen Reglement", 22-27.

[24] Rasker, *De Nederlandse Hervormde Kerk*, 156-158.

would allow the orthodox party, led by the historian Guillaume Groen van Prinsterer, to either take over the church or to rent it by schism, all the while allowing ultramontanism to go unchecked, free from any kind of state oversight.[25]

This apprehension became evident in the spring of 1853. Judging by the relatively small numbers of their publicists, Dutch Roman Catholics broadly supported Thorbecke's reforms of 1848, since they promised, at least in theory, a state that regarded them as possessing the same rights and enjoying the same access to itself as their Protestant fellow citizens. There was one major exception to this rule: the constitutional restriction on Catholic processions. Initially, Thorbecke had wanted to do away with restrictions on processions altogether, but a Protestant backlash made this politically impossible, and the new constitution now stipulated that processions could be held outside the church only in those localities where they were specifically permitted. The liberal constitution of 1848, then, did not wholly put an end to state restrictions on Catholic freedom of worship.

At the same time, though, the new liberal constitutional regime crucially opened the way for the return of the Roman Catholic hierarchy to the Netherlands. In rejecting the principle of a concordat, or any kind of state treaty with the Holy See, the Thorbecke government in effect allowed for the return of Catholic bishops to the Netherlands after an effective absence of some 275 years. This restoration of the Catholic bishoprics - with the symbolically laden return of an archbishop to Utrecht, a city in the country's Protestant heart - was met with dismay by many Dutch Protestants. It did not help that the papal nuncio in charge of the negotiations made cutting remarks about the Calvinist heresy, but the possible return of the hierarchy was bound in any circumstances to evoke and mobilise Protestant anger. A stunning number of Dutch citizens - some 200,000 of them - signed a protest petition in the spring of 1853, organised by the Reformed consistory of Utrecht, in what is called the April Movement.[26] The Thorbecke government fell as an indirect result of the protest, but the movement could not prevent the restoration of the episcopate. But it did compel the new conservative government to pass a Law on the Denominations (*Wet op de kerkgenootschappen*) in 1853. It contained some restrictions on worship aimed at the Catholics - most notably the prohibition of (Catholic) clerical garb in public, so as to make processions even more difficult than they already had been to organise. It also required government permission for the establishment of church offices in a particular town (the government thus claiming, for instance, the right to prevent the new Catholic archbishop from residing in Utrecht, though in the end it did not so do).[27] The perceived threat to the Netherlands as a Protestant country in the wake of disestablishment and restoration did, however, unleash a torrent of Protestant activism that would profoundly affect Dutch politics and civil society.[28]

131

---

[25] Vree, "De herziening van het hervormde Algemeen Reglement", 39-42.
[26] Vis and Janse, *Staf en storm*.

[27] Aalders, "De Wet op de Kerkgenootschappen", 118-119.
[28] Houkes, *Christelijke vaderlanders*, 44-46.

The Separation of Church and State in Practice (1853-1922)

The Reformed opposition to the political developments at the mid-point of the nineteenth century, and the technical complications arising from the separation, meant that Thorbecke's reform efforts to further separate church from state proceeded slowly. There was never a political consensus either over how to cut off state financing to the Reformed Church or how to make it more equitable. But the disengagement of the state from ecclesiastical affairs was unmistakeable, and church-state relations henceforth seldom played an important role in political debate. That does not mean that all Reformed were reconciled to disestablishment; theologians like Philip Hoedemaker held at the end of the nineteenth century that the Reformed Church had a special mission to the state and to the Dutch people, and that it ought to be a privileged church. This vision for a 'theocracy', as this strand of thought became known in the Netherlands, would remain significant in some Reformed circles until the present day, and would particularly enjoy a renaissance immediately after the Second World War. It would also find resonance in Protestant parties founded in the early twentieth century such as the Christian Historical Union (formally founded in 1908), a party which held to the view that the Netherlands was a Protestant country and the Reformed Church the most natural expression of that fact, or the small, restorationist State Reformed Party (*Staatkundig Gereformeerde Partij*, founded in 1918), which called for the reinstatement of the confessional state.[29] But these various articulations of a 'theocratic' ideal did not result in any change to the church-state relationship as it developed in the late nineteenth century.

The government ministries for worship (still divided between one for Catholics and one for all the rest) would in various organised forms continue to function until the end of 1870, with more conservative cabinets recognising separate ministries, and more progressive cabinets demoting them to departments of other ministries. But, from 1871 on, the government no longer retained a special agency for religious affairs. In the light of these changes, the government released the religious bodies with which they had made *reglementen* from all restrictions, for the Lutherans in 1857 and for the Jews in 1870. Although new regulations in 1852 largely freed the Reformed Church from government control, the government retained eleven remaining restrictions on the church's freedom of movement (including those concerning the management of property, the notification of clerical appointments and, notably, the denial of the church's right to determine Reformed Church policy in the colonies). The ties between church and state were too intricate, and the concerns about the effects of rapid disestablishment too great, for the state to immediately abandon all responsibility for the Reformed Church.

[29] Van der Zwaag, *Onverkort of gekortwiekt?*, 352-404.

132

J.H. Neuman, Johan Rudolf Thorbecke, *oil on canvas, 1852.*
[Amsterdam, Rijksmuseum: SK-A-4120]

But these restrictions, too, came to an end in 1870.[30] In the 1850s the crown formally relinquished the right to administer the church; in the 1860s it formally renounced its claim to manage church properties. Only with a legal reform in 1922 were the last rights of secular authorities to appoint local clergy abolished.[31]

Although the state now renounced any special relationship with any and all churches, the constitution of 1848 made provision for state subsidies to churches to continue. Because the state was not *obliged* to support any church, the continued payments were justified as the compensation of churches for properties once taken from them, either during the Reformation or the Batavian Revolution, or because local congregations simply required the funding. The state continued to pay something more than 1 million guilders a year to the Reformed Church (about £85,000 in 1900), an amount that was annually sustained, but did not appreciably increase until the termination of these modest payments in the early 1980s. Thorbecke himself was in no hurry to end the subsidies; in 1869 he opined as prime minister that real hardship in local church situations might justify the continued state expenditures.[32] Churches could request, often via parliamentarians, small subsidies from the Dutch government (sometimes matching funds were required), such as paying the salary of an additional clergyman in a given city. And, to show its impartiality, the state showed a willingness to fund other churches as well; by 1907, the Roman Catholic Church received half a million guilders a year. Denominations received small lump sums from the government at irregular intervals. And the state continued to pay for the theological education of the traditional Protestant denominations, even after 1876, when ecclesiastical training was formally separated from the now purely 'scientific' faculties of theology at the four Dutch universities.

These pragmatic arrangements, then, were neither conceptually elegant nor wholly consistent. The Reformed Church had difficulties functioning financially as a free church, but it possessed enough clout to block the termination of funding to itself, and to prevent the reallocation of church funding on a fully equitable basis. Many Reformed continued to resist the consequences of the separation of church and state, holding fast to the notion of the Reformed Church's special mission to the Dutch nation. This was all to the annoyance of both radical liberals and orthodox Calvinists of the free churches, who, like some of their counterparts in other countries, saw church subsidies as contrary to their notions of what both church and state must be.[33] But no consensus on an equitable solution could be found, and the modest levels of money involved made resolution no pressing matter.

What led to far sharper confrontation was the one major area where government control of religious activity increased in the period of early disestablishment: the restriction on Catholic processions. Already in 1848 and in 1853, as noted above,

---

[30] Diepenhorst, *De verhouding tusschen kerk en staat*, 82; de Visser, *Kerk en staat*, 379-383.
[31] Faber, "De afschaffing van de collatierechten", 88-89.

[32] De Visser, *Kerk en staat*, 422; Kromsigt, *De leuze "Scheiding van Kerk en Staat"*.
[33] For an influential free church critic see Kuyper, *De gemeene gratie*, 247-267.

Protestant fears had resulted in new restrictions on Catholic processions, which for a time effectively curbed Catholic religious presence in the streets. In the 1870s, however, the law resulted in a series of new confrontations, as Catholics, partly inspired by Catholic activists who had fled German persecution in the *Kulturkampf*, began to assert their right to hold processions. This resulted in government crackdowns, a number of arrests and the further politicisation of Dutch Catholicism. Within a few years, however, the government - realising that processions were theoretically difficult to define and practically difficult to prohibit - retreated from a zealous enforcement of the law, and Catholics - in part facilitated by the advent of train travel, which redefined the nature of pilgrimages - found ways to organise processions in ways that avoided conflict.

It is not surprising, then, that the political reforms of mid-century did have important effects on church bodies themselves. The return of the Catholic hierarchy revolutionised the political orientation and social mobilisation of Dutch Catholics, precisely at a time when Pius IX was transforming the Catholic Church into a truly international body. The separation of church and state forced the Reformed Church, however reluctantly, to seek financial and administrative support from local church bodies, partly by, as briefly noted above, congregationalising a once-hierarchical church. By 1867, Reformed congregations gained the right to select their own clergy, a provision that mobilised both progressive and especially orthodox church members.[34] Furthermore, the legal changes of 1848 lowered the bar for other forms of religious expression. New ecclesiastical bodies could emerge at will; in 1886, an orthodox Reformed group, led by the intrepid politician-theologian Abraham Kuyper, left the Reformed Church; ultimately, this offshoot Reformed Churches in the Netherlands would constitute about 8% of the Dutch population. After the 1880s, too, a significant number of Dutch would abandon the institutional church altogether - more than 14% of all Dutch by 1930, a large percentage by European standards. Many of them came out of the Reformed Church, and a good number left in the 1920s, when the church - in an effort to solicit additional funds from its members - increased the size of the contribution it requested.[35]

All these were indications of the eclipse of the churches as the predominant religious institutions of Dutch society. In the course of the late nineteenth and twentieth centuries, they would increasingly be passed by other, often more dynamic institutions of Christian civil society. It meant, too, that the fight over the place of religion in public life would take place over other issues, and in the long run it would not be over the state's financial support of the church, but the state's financial support for Christian associations.

135

---

[34] Houkes, *Christelijke vaderlanders*, 145-183.

[35] For related financial difficulties facing the Reformed Churches around 1920, see den Ouden, *De ontknoping van de zilveren koorde*, 135-140.

Poor Relief and Education
New Reform Efforts (1848-1917)

Not only disestablishment and a liberal constitution, but the increasing complexity of society and the need for better quality of services, both in caring for the indigent and in educating the young, raised new questions about which agencies of society should carry the primary responsibility for these tasks, and which reforms were necessary to ensure these responsibilities.

As in other parts of (Western) Europe, Dutch society was characterised by two contrasting developments. The first was the increasing power of the state, and the areas of life that the state claimed for itself. From the 1860s and 1870s, Dutch liberalism, the dominant ideological current of that period, was increasingly shaped by a more activist stance in respect to the labour market, infrastructure and education, seeing it as the state's responsibility to provide the minimal conditions for a 'modern' society of the kind they wanted the Netherlands to be. At the same time, the nineteenth century witnessed a crescendo of voluntary associations across both Europe in general and the Netherlands in particular.[36] Many were not focused on reform of any kind; many were not religious in composition or in purpose. But the expansion of civil society, in which citizens and citizens' groups made their own claims on public life and articulated their own visions of the future, sometimes conflicted with state prerogatives. In this case, the explosion of religiously-based associations in the late nineteenth and early twentieth centuries, with their own visions of reform, sometimes collided with a liberal vision of state and society. It is not that these new religious groups were necessarily hostile to the state; as we shall see, for they would prove to be willing to use the state's power of the purse to suit their own goals. But it did mean that there were differing views of how a modern society should be structured, and what role, if any, religious organisations, should play.

The two areas of reform which defined the relationship between religious groups and the state in this period had to do with the care for the poor, and above all, the organisation of schools.

Poor relief, one of the classic *res mixtae*, had already been a point of friction between church and state in the *ancien régime* and between 1795 and 1848. Prior to 1795, the diaconal work and other organisations aimed at assisting the poor had been a patchwork of local provisions, with the poor more or less falling under the care of the religious communities with which they came to be associated, often in cooperation with municipal initiatives. The Batavian Revolution had preached the equality of all citizens, but the role of the state in regulating this fragmented system of poor relief remained quite limited. A law promulgated in 1800, which declared care for the poor

---

[36] Janse, *De afschaffers*; Hoffman, *Civil Society and Democracy*.

to be a public service and which attempted to centralise local funding agencies, soon foundered through the opposition of the local providers, who saw their charity as not belonging to the realm of the state at all. Churches in practice were required by local authorities to take care of their own poor, a practice codified into law in 1818, which also prescribed several measures by which churches were to implement their care, including a residency requirement for the indigent (four years) and the requirement that local charitable agencies report their activities to the central government.

The points of contention increased after 1848, with the implementation of a liberal constitution. The 1840s witnessed two opposing reform movements: the first to make care of the poor a formal task of government and assistance the right of the citizen; the second to strengthen the place of the church and other private organisations, particularly in freeing them to pursue their own charitable policies. With the separation of church and state in 1848, churches and local governments were obliged to work more independently of each other, though that was not supposed to bring an end to cooperation. In 1851 Thorbecke's liberal government attempted to rationalise the laws regarding local poor relief by setting the level of payments recipients ought to receive on the basis of age and family size; like the Batavian reformers, he saw assistance to the poor as a public service. This reform, aimed at strengthening state oversight over the practice of private initiative, failed to become law. Parliament found Thorbecke's plan too radical, and the successful resistance to Thorbecke's reforms had to with the resistance of local administrators of local agencies who preferred the status quo to the centralised reforms of the state.

Resistance to Thorbecke also had to do with the movements within churches and local philanthropic bodies, who understood assistance to the poor more than ever in voluntary and moral terms. Prior to Thorbecke's reforms, the *Reveil* movement in the Netherlands had been active in launching new projects to help the poor, led by Otto Heldring, a Reformed Church pastor who was highly successful in launching new initiatives to assist the destitute. Churches and charitable agencies argued that they must be free to determine which applicants were morally worthy or not, and how they could best be helped, and that the state should not intrude on these prerogatives. The Poor Law of 1854 gave churches the right to regulate their own affairs in respect to the poor and indigent of their own persuasions, with direct government aid given only to those who could not make a successful appeal to their own (or any) church.

The churches and many Christian agencies welcomed the law of 1854 which expanded their scope of action. They could become choosier in their acceptance of indigence, requiring more than ever before proof of active membership or morally reputable behaviour.[37] Local churches and other private charitable organisations would continue to take pride of place in the country's system of poor relief. Religious groups were successful at checking reform efforts, particularly active in two decades

137

---

[37] Spaans, "Kerkelijke en publieke armenzorg", 130-131.

Profijtelijk akkoord.

Teekening van ALBERT HAHN

Voor het kiesrecht zijn wij koud, in alle rangen en standen!

A. Hahn, Profitable agreement, *cartoon, 1913.*
Protestants and Catholics were coming to terms in
several areas of reform, e.g. concerning universal
suffrage.
[Amsterdam, Internationaal Instituut voor Sociale
Geschiedenis]

138

before the First World War, to give the state a greater role in coordinating and executing poor policy. The Poor Law of 1912 sustained the primacy of particular initiative, and formally allowed an emergent practice: the state to supplement the payments handed out by churches and other private organisations.[38] This arrangement reflected both the increasing power of religious blocs, orthodox Protestants and Catholics, to implement the state in the defence and preservation of religious institutions, in this case, by subsidising private poor relief efforts.

At the same time, the new emphasis on moral conduct emphasised by the churches paved the way for a new place for the state, which took on increasing numbers

---

[38] Van Leeuwen, "Armenzorg".

of people whose applications had been rejected by churches and other private agencies. The increased role of local government on this count went hand in hand with the ability of the state to generate more financing for the poor than private giving could provide. Before 1848, local poor councils had drawn from both private and public sources of funding in assisting the poor. At the time of the separation of church and state in 1848, it is estimated that the government financing in assisting the poor had already exceeded that of the churches. The state's actual role in poor relief increased substantially thereafter; municipalities, benefiting from reliable tax incomes and from the professionalisation of an emerging bureaucracy, developed social policies and services to the poor that were often of higher quality and certainly better financed; church expenditures on the poor steadily declined in relative terms throughout the last half of the nineteenth century and first two decades of the twentieth.[39] Increasingly, even private agencies and churches were dependent on government for extra funds, but these private bodies remained the leading institutions of poor relief in the Netherlands. Those supporting the prerogatives of the churches had won in political terms, but not in a way that stopped the increasing marginalisation of churches as the leading agents in poor relief.

Much more successful were efforts by religious groups to construct a sustainable network of Catholic and Protestant schools. The 'school question', as it was called, mobilised religious voters like no other issue, and was most responsible for the ultimate creation of politically powerful religious subcultures in the Netherlands.

As with other issues, the political struggle over the Dutch education system came subsequent to the constitution of 1848. Two issues soon required resolution. The first was whether citizens had to be required to attend public as opposed to private schools. After 1815, special permission had to be granted by the government before private or religious schools could be established, to which the government sometimes acceded, as in the case of Jewish schools, which it subsidised. The second issue concerned the religious basis, if any, that public schools should possess. As noted above, the law of 1806 had stipulated a non-doctrinaire Christianity as the moral basis for the public school, but after 1848 there were already voices who found such a formulation either not sufficiently Christian or not sufficiently secular and neutral. The first effort at school reform, passed in 1857, laid an important basis for the next twenty years: private schools were to be allowed, but not subsidised, by the state, and public schools were to retain the same broad religious spirit mandated by the law of 1806. Some orthodox Protestants like Groen van Prinsterer objected strongly to this law, preferring as he did public schools with a strong confessional identity, either Protestant or Catholic, according to local conditions. But in the 1860s, Groen abandoned this vision, and came to believe that the only way forward was if Christians opted for private schools, the Christian public school now given up as a hopeless cause. Groen

139

---

[39] Van Doorn, "De strijd tegen armoede en werkloosheid", 17.

and his fellow travellers, known as Anti-Revolutionaries (because they opposed the spirit of the French Revolution) were joined by the Catholic episcopate who, influenced by the anti-liberalism of Pope Pius IX, called for the creation of parochial Catholic schools in 1868. Neither Groen nor the bishops found univocal or immediate support among their co-religionists. Many Protestants and Catholics alike felt sufficiently at home in the local public school, over which they continued to exercise some control, and many Protestants in particular distrusted religious schools either for their ostensible sectarian spirit or, in the case of Catholic schools, for the clerical domination that would inevitably colour parochial education.

As it turned out, it was ambitious liberal efforts at further reform of the public schools in the 1870s that would decisively tip the balance in favour of the campaign to unite large sections of confessional leaders and voters in favour of private religious schools. Dutch liberalism in the 1870s, even if did not engage in a *Kulturkampf*, was, like other liberal movements in Europe of the time, more secularist and anticlerical than it had been before, more forcefully committed to the march of science and progress, and more critical of religious forces that might stand in the way, such as Catholic ultramontanists or, to a lesser extent, the orthodox Calvinist Anti-Revolutionaries. It was in this context that the liberal government of Johannes Kappeyne van de Coppello sought in 1877 to modernise the Dutch educational system. The national government would invest heavily in education, and raise the standards of all schools. Public education was to be made free, and religious education was to be made strictly optional, though churches could make free use of public school facilities to teach religion after school hours. Kappeyne's School Law, passed in 1878, had attenuated the notion that Dutch public schools were Christian institutions. But perhaps more important to most believers, his law also additionally disadvantaged private schools. These schools were now required by law to meet new, higher standards, but to do so they would have to raise their tuition fees so much as to make it unaffordable to many families. These reforms were completely unpalatable for hundreds of thousands of citizens.

This expressed itself in the petition drive of 1878, directed at the king, asking that he would not sign the recently passed education law. Over 300,000 Dutch citizens signed the petition, again, as had been the case in 1853, a number without precedent. The king was in no position to honour the petitioners' request, and the law was enacted. But the mobilisation necessary for the campaign served as an important impulse for further confessional activity, both on the side of Catholics but particularly on the part of the orthodox Protestants, who established the Netherlands' first modern political party, the *Antirevolutionaire Partij* (ARP).

The School Law of 1878 changed the terms of the debate over education for the next decades. The debate no longer focused on the nature of the public school (confessional, Christian, religiously neutral), but on whether the government should subsidise private education or not. Most liberals (and later, social democrats) were opposed to the notion of subsidies, because they regarded such a concession as the end of laudable state ambitions to shape and improve the public sphere. On the confessional side, too, there were those who were wary of the effects of state subsidies on private schools.

But by and large Roman Catholics and orthodox Protestants after 1878 came to regard a subsidy for Christian schools as the central reform they sought to enact in the political realm.

The political mobilisation of the orthodox Protestants to this end took place earlier than among Catholics, and it also took years before a sustained degree of cooperation was achieved between these two historically opposed confessional blocs. The first important sign of their success were the elections of 1888, which resulted in the first confessional cabinet of Anti-Revolutionaries and Catholics. Though of short duration (1888-1891), the government in 1889 passed its own reform of the 1878 law, which allowed private schools to receive about 30% of the funding given to public schools for each child enrolled. Subsequent confessional governments led by the Anti-Revolutionary leader Abraham Kuyper (1901-1905) and by Theo Heemskerk (1908-1913) would ensure that the government provided additional financial supports to private education. Under these conditions, the number of private schools grew, with about 40% of Dutch pupils attending them by the beginning of the First World War. A commission appointed in 1910 by a confessionally-led government recommended that private schools be fully funded by the government. But it was not until 1917 that the liberal government of Pieter Cort van der Linden negotiated a constitutional change that guaranteed equal financing of private (and thus also religious) schools by the state (and subsequently implemented on the primary level by the law of 1920). The tensions of the First World War played a role in the parliament's acceptance of this provision, the Cort van der Linden government also introducing other key reforms, such as the universal franchise, and proportional representation.

141

Many scholars see 1917 as the end of a political era of change, and of reform.[40] In the end, though, the strength of religious parties in a new era of mass politics proved decisive, just as it had in Belgium, where the Catholic party was in the ascendant after 1880. After decades of struggle, Protestant and Catholic parties finally had their way in the passage of the educational law of 1920: state neutrality meant state subsidies to *all* schools, on the basis of financial parity with public schools. Reforms in the form of separation of church and state had meant in France the secularisation of the state by the early twentieth century, Hugh McLeod notes, but in the newly-independent Ireland and in the Netherlands separation meant, in the long run, just the opposite: a state in the control of those who were sympathetic to, and financially supportive of, various forms of religious endeavour.[41] The state remained an important player in fields like education and the media, but now primarily as the financial underwriter and facilitator of private and religious initiative. In the 1920s, that would lead to, for example, the partial public funding of radio corporations that respectively represented Catholics, socialists, liberal and conservative Protestants and liberal-leaning 'neutral'

---

[40] De Haan, *Het beginsel van leven en wasdom*; de Rooy, *Republiek van rivaliteiten*.

[41] McLeod, *Secularisation in Western Europe*, 56. McLeod sees Britain and Germany taking a middle position between France on the one side and Ireland and the Netherlands on the other.

associations that together constituted Dutch national radio.[42] It was an arrangement that would come under serious attack only in the 1960s.

For the first part of the period under study, contesting visions of religious reform had focused on whether the church should be cut loose from the state, or be tied more effectively to it. After the mid-nineteenth century, this issue lost much of its importance. The issue then became to what extent, and in which ways, a liberal state could make allowance for religious groups in projects that it increasingly tended to claim for itself, most notably poor relief and education. In seeking state funding of their religious schools - a goal fully achieved by 1920 - confessional political groups were able to reform the state's relationship to religion in a way that was, in its 'principled pluralism', quite different from what either the Batavian reformers, Willem I or Thorbecke could have predicted, or would have desired. In this new situation, the state's role shifted from the creator of state institutions into a supporter and facilitator of private (especially religious) initiative. The state was, in many cases, there to help ensure that private organisations - not least Protestant and Catholic ones - could optimally function according to their own principles. In being cut free from state oversight, religious bodies - now more differentiated than ever before - were able to shape and reform the state, and transform society, in ways that were unimaginable in 1800 or 1850.

---

[42] Hiemstra, *Worldviews on the Air.*

Bibliography[*]

Belgium

Aubert, Roger. "Kirche und Staat in Belgien im 19. Jahrhundert" in: Werner Conze, ed. *Beiträge zur deutschen und belgischen Verfassungsgeschichte im 19. Jahrhundert* Stuttgart, 1967, 5-25.

Chappin, Marcel. "Entre dogme et diplomatie: La Curie romaine et le problème de la tolérance civile à propos de la 'Déclaration' de F.A. de Méan, 1817" in: R. Crahay, ed. *La tolérance civile.* Brussels, 1982, 217-234.

Claeys Bouuaert, Ferdinand. *Les déclarations et serments imposés par la loi civile aux membres du clergé belge sous le Directoire (1793-1801).* Gembloux, 1960.

De Pooter, Patrick. *De rechtspositie van erkende erediensten en levensbeschouwingen in Staat en maatschappij.* Brussels, 2003.

De Vleeschouwer, Robert. "Le cas de la Belgique" in: *Occupants - Occupés, 1792-1815.* Brussels, 1969, 43-65.

Dhondt, Luc. "La guerre des paysans et le processus révolutionnaire en Belgique". *Études sur le XVIIIe siècle*, 16 (1987), 103-117.

Gérin, Paul. "La démocratie chrétienne dans les relations Église-État à la fin du XIXe siècle. L'action de Mgr Doutreloux" in: Gaston Braive and Jacques Lory, eds. *L'Église et l'État à l'époque contemporaine. Mélanges dédiés à la mémoire de Mgr Aloïs Simon.* Brussels, 1975, 255-288.

Haag, Henri. *Les origines du catholicisme libéral en Belgique (1789-1839).* Leuven, 1950.

Hasquin, Hervé, ed. *La Belgique française.* Brussels, 1993.

Hasquin, Hervé. *Joseph II, catholique anticlérical et réformateur impatient, 1741-1790.* Brussels, 2007.

Hemblinne, Jean-Pierre. *Chouannerie et contrerévolution en Belgique, 1791-1815.* Braine-l'Alleud, 1990.

Lamberts, Emiel. *Kerk en liberalisme in het bisdom Gent (1821-1857). Bijdrage tot de studie van het liberaal-katholicisme en het ultramontanisme.* Leuven, 1972.

Lamberts, Emiel. "Les sociétés pilarisées: l'exemple belge" in: Gerard Cholvy, ed. *L'Europe. Ses dimensions religieuses.* Montpellier, 1998, 221-236.

Lamberts, Emiel and Lory, Jacques, eds. *1884: Un tournant politique en Belgique.* Brussels, 1986.

Lory, Jacques. *Libéralisme et instruction primaire, 1842-1879. Introduction à l'étude de la lutte scolaire en Belgique.* Leuven, 1979.

Markowitz, Marvin. *Cross and Sword: The Political Role of Christian Missions in the Belgian Congo (1908-1960).* Stanford, 1974.

Miroir, André. "L'État et les cultes en droit belge. Réflexions sur la nature de leurs rapports". *Res Publica*, 15 (1973), 725-744.

Pirenne, Henri and Vercruysse, Jeroom. *Les États Belgiques Unis: histoire de la révolution belge de 1789-1790.* Paris, 1999.

Polasky, Janet. "The Success of a Counter-Revolution in Revolutionary Europe: the Brabant Revolution of 1789". *Tijdschrift voor Geschiedenis*, 102 (1989), 413-421.

Roegiers, Jan and Van Sas, N.C.F. "Revolution in the North and South, 1780-1830" in: Hans Blom and Emiel Lamberts, eds. *History of the Low Countries.* New York-Oxford, 2006, 275-318.

Shelley, Thomas. "Mutual Independence: Church and State in Belgium, 1825-1846". *Journal of Church and State*, 1 (1990), 49-63.

Simon, Aloïs. *Le cardinal Sterckx et son temps.* Wetteren, 1950, 2 vols.

Terlinden, Charles. *Guillaume Ier et l'Église catholique en Belgique.* Vol. 2. Brussels, 1906.

143

[*] Note that Belgian authors are listed alphabetically according to the prefix 'De' or 'Van', Dutch authors according to the main part of the surname.

Tihon, André. "Les religieuses en Belgique du XVIIIe au XXe siècle. Approche statistique". *Revue belge d'histoire contemporaine*, 7 (1976), 1-54.

Vanthemsche, Guy. *La Belgique et le Congo. Empreintes d'une colonie, 1885-1980.* Brussels, 2007.

Wagnon, Henri. "La reconduction du concordat de 1801 dans les provinces belges du Royaume-Uni des Pays-Bas (1814-1817)" in: *Scrinium Lovaniense: mélanges historiques Étienne van Cauwenbergh.* Gembloux-Leuven, 1961, 514-542.

Wagnon, Henri. "Le congrès national belge de 1830-1831 a-t-il établi la séparation de l'Église et de l'État?" in: *Études d'histoire du droit canonique dédiées à G. Le Bras.* Vol. 1. Paris, 1965, 753-781.

Wagnon, Henri. "Le concordat de 1801-1827 et la Belgique indépendante" in: Gaston Braive and Jacques Lory, eds. *L'Église et l'État à l'époque contemporaine. Mélanges dédiés à la mémoire de Mgr Aloïs Simon.* Brussels, 1975, 547-561.

Witte, Els. *La construction de la Belgique (1828-1847).* Brussels, 2005.

The Netherlands

Aalders, M.J. "De Wet op de Kerkgenootschappen van 10 september 1853" in G.J. Schutte and J. Vree, eds. *Op de toekomst van het protestantse Nederland. De gevolgen van de grondwetsherziening van 1848 voor kerk, staat en maatschappij.* Zoetermeer, 1998, 91-127.

Aerts, Remieg, ed. *De Gids sinds 1837: de geschiedenis van een algemeen-cultureel en literair tijdschrift.* Amsterdam, 1987.

Alting van Geusau, W.H. *Neutraliteit der overheid in de Nederlandsche koloniën jegens godsdienstzaken.* Haarlem, 1917.

Berg, Henk van den. *In vrijheid gebonden. Negentiende-eeuwse katholieke publicisten in Nederland over geloof, politiek en moderniteit.* Nijmegen, 2005.

Beyen, Marnix and Majerus, Benoît. "Weak and Strong Nations in the Low Countries: National Historiography and its 'Others' in Belgium, Luxembourg and the Netherlands in the Nineteenth and Twentieth Centuries" in: Stefan Berger and Chris Lorenz, eds. *The Contested Nation: Ethnicity, Class, Religion and Gender in National Histories.* Basingstoke, 2009, 283-310.

Bornewasser, J.A. "Twee eeuwen kerk en staat; een veelledige confrontatie met de moderniteit" in: J. de Bruijn, ed. *Geen heersende kerk, geen heersende staat: de verhouding tussen kerken en staat, 1796-1996.* Zoetermeer, 1998, 29-60.

Bos, David. *In dienst van het koninkrijk. Beroepsontwikkeling van hervormde predikanten in negentiende-eeuws Nederland.* Amsterdam, 1999.

Carlson-Thiess, Stanley. *Democracy in the Netherlands: Consociational or Pluriform?* Toronto, 1993.

Clemens, Theo. "Confessie, kerk, natie en staat in Nederland" in: J. de Bruijn, ed. *Geen heersende kerk, geen heersende staat: de verhouding tussen kerk en staat, 1796-1996.* Zoetermeer, 1998, 145-176.

Coninck, Pieter de. *Een les uit Pruisen. Nederland en de Kulturkampf 1870-1880.* Hilversum, 2005.

Diepenhorst, I.A. *De verhouding tusschen kerk en staat in Nederland.* Utrecht, 1946.

Doorn, J.A.A. van. "De strijd tegen armoede en werkloosheid in historisch perspectief" in: W.P. Blockmans and L.A. van der Valk, eds. *Van particuliere naar openbare zorg en terug? Sociale politiek in Nederland sinds 1880.* Deventer, 1992, 1-30.

Dorsman, Leen. "C.W. Opzoomer en de 'Scheiding van kerk en staat' (1875)" in: F.G.M. Broeyer and D.T. Kuiper, eds. *Is 't waar of niet? Ophefmakende publicaties uit de 'lange' negentiende eeuw.* Amsterdam, 2005, 215-234.

Eijnatten, Joris van. *Preaching, Sermon and Cultural Change in the Long Eighteenth Century.* Leiden, 2009.

Faber, S. "De afschaffing van de collatierechten" in: G.J. Schutte and J. Vree, eds. *Op de toekomst van het protestantse Nederland. De gevolgen van de grondwetsherziening van 1848 voor kerk, staat en maatschappij*. Zoetermeer, 1998, 81-90.

Haan, Ido de. *Het beginsel van leven en wasdom. De constitutie van de Nederlandse politiek in de negentiende eeuw*. Amsterdam, 2003.

Hiemstra, John. *Worldviews on the Air: The Struggle to Create a Pluralist Broadcasting System in the Netherlands*. New York, 1997.

Hoffman, Stefan-Ludwig. *Civil Society and Democracy in Nineteenth Century Europe: Entanglements, Variations, Conflicts*. Berlin, 2005.

Houkes, Annemarie. "Het succes van 1848: politiek in de Aprilbeweging" in: Jurjen Vis and Wim Janse, eds. *Staf en storm: het herstel van de bisschoppelijke hiërarchie in Nederland 1853: actie en reactie*. Hilversum, 2002, 87-104.

Houkes, Annemarie. *Christelijke vaderlanders. Godsdienst, burgerschap en de Nederlandse natie (1850-1900)*. Amsterdam, 2009.

Janse, Maartje. *De afschaffers: publieke opinie, organisatie en politiek in Nederland 1840-1880*. Amsterdam, 2007.

Jong, O.J. de "Uitkeringen aan kerken" in: J. de Bruijn, ed. *Geen heersende kerk, geen heersende staat: de verhouding tussen kerk en staat, 1796-1996*. Zoetermeer, 1998, 203-250.

Joor, Johan. *De Adelaar en het Lam. Onrust, opruiing en onwilligheid in Nederland ten tijde van het Koninkrijk Holland en de inlijving bij het Franse Keizerrijk (1805-1813)*. Amsterdam, 2000.

Kloek, Joost and Wijnand, Mijnhardt. *Dutch Culture in a European Perspective: Blueprints for a National Community*. New York, 2004.

Kromsigt, P.J. *De leuze "Scheiding van Kerk en Staat" een gevaar voor de Hervormde Kerk*. Rotterdam, 1921.

Kuyper, Abraham. *De gemeene gratie*. Vol. 2. Kampen, 1902.

Leeuwen, Marco H.D. van. "Armenzorg 1800-1912: erfenis van de republiek" in: Jacques van Gerwen and Marco H.D. van Leeuwen, eds. *Studies over zekerheidsarrangementen. Risico's, risicobestrijding en verzekeringen in Nederland vanaf de Middeleeuwen*. Amsterdam, 1999, 276-316.

Margry, Peter Jan. *Teedere Quaesties: religieuze rituelen in conflict. Confrontaties tussen katholieken en protestanten rond de processiecultuur in 19-eeuws Nederland*. Hilversum, 2000.

McLeod, Hugh. *Secularisation in Western Europe, 1848-1917*. Basingstoke, 2000.

Melief, P.B.A. *De strijd om de armenzorg in Nederland. 1795-1854*. Groningen, 1955.

Noordeloos, Pieter. *De restitutie der kerken in den Franschen tijd*. Nijmegen, 1937.

Ouden, Willem Hendrik den. *De ontknoping van de zilveren koorde. De geschiedenis van de rijkstractementen in de Nederlandse Hervormde Kerk*. Zoetermeer, 2004.

Rasker, A.J. *De Nederlandse Hervormde Kerk vanaf 1795*. Kampen, 1981.

Rooden, Peter van. "Long-term Religious Developments in the Netherlands, 1750-2000" in: Hugh McLeod and Werner Ustorf, eds. *The Decline of Christendom in Western Europe, 1750-2000*. Cambridge, 2002, 113-129.

Rooy, Piet de. "Armenzorg in Nederland" in: Bernard Kruithof, Jan Noordman and Piet de Rooy. *Geschiedenis van opvoeding en onderwijs. Inleiding, bronnen, onderzoek*. Nijmegen, 1982, 96-104.

Rooy, Piet de. *Republiek van rivaliteiten. Nederlands sinds 1813*. Amsterdam, 2002.

Samkalden, Channah. *Believing in Secular States: Freedom of Religion and Separation of State and Religion in Legal Concepts in Europe*. Diss. Florence, 2009.

Schilling, Heinz. *Religion, Political Culture, and the Emergence of Early Modern Society: Essays in German and Dutch History*. Leiden, 1992.

Snouck Hurgronje, C. *Nederland en de Islam: vier voordrachten gehouden in de Nederlandsch-Indische Bestuursacademie*. Leiden, 1911.

145

Spaans, Joke. "Kerkelijke en publieke armen-zorg voor en na de scheiding tussen kerk en staat" in: J. de Bruijn, ed. *Geen heersende kerk, geen heersende staat: de verhouding tussen kerken en staat, 1796-1996*. Zoetermeer, 1998, 127-145.

Steenbrink, K.A. "Staat en religies in koloniaal Nederlands Indie" in: J. de Bruijn, ed. *Geen heersende kerk, geen heersende staat: de verhouding tussen kerken en staat, 1796-1996*. Zoetermeer, 1998, 177-202.

Vis, Jurjen and Janse, Wim, eds. *Staf en storm: het herstel van de bisschoppelijke hiërarchie in Nederland 1853: actie en reactie*. Hilversum, 2002.

Visser, J. Th. de. *Kerk en staat. Nederland van 1796 tot op heden*. Vol. 3. Leiden, 1927.

Vree, J. "De herziening van het hervormde Algemeen Reglement" in: G.J. Schutte and J. Vree, eds. *Om de toekomst van het protestantse Nederland. De gevolgen van de grondwetsherziening van 1848 voor kerk, staat en maatschappij*. Zoetermeer, 1998, 22-63.

Wallet, Bart. *Nieuwe Nederlanders. De integratie van de joden in Nederland 1814-1851*. Amsterdam, 2007.

Wintle, Michael J. *Pillars of Piety: Religion in the Netherlands in the Nineteenth Century, 1813-1901*. Hull, 1987.

Zwaag, Klaas van der. *Onverkort of gekortwiekt? Artikel 36 van de Nederlandse Geloofsbelijdenis en de spanning tussen overheid en religie. Een systematisch-historische interpretatie van een 'omstreden' geloofsartikel*. Heerenveen, 1999.

GERMANY

The German section has been written by two authors who have approached their task from different disciplinary backgrounds: Heiner de Wall is primarily an ecclesiastical lawyer and Andreas Gestrich a social historian. Nevertheless, this contribution has been conceived as a single piece. Differences of approach, under editorial guidance, have been worked through in the composition so that both legal and political perspectives receive interlocking attention. A single section, treated in this manner, makes it easier, though far from simple, to tackle the complexity that was 'Germany' in this period. There can be no pretence that 'Germany' exhibited a uniformity of constitutional arrangements in matters of church and state. The narrative that follows, however, aims to avoid the twin dangers that can easily trap writers on this topic. It seeks to avoid a descent into a mere catalogue of peculiarities by drawing attention to the structures of Prussia and Bavaria, in particular, as to some extent 'models', while not neglecting to observe that Oldenburg, for example, was not Mecklenburg. There was no universal template. But that is not to say that in these matters there was no such thing as 'Germany'. The confessional divide, and the entrenched weight of history which it carried, existed, in different balances, as the inescapable 'German' fact. How it played out, at different points in time and in changing territorial configurations, is a central theme in this section.

Constitutional Complexity and Confessional Diversity

Heiner de Wall & Andreas Gestrich

The political and legal relationship between church and state was particularly complex in Germany as so many core parameters of this relationship kept changing. In the early nineteenth century the political map of Germany altered profoundly. At its outset, many member states of the former Holy Roman Empire disappeared completely or lost their status as autonomous political units, a few also did so later. Others grew through the incorporation of these formerly independent territories. Through these changes in the political landscape previously mono-confessional states frequently became multi-confessional.

The successor formations of the Holy Roman Empire also changed. The German Federation of 1815 more or less comprised the same geographical territory as the Empire. The Prussia-dominated new German Empire of 1871 was not only much smaller, but also quite different as far as the balance and political influence of different churches or religious denominations was concerned. With the Habsburg monarchy and its German territories excluded from the new Empire and all former Catholic prince-bishoprics and most monasteries dissolved, the Catholic Church not only lost important political allies in Germany, but also much of its financial basis. This altered the political framework of former established churches and rendered the redefinition of church-state relationships almost inevitable.

The main political issues of the time were national unity and political democratisation. Traditional German federalist structures survived 1871. The new Empire was itself a federation of states with a large degree of autonomy, particularly in cultural and religious matters. Both, the German Confederation of 1815 and the new German Empire of 1871 left the regulation of religious matters to their individual member states.

Thus, even though there might be many common characteristics in the way these federal states reformed church-state relationships, there were also many differences in the details and timing of reforms which an overview like this can only hint at. It was only after the First World War that the constitution of the Weimar Republic was able to create a general framework for all churches and religious associations within what continued to be called the German Empire.

The revolution of 1848 failed and with it not only democratic reforms of the political system, but also attempts to radically disentangle church-state relationships and to give all churches and religious associations the freedom to regulate their own affairs and, for example, democratise their own internal structures. This is particularly true for the Protestant churches, which continued to acknowledge monarchs as their heads right through the nineteenth century. Debates on the political and administrative structure of the churches remained entangled with general discussions on questions of constitutional political change.

In terms of arrangement, the first sections of this chapter will consider, chronologically, the main stages of the relationship between churches and states in Germany, focusing primarily on constitutional debates and regulations. As most of the problems of the Catholic Church after 1815 were quite distinct from those of the Protestant churches, the Catholic and Protestant Churches are dealt with separately in this overview. It also needs to be selective as far as the church politics of individual German states is concerned. Prussia, as the largest and politically dominant, is always an obvious choice, and Bavaria can often serve as an interesting counterpoint, but other states will also be taken into account. The later sections consider general topics which featured prominently in debates on legal and political church reform: church financing, the legal position of religious minorities, the position of the churches in a changing secular welfare system and the position of monarchs within the churches. The chapter concludes with a discussion of church and state as set out in the post-First World War 'Weimar' Constitution.

The Holy Roman Empire and its Churches

The history of the relationship between state and church in Germany is shaped by two important factors: the religious divide and the lack of national unity. In contrast to the Lutheran countries in Northern Europe and the Catholic countries in Western and Southern Europe or to the very different religious landscape in Britain, in the centre of the continent and especially in the territories of the Holy Roman Empire, the Catholic and Protestant Churches were more or less equally strong in numbers and had to coexist. In these circumstances the question of religious equality gained particular significance. It was not a problem of the emancipation of small religious minorities, but of the balance of two equal weights. A solution could only be found if the characteristics of both confessions and especially the principles of their church constitutions and law were taken into account.

Until the beginning of the nineteenth century the Holy Roman Empire was the political and constitutional framework of Germany. It was not a state with a central government. However, institutions such as the *Immerwährender Reichstag* (Imperial Diet) in Regensburg, the *Reichshofrat* (Imperial Aulic Council) in Vienna and the *Reichskammergericht* (Imperial High Court) in Wetzlar provided a legal and political framework for more than 300 more or less independent political units. These were of different importance, size of territory and population, had different constitutions and also differed in their degree of independence from the emperor. Some of the larger so-called territories (*Territorien*) of the Empire, such as Prussia or Bavaria, were more or less sovereign states. Brandenburg-Prussia and Austria-Habsburg played their own independent role among the pentarchy of the European powers alongside Russia, Britain and France. The majority of the Empire's territories, however, could hardly be compared with these important powers. Whereas, for the larger states, the Holy Roman Empire was only one factor among others in their politics, for the many tiny principalities and free cities, it was central to their existence and political independence. The role of the house of Habsburg as emperors on the one hand, and as princes of important territories inside and outside the Empire on the other, resulted in a complex mixture of interests.

151

In the constitution of the Holy Roman Empire the principle of the coexistence and the equality of the major Christian traditions was crucial. Confessional conflicts could only be settled by *amicabilis compositio*, an amicable agreement among the parties. However, the right to determine the religion of their territories and the constitution of the churches lay in the hand of the princes. This meant that the principle of coexistence and equality was only put into effect on the imperial rather than the territorial level. According to one of the Basic Laws of the Empire, the Peace of Augsburg of 1555, it was the princes, not the people, who had the freedom to choose their own religion and that of their country. Even though this rule was slightly changed during the following centuries and tolerance of different confessions within a territory became more common within the Empire, it was still restricted to those religious beliefs included in the Augsburg peace treaty and the subsequent Peace of Westphalia (1648), that is to say to Lutheran and Reformed Protestantism and Roman Catholicism.

In the Holy Roman Empire detailed legislation concerning the churches was not a matter for the imperial diet but rested with the princes and municipalities. There were, however, significant differences between the possibilities open to a prince in regulating the Catholic and the Protestant Churches. The legal status of the Protestant churches was based on the *Landesherrliche Kirchenregiment* (princely rule over the church). It included the princes' right to determine the constitution of the Protestant churches within their territories as well as to exercise the main governing power over and within these churches. However, the legal status of the Catholic Church was not based on this principle. It continued to be governed by the bishops and remained within the hierarchical and legal framework of the Roman Catholic Church as a whole. Nevertheless, over the centuries, and particularly in the eighteenth century, there were many attempts by the secular authorities and even by Catholic princes to gain power over the affairs of the Catholic Church in their respective territories. As a result, despite the basic legal difference between the regulations applying to the Protestant and the Catholic Churches, the princes were able to gain considerable influence in the affairs of both churches.

An institution peculiar to the Catholic Church in Germany was that of the prince-bishoprics. Here, Catholic bishops not only held their ecclesiastical office but were also the territorial lords and as such princes of the Empire. Three of the seven or eight electors of the Empire were prince bishops, namely the prince bishops of Mainz, Cologne and Trier. They were the highest dignitaries of the Empire.

Freedom of Religion - and its Limits

As far as the rights of the individual were concerned, neither freedom of religion nor religious equality were granted by the political order of the Holy Roman Empire. It was the princes and the councils of the Free Imperial Cities who had the right to determine the confession of their territory or cities. And even they were not free to choose whatever religion they wanted but were restricted to those three confessions recognised by the Empire, i.e. Catholicism, Lutheran and Reformed Protestantism. According to the Peace of Augsburg of 1555 the individual citizen had the right to emigrate for religious reasons, but not to choose a religious belief or church different from that of the territorial lord. After the middle of the seventeenth century, the right of families to practise their religion within their homes, but not publicly, was guaranteed by the treaty of Westphalia. In the course of the seventeenth and eighteenth centuries, in many parts of Germany, further toleration of different confessions was granted as a result of princes gaining territories with inhabitants of confessions other than their own. The Peace of Westphalia guaranteed that every confession which was legal in a territory or state in the year 1624 had to be henceforward accepted by a prince irrespective of his right to determine the religion of the country. If, for example, a Catholic prince conquered a Protestant city, he had to tolerate Protestant inhabitants holding services publicly. This was a considerable step towards religious freedom and equality. In the eighteenth century, some princes turned to a policy of toleration. In some cases the reasons for this were mainly economic. In Prussia and other territories, for example, Huguenot immigrants from France were invited to settle because their skills as craftsmen would help the economic development of the country. But the ideas of the Enlightenment also made way for real toleration of other churches and religions. In Austria, for example, Emperor Joseph II passed a bill of toleration which gave legal guarantees to Protestants. Bavaria followed suit at the beginning of the nineteenth century. In the same context the legal position of Jews was also improved.

The ecclesiastical policy of the enlightened absolutism of the middle and late eighteenth century was, however, ambiguous. There were tendencies towards toleration and freedom on the one hand, but on the other hand governments tried to gain control over the whole of their societies and especially over the churches. The states saw the churches primarily as another means of providing public welfare, an attitude which led in Austria under Emperor Joseph II to only those religious orders being tolerated which did useful work, such as nursing or teaching, while those whose sole purpose was religious devotion were forbidden. The state was also considered the only institution which could enforce legal rules. Every other community or association within the state, even the church, could only have the status of a private corporation with little right to self-determination and no legal autonomy. This idea obviously did not fit the reality of the canon law of the Catholic Church. The German legal term *Religionsgesellschaft* (religious association), which was used in the Prussian *Allgemeine Landrecht* (General Law Code of 1794) and which is still in use in the present constitution of Germany, is a heritage of this epoch. The integration of church authorities into the ministries of the state, which took place in some German countries at the beginning of the nineteenth century, further exemplifies this tendency on the part of states. The Prussian General Law Code was drafted during the last years of Frederick II's enlightened despotism. In Austria, this mixture of toleration control and the idea that the church had to serve the common welfare of the state took its name Josephinism from the reform politics of Emperor Joseph II.

Any outline of the legal position of the churches in the late eighteenth century must not ignore the relationship between local authorities and local congregations. The political order of the Holy Roman Empire conferred political power not only on the princes, but also on subordinate and intermediate levels, such as lords of the manor or city councils. They, too, had their limited rights to rule in local affairs. Among the many different types of such rights, patronage is of special importance. Typically, the patron had the obligation to maintain the church building and the right to appoint the vicar. In many cases, the local council, the lord of the manor or the prince himself held the patronage over a parish. As a consequence there was a special set of legal rules applying to those parishes which had patrons. This distinguished their position from that of other congregations to which the common church law applied.

Secularisation, and the End of the Holy Roman Empire

The political and cultural changes of the French Revolution and Napoleonic rule also resulted in far-reaching political reforms in Germany. Although these changes did not lead to a democratic republic, they can still be considered revolutionary in that they brought the Holy Roman Empire, which had lasted for nearly a thousand years, to an end in 1806. Its special law concerning the churches ceased to exist. However, since the territorial princes already exercised supreme authority over the Protestant churches its lapse almost exclusively affected the Catholic Church. The reforms of the legal position of the Catholic Church were brought into effect by the *Reichsdeputationshauptschluss* (Principal Decree of the Imperial Deputation). This decree may be seen as the last attempt to save the Holy Roman Empire by means of reform, although the word 'reform' understates what actually happened to the church and its legal position.

153

The *Reichsdeputationshauptschluss* was a consequence of the Peace Treaty of Lunéville (1801) which ended the Empire's war against Napoleonic France on terms which greatly favoured the latter. Napoleon himself forced the *Reichstag* (Imperial Diet) to set up a committee (*Reichsdeputation*) in order to work out a plan to compensate the German princes allied to Napoleon for their losses to France on the west bank of the Rhine. To provide this compensation, the prince-bishoprics were secularised and the rights to rule over them were transferred to the secular princes. In the same way, several free cities and smaller territories lost their independence and were incorporated into the territories of the states which had to be compensated. This was called mediatisation as these political entities lost their political position of being immediate to the emperor. Prince bishops and abbots lost both their territories and their positions as imperial princes. The rights and entitlements which applied to their lands were transferred to the new territorial lords who were also permitted to expropriate church property in their new territories except for the assets of the local parishes. As a result of the secularisation of former church territories, more than 2.4 out of about 20 million Germans were made subjects of new territorial lords and came under new governments.

These transfers meant that the Catholic Church lost a great part of its wealth in Germany. Although the princes were ordered to compensate the church for some of its losses, such compensation was made only reluctantly and was by no means adequate. It formed the basis of a complex system of payments by the various German states to the church. The details of these payments had to be settled by contracts and bills through the nineteenth and twentieth centuries, and the 1803 regulation still forms the historical basis of ongoing subsidies by the present German *Länder* (states) to the Catholic Church.

Just as important as the loss of its wealth were the changes in the political position of the Catholic Church within the Empire. The end of the prince-bishoprics also meant the end of the *Reichskirche* (Imperial Church) with its special constitutional position. The bishops no longer held secular power. Church interests and political interests were no longer intertwined. This was important for the independence of the Catholic Church and the image of its position within society. It no longer served as a kind of reservoir of posts for the younger sons of the princely houses in Germany, men who had no right of succession to the family's princely title. Until the beginning of the nineteenth century, the bishops of the Catholic Church in Germany were drawn from the nobility. After the *Reichsdeputationshauptschluss*, the social background of the German episcopate changed radically. The fact that they were no longer powerful princes of the Empire also strengthened the influence of the Holy See over the Catholic Church in Germany. Together with various movements towards a spiritual renewal, which are dealt with in other volumes of this work, this led to profound changes in the image of the Catholic Church. Instead of its worldly power, its quality as a religious community and its spiritual tasks now came to the fore.

C. Bourgeois du Castelet & J.B. Debret, Prince-
bishop Theodor von Dalberg, primate of the
Confederation of the Rhine, receives Napoleon at
Schloss Johannisburg in the city of Aschaffenburg,
oil on canvas, 1812.
[Versailles, Châteaux de Versailles et de Trianon;
© RMN (Château de Versailles)]

Restauration - up to a point

The German Confederation

The political developments which followed the Napoleonic Wars between 1806 and 1812 and the subsequent *Befreiungskriege* (Wars of Liberation), made it necessary to re-organise Germany, with respect to the borders of its remaining territories and to its political constitution. This task was carried out by the Congress of Vienna in 1815. Despite the name which was given to the decades which then followed, the *Restauration*, the *ancien régime* was not restored. Only 39 of the more than 300 territories of the Empire remained. They now became sovereign states. The *Deutscher Bund* (German Confederation) which was established in 1815 consisted of 35 states (kingdoms and principalities) and 4 free cities (Frankfurt, Hamburg, Bremen, and Lübeck). A united Germany, with a democratic constitution, was not achieved, despite the endeavours of liberals and nationalists. Once again monarchies were established. To protect them, the *Deutscher Bund*, led by the Austrian statesman Metternich, suppressed all democratic and nationalist activities.

156 After the end of the Imperial Church and the constitutional order of the Empire, the relationship between the church and the state was now a matter for the individual German states. The German Federal Act contained only one paragraph (Art. 16) dealing with religious affairs. It guaranteed the equality of the citizens of the federal states irrespective of their religion - again only the three traditionally acknowledged confessions were covered by this guarantee. Additionally, a promise to begin negotiations about an improvement of the legal status of the Jews was included. All remaining religious matters were to be handled by the individual states.

One of the few concessions that were made to the constitutional movement was the promise contained in Art. 13 of the German Federal Act that a constitution with the political representation of Estates (*Landständische Verfassung*) would be introduced in all member-states. This promise was only reluctantly fulfilled by the *Restauration* governments. The first constitutions were introduced in the South German monarchies of Bavaria, Württemberg and Baden at the end of the second decade of the nineteenth century. These monarchies were among those to have gained from secularisation and from subsequent territorial expansion. In the course of this enlargement the former almost exclusively Catholic Bavarian monarchy and the mainly Protestant territories of Württemberg and Baden now included considerable minorities who were members of other churches. The integration of these new subjects made it necessary to respect their religious affiliations and to recognise them in a similar way as the established churches of the country. Therefore, freedom and equality of religion were of special significance for these states and were granted by their early constitutions - although the established churches were still privileged. However, these constitutions provided only guarantees of the religious rights of individuals, not of the churches and religious communities as such. Thus the claim that the churches should be considered and treated as independent bodies separate from the state and be given autonomy, stayed an issue in early-nineteenth-century political debates in Germany. It was not until mid-century that the rights of the churches and religious communities to autonomy were introduced into the constitutional enactments of member states of the *Deutscher Bund*.

Since the legal status of the Protestant and Catholic Churches was quite different, developments in their respective relationships with the state are treated separately in what follows.

Compacts, Compromises and Controls: Rulers and the Catholic Church

Even after the end of the Holy Roman Empire and during the course of the political re-shaping of Germany, attempts were made to restore or establish the Catholic Church as an Imperial Church and to strengthen the position of the bishops. The activities of the last remaining prince bishop, Theodor von Dalberg, and of his pupil and vicar-general, afterwards bishop of Constance, Ignaz von Wessenberg, should be mentioned in this connection. But these attempts failed.

In their newly shaped and constituted countries, some princes, who had achieved sovereignty and could legislate on the relationship between state and church, tried to establish a control over the Catholic Church similar to that common over the Protestant Church. Control in such instances, however, meant two different things. Where the prince was Protestant, he claimed and exercised supervision both over the Protestant churches (which were under the control of the state authorities anyway), and over the Catholic Church. Usually, however, a difference was made between the two churches. In the case of the Catholic Church, the state only had control over external affairs, the *iura circa sacra*. This comprised the regulation of clerical salaries and the upkeep of church buildings, but also of the academic requirements for admission to church offices or the basis on which pastors and priests could partake in politics and public life. In the case of the Protestant churches, however, through its church government, the state was entitled even to control the *iura in sacra*. It therefore could also regulate the internal affairs of the church, i.e. even interfere on questions of church doctrine. In early-nineteenth-century Württemberg, however, attempts were made to establish for the Catholic Church a state-run church authority, a *consistorium*, on the model of that for the Protestant churches.

The new borders of the German states and the rule of the state over the Catholic Church also required a re-shaping of the borders of the dioceses. The spatial definition (the so-called *circumscription*) of the dioceses depended on the consent of the Holy See. Negotiations had, therefore, to take place between the German states and the Holy See. The decline of the position and power of the bishops since the *Reichsdeputations-hauptschluss*, together with other factors, strengthened the position of the Holy See in Germany, both within and outside the church. Equally, agreements initiated by the Holy See with the princes gained in importance. A number of such agreements were signed in the early nineteenth century. They dealt with the spatial definition of the dioceses, compensation as a result of the *Reichsdeputationshauptschluss*, or with state influence on the election of bishops. The Bavarian concordat of 1817 deserves particular mention in this context.

In other German states these questions were also settled by way of compromise and contract with the Holy See. Formally, however, the resulting agreements were not laid down in concordats but in papal Bulls of Circumscription (*De salute animarum* in 1821 for Prussia, *Impensa Romanorum Pontificum* in 1824 for Hanover, *Provida solersque* in 1821 for the newly established Ecclesiastical Province of the Upper Rhine), which were approved and sanctioned by the respective state governments. These new regulations for the Ecclesiastical Province of the Upper Rhine are a good example of the tension between the Catholic Church and the state in the early nineteenth century. The south-western states of Germany (Baden, Württemberg, Hessen and Nassau) coordinated their church policy and cooperated in the negotiations with the Holy See. After Pius VII had promulgated *Provida solersque*, but before any consensus was reached on the question of how bishops were to be elected, these governments in 1823 agreed on a *Kirchenpragmatik*, a law for the Catholic Church in their respective territories. It stipulated state supervision over the church and the right of the states to propose a new bishop in the event of an episcopal vacancy. Subsequently, however, the bishops put forward in this manner were not in fact installed by the pope. Even after a compromise was found in 1827, conflicts about the appointment of bishops continued in South-West Germany and in other German states.

Meeting Opposition: Ultramontanism

Any discussion of Catholicism, however, has to take into account the emergence, particularly in the dioceses of Mainz and Trier, of ultramontanism. States in Germany, as elsewhere, found themselves engaged with Catholics who rejoiced, with increasing enthusiasm, in the external authority of the Papacy. The spread of ultramontanism was underpinned by a so-called *Katholische Bewegung* (Catholic Movement). This had many parallels and links with the revivalist movement of popular pietism in the Protestant Church which emerged at about the same time. In Bavaria the Catholic theologian, Johann Michael Sailer (1751-1832), made impassioned appeals for a Catholic revivalist movement. Since 1838 Joseph Görres (1776-1848), a historian at Munich University and active publicist, had been publishing the *Historisch-politische Blätter* as the mouthpiece of a new Catholicism that was also politically aware. In other Catholic regions of Germany and Europe there were influential figures similar to Sailer and Görres, e.g. Fürstin Amalia von Gallitzin, who inspired the Catholic pietism movement in Westphalia as Sailer had done in Bavaria. In France, Joseph de Maistre (1754-1821) had strongly argued for the re-establishment of the pope's religious and secular power. His most important work, which had greatly influenced the originally radical liberal Joseph Görres, was his book *Du Pape*, published in 1819. This book became a standard

work of ultramontanism, and in Germany Görres became the most important dissemi-
nator of ultramontane beliefs.

An early test case for ultramontanism were the *Kölner Wirren* (Cologne Distur-
bances). Prussia after 1815 had gained considerable new territories with a Catholic
majority in the Rhineland. There, a conflict arose over the question of which law was
to be applied to mixed marriages between Protestants and Catholics. According to
the Catholic Tridentine law of matrimony, the marriage of a Catholic and a Protestant
required a dispensation by the bishop, something only to be granted if both spouses
promised to raise their children as Catholics. According to Prussian law, however, sons
had to be educated in the religion of their father. The position was aggravated when
the Prussian government changed the law, ruling that the father had the right to decide
the confession of daughters as well as sons. After the Prussian state and the Catholic
bishops had agreed on a compromise without informing the Holy See, the controversy
escalated when in 1835 Clemens August Freiherr von Droste-Vischering became archbishop of Cologne and - with the support of the Holy See - began to enforce canon
law rather than Prussian state law in this question. The struggle culminated in the
removal of Droste-Vischering as archbishop and his imprisonment by the Prussian
government. It was not only the pope who protested against these measures. They
also caused massive protests by the Catholic public. So-called political Catholicism,
very influential in Germany until the mid-twentieth century, can be dated from this
point. Only after Friedrich Wilhelm IV became king of Prussia in 1840 did matters
calm down. Prussian church policy became less state centred than it was under his
predecessor, and Droste-Vischering was rehabilitated, though he did not return to his
office as archbishop. The question of mixed marriages, however, was now handled in
Prussia according to Catholic canon law. This outcome and the whole struggle meant
a success for the Catholic Church, as it had gained much support from the laity. In the
following period, Catholics in Prussia and in the rest of Germany continued to lobby
for 'religious freedom'. This became especially clear in 1848 during the discussions in
the Paulskirche on whether the state should take over from the church the supervision
of the school system, and on whether the Jesuit order should be banned.

At the same time, however, there were Catholics who did not favour uncondi-
tional orientation towards Rome and wanted to set up a national church along the
lines of the Gallican church in France in the early modern period. In Germany these
people called themselves 'German Catholics'. During the time of the 1848 revolution
in particular they attracted considerable support, but were subsequently marginalised
by the dominance of ultramontane Catholicism and failed to develop any real political
influence.

In March 1848 so-called *Piusvereine* (Pius Associations), named after the new
pope Pius IX who had taken office in 1846, emerged all over Germany. He was originally sympathetic to liberalism, and had come to Rome as a reformer. The Pius Associations had no clear position in the political spectrum of the German associations and
parties of 1848-1849. They recognised, and welcomed, that liberals would be likely to
support liberation of the church from state control, but they objected to liberal support

159

Erzbischoff von Köln.

Abführung nach Minden.   *Aufenthalt in Minden.*

Clemens August Freiherr von Droste-Vischering,
archbishop of Cologne, imprisoned by the Prussian government in the fortress city of Minden,
pamphlet, 1837.
[*Münster, Westfälisches Archivamt, Gräflich Droste
zu Vischering'sches Archiv Darfeld: Avg 364*]

for the secularisation of the state and the nationalisation of the school system. For
this reason, in the Paulskirche, where the revolutionary parliament assembled in 1848,
many prominent representatives of political Catholicism took sides with the extreme
right-wingers. In questions of religious policy the Catholic deputies were united in
the *Katholischer Club* (Catholic Club), which sought to protect the right to religious
freedoms in the spheres mentioned. However, since the Pius Associations were strongly orientated towards Rome, in other words belonged to the ultramontane camp, they

were also automatically influenced by Pope Pius IX's rejection of liberalism and his defection to the reactionary side.

The Pius Associations were organised all over Germany. In October 1848 there were reportedly already 400 of them in Baden, with around 100,000 members. They were equally strongly represented in the Catholic Rhineland, in Bavaria and in Silesia. In October 1848 a general assembly of the Pius Associations took place in Mainz. This assembly is regarded as the original German *Katholikentag*. It dealt quite specifically with political issues, to some extent prescribing how the Catholic deputies should vote in the Paulskirche and in the regional parliaments, and also submitted its own petition to that gathering.

Pius Associations cannot automatically be compared with other political associations. While the other associations concentrated on far-reaching political objectives, the Pius Associations focussed on the relationship between church and state. The extent to which the population was concerned with religious issues in 1848-1849 is illustrated by the huge number of signatures on petitions to the National Assembly on this subject. Of the 2,000 or so petitions received from the Prussian Rhine Province, those concerned with religious issues had about 163,000 signatures; on economic matters it was about 54,000 and on general political issues around 20,000.[1] A similar interest in matters of religious policy can be observed in other territories.

After the 1848 revolution, Catholicism became even more politicised, firstly due to the massive anti-modernist and anti-liberal policy of the Vatican, which led to an enduring conflict not only with political liberalism, but also, to a degree, with conservative Protestantism. The dogma of the immaculate conception promulgated in 1854, the *Quanta Cura* encyclical of 1864 with its syllabus of errors, the dogma of infallibility, proclaimed on the day before the outbreak of the Franco-Prussian war, as well as the doctrine of papal supremacy proclaimed at the First Vatican Council, were perceived in Germany as direct attacks on the modern national state and its liberal-Protestant protagonists. And, within the Catholic Church itself, the doctrine of papal supremacy resolved a centuries-long conflict concerning its internal structure.

Kept under Control: Prussia, Bavaria and the Protestant Churches

At first glance, despite the political changes of the early nineteenth century, the legal status of the Protestant churches in Germany appears to have remained basically unchanged. State rule over the Protestant churches was neither affected by the Principal Decree of the Imperial Deputation (RDH) nor by the end of the Holy Roman Empire or the German Federal Act of 1815. However, the decline of the number of principalities and free cities from more than 300 to 39 required the re-structuring and re-organising

---

[1] Langewiesche, "Die Anfänge der deutschen Parteien", 348.

also of the Protestant churches within the new and enlarged territories of the German states. A reform of general government, which still tended to be based on regulations from the seventeenth and eighteenth centuries, became necessary in many of these enlarged and reshaped states of the early nineteenth century. Such general reforms also necessarily affected the churches. Finally, changes in the legal framework of the churches were also influenced by broader religious and political motives. In what follows, Prussia and Bavaria will serve as examples of these complex reform processes as they affected nineteenth-century Protestant churches and their law.

In the Prussian territories, in the course of the sixteenth and seventeenth centuries, consistories were introduced as permanent governing bodies of the churches with ministers, theologians and lawyers as their members. Even though consistories were the most important institutions of state government of the church, they were originally kept separate from the other government institutions. However, as state control over the churches grew during the seventeenth and eighteenth centuries, and as churches were increasingly considered part of the state's sovereignty, in several states the consistories became part of, or were controlled by, the common state government. The Prussian Common Law Code of 1794 (*Allgemeines Landrecht für die Preußischen Staaten*) is a prime example of this tendency when it rules that "All consistories of the Protestants are under the direction of the authorised department of the state's ministry" (II,11 §146). However, this was only the beginning of an even tighter control of the Protestant churches which the Prussian state introduced in the first half of the nineteenth century.

The historical background to the complete integration of the Protestant consistories into the Prussian government apparatus at the beginning of the nineteenth century was the collapse of the Prussian state after its army was defeated by Napoleonic troops at the Battle of Jena and Auerstedt in October 1806. This crushing defeat made it clear that both the military and the civil government of Prussia urgently needed reform. The widespread discussion on this problem also included church reform. However, there were many conflicting views on how this should be done. In 1808 the eminent Berlin theologian Friedrich Daniel Ernst Schleiermacher published his *Suggestions for a New Constitution of the Protestant Church in the State of Prussia*.[2] In line with the spirit of the time and also with some of the reforms initiated by Baron vom Stein on municipal reform, Schleiermacher argued for a careful democratisation of the church by introducing presbyteries on the parish level and synods on an intermediary district (*Kreis*) level and a collegial board and a bishop at the top of every province of the kingdom.

However, due to French pressure, Stein had to be dismissed. As a consequence, reform in Prussia came to place a heavy centralising emphasis upon the state. Schleiermacher's plans were not put into effect and church government came under the

162

[2] Schleiermacher, *Vorschlag zu einer neuen Verfaßung der protestantischen Kirche im preußischen Staate.*

complete control of the state authorities. The separate consistories of the Reformed and Lutheran Churches in Prussia were dissolved and their tasks transferred to the Ministry of Internal Affairs. This ministry not only had the task of supervising external church matters such as church building, salaries or sufficient training of priests, the so-called *iura circa sacra*, which the king of Prussia as the territorial lord had over every religious community, including the Catholic Church. In the case of the Protestant churches the ministry now also had the right to rule over their internal matters - the *iura in sacra*. At the provincial level, their consistories were also dissolved and ecclesiastical matters were dealt with by the provincial governments. This signified in essence the end of a separate church government both in the Prussian state as a whole and in its individual provinces. The government of the churches had entirely become a state affair.

This state control of the Protestant churches in Prussia was deeply criticised by some of Germany's leading Protestants. Their appeals for an independent church were not restricted to demands to reinstate the consistories as independent church authorities and separate them from the state authorities. They made far-reaching suggestions to constitute the church on a completely renewed basis with presbyterian structures on the local level and with independent synods as legislative bodies at the top. As will be shown below, the chances of such appeals being granted increased as a consequence of the territorial gains of Prussia in 1814-1815. At first, however, the Prussian government only reacted to these protests by introducing a new form of consistories whose only task was to advise the government. Church affairs continued to be governed by the state ministry. However, a government ruling of 3 November 1817, acknowledging the importance and the dignity of ecclesiastical matters, and related questions of education and schooling, made provision for a special ministry to deal with them. This act established the tradition of *Kultusministerien* in Germany (i.e. ministries of religious affairs) which still exist in a number of present-day German *Länder* and which are still in charge of schools, education and the relationship between state and church.

Discussions about a reform of the church went further. There were debates about the introduction of synods, and even about the complete separation of the state and the Protestant churches. In such an eventuality, the latter would then have independent church constitutions based on presbyterian structures. As a result of these discussions, 1816 saw the introduction of presbyteries in the parishes, followed in 1817 and 1818 by synodal meetings at the *Kreis* (local district) level and, in 1819, even at the provincial level. These synods consisted of superintendents, the leading clerics. Laymen did not participate. A decision was made to call for a meeting of a general synod for the whole Prussian state in 1825. But with the advent of *Restauration*, development towards a new church order was halted until the middle of the century.

The Rhenish-Westphalian church order of 1835 was an exception to the policy of *Restauration* in this period. It contained trend-setting elements of constitutionalism in the church and became a model for church constitutions from the middle of the nineteenth century onwards. After 1815, Prussia had gained considerable territories in the western part of Germany which, together with lands which it already held, now formed the western Prussian provinces of the Rhineland and of Westphalia. In these

163

new Prussian territories, there were autonomous Lutheran and Reformed Churches, whose legal status had previously been that of tolerated churches of a Protestant minority in Catholic countries under Catholic princes. In these territories, there had been no state rule over the church and it had been governed by presbyterian structures and synods. Therefore, the introduction of consistories and state rule according to the Prussian model met with considerable resistance. The church order established by the Prussian monarch in 1835 was a compromise between the Rhenish-Westphalian tradition of presbyteries and synods and the state rule over the church by consistories. The parishes were organised according to the presbyterian tradition. The synods of the province were given the right to legislate in the provincial church. They did not only consist of clerics but also of churchwardens or presbyters, who were to be elected as members of the synod. The consistories had the right to supervise and approve. They were also in charge of the day-to-day operations of the church government.

Where the history and the legal status of the Protestant Church in Prussia is concerned, another issue played an important role in this period: the project of uniting the two Protestant confessions, the Lutheran and the Reformed, encouraged by King Friedrich Wilhelm III. In Prussia, there were three different Protestant churches - the Lutheran Church, the German Reformed Church and the French Reformed Church of the Huguenot immigrants. The new territories, with their strong Reformed tradition, strengthened the Reformed Church and therefore consolidated the existence of two different Protestant denominations in Prussia. Although this division was increasingly criticised, attempts by Friedrich Wilhelm III to establish a Union, finally declared in 1817 - three hundred years after the Reformation - were met with scepticism and resistance. Implementing this union could only be achieved very slowly and incompletely. In Prussia, while agreeing to certain common local administrative arrangements, Lutherans and Reformed could not agree on a single confession and form a single Uniate Church. Thus the Prussian Union, which intended to unify the two Protestant branches, in fact resulted in a third Protestant denomination. A further project of King Friedrich Wilhelm III, to introduce a new liturgy, also led to a dispute: his claim of a *ius liturgicum* was the subject of the *Agendenstreit*, a controversy which lasted a decade.

These different questions illustrate the complexity of Prussian church policy in this period: effective government for the three denominations Lutheran, Reformed and Catholic, integration and organisation of the churches in the new Prussian territories, theological and ecclesiastical ideas originating in the monarch, and the possible separation of state and church, with presbyterian structures for the latter. They not only caused tension between the state and the churches, but also within the churches themselves. Politicians joined in. Instituting synods might seem a step towards independence of the church on the one hand, but, on the other, it could be an attempt to increase clerical influence. It might turn the church into a political organisation. In the end, the importance of the individuals who acted in church policy should not be underestimated - the different strategies of Friedrich Wilhelm III and Friedrich Wilhelm IV being a case in point. After the coronation of the new king in 1840, the question of the independence and the constitution of the Prussian Protestant Church was on the

K.A. Lebschée, The Evangelische Matthäus-Kirche
in Munich, *lithograph, c.1830. This first evangelical
church in Munich, designed by Johann Nepomuk
Pertsch, was built in 1827-1833 and demolished in
1938 by the Nazis.*
*[Munich, Bayerische Staatsbibliothek, Porträt- und
Ansichtensammlung]*

political agenda again. The policy and the discussion were of course influenced by the
political developments of the late 40s.

Under *Kultusminister* Eichhorn, the district synods (1841) and the provincial
synods (1844) were reinstated. In 1846, for the first time a general synod for the whole
Prussian monarchy was held. This general synod included laymen as well as clergy.
It drafted a constitution for the Prussian church which - just like the church order of
the Rhineland and Westphalia - combined the presbyteries and synods as elements of
church autonomy, and the consistories, the instruments through which the state ruled
the church. However, the king rejected this constitution. It was only under his successor, Wilhelm I, that a church constitution of this type came into force. The general
synod of 1846 remained a one-off event for two decades.

The historical background of Protestantism in Bavaria was quite different from
that of Prussia. It was only at the beginning of the nineteenth century, that the electorate (and later kingdom) of Bavaria gained territories with a considerable Protestant
population. Bavaria was one of the biggest winners of the Principal Decree of the Imperial Deputation. By this and by other developments in the first two decades, Bavaria

gained formerly free cities and principalities with a Protestant population, such as Nuremberg, Augsburg and Rothenburg, together with the margravates of Bayreuth and Ansbach. From that time on, Protestants have constituted around a quarter of the Bavarian population. The task, therefore, was to forge the Protestant churches of these cities and principalities into a new Bavarian church. This new Bavarian Protestant Church would in turn cement the loyalty of the new Protestant population towards the Bavarian monarchy.

As usual under state rule over the Protestant churches in Germany, the Bavarian monarch as sovereign was *summus episcopus*, the highest bishop of the Protestant Church. One peculiarity of the Bavarian Protestant Church constitution was, however, that the king was not a member of this church. Besides the Habsburgs, the reigning house of Wittelsbach and its Bavarian princes had traditionally been among the most important supporters and princes of the Catholic part of the Holy Roman Empire. They remained Catholic after it came to an end. The case of a Catholic prince as the highest bishop of a Protestant Church had already occurred in the seventeenth and eighteenth centuries. The best-known examples are the electors of Saxony, the country in which the Reformation first took place, since Elector August had turned to Catholicism in order to get the Polish crown. In Saxony, however, the Catholic electors did not claim in person to execute their episcopal rights over the Protestant Church. They were performed by a committee of state officials, who had to be Protestant.

At the end of the eighteenth century, the leading Bavarian statesman and state minister, Count Maximilian von Montgelas, had not only proclaimed tolerance and equality between the denominations as guidelines of his policy, but also control over church affairs by the state government. One aim of this policy was to improve the economy by accepting Protestant merchants and entrepreneurs. By the Bavarian Toleration Act of 26 August 1801, and the Act on Religion of 10 January 1803, equality of the three denominations acknowledged by imperial law (Lutheran, Reformed, Catholic) was guaranteed. This was confirmed by the 'Act on the external legal matters of the inhabitants of the kingdom of Bavaria concerning religion and religious communities' (*Religionsedikt*) of 24 March 1809.

The organisation of the Protestant Church was settled by two acts in 1808 and 1809. In 1808, a special department within the State Ministry of Internal Affairs was introduced, which had the task of controlling the external affairs of the Protestant and Catholic Churches, thus to execute the *iura circa sacra* in the aforesaid sense. This department had Catholic and Protestant advisors. However, this department was also entitled to care for the *iura in sacra* of the Protestant Church, the internal church affairs, including the organisation and the government of the church. In this capacity it acted as 'General Consistory' of the Bavarian Protestant Church. Just as in Prussia, the State Ministry of Internal Affairs also ruled over the internal affairs of the Protestant Church of Bavaria.

The Bavarian constitution of 1818 brought with it a step towards the emancipation of the Protestant Church. As attachments to the constitution, two acts were released, the act on religion which contained general provisions concerning religious freedom, and the *Protestantenedict* (Protestant Act). By the latter, a new *Oberkonsistorium* (Upper Consistory) was instituted, which was no longer a department of the state ministry, but an independent state authority. The *Oberkonsistorium* was in charge of the internal affairs of the Protestant Church and the *iura in sacra* of the king. The task of supervision over the external affairs remained with the State Ministry of Internal Affairs. The separation of *iura in sacra* and *iura circa sacra* was the basis of this design, although the Ministry of Internal Affairs was still given some rights of control over the Upper Consistory. The relationship between these two authorities, Upper Consistory and State Ministry, was full of tension. Because of persistent dissent and conflict, and after remonstrance by the Upper Consistory, in 1831 the king was forced to explain that he would not tolerate any violation of the constitutional rights of the Upper Consistory. After further conflicts about the church policy followed by the decidedly Catholic minister Abel after 1837, the Ministry of Internal Affairs was denied its right of control over the Upper Consistory, which instead was given to the newly instituted *Kultusministerium*. Because it had committed men of strong conviction and high reputation, the Consistory was able to defend its position against the state authorities.

According to § 7 of the Protestant Act, which not only maintained the synods at *Kreis* level but instituted three on a higher level, between the districts and the Bavarian monarchy as a whole. These synods were to meet every four years. The two synods of the parts of Bavaria east of the Rhine (*Bayern rechts des Rheins*) met in a joint session in 1849 under the name of United General Synod (*Vereinigte Generalsynode*), which had been permitted since the previous year. In 1881 they were allowed to meet as a united general synod without having to apply for a joint session.

The parts of the Bavarian monarchy on the west bank of the Rhine did not belong to the Bavarian heartland. However, they had been under the rule of the house of Wittelsbach, which was the house of the Bavarian electors and kings, for a long time. They had been integrated into the Bavarian state by the Congress of Vienna. The Palatinate had a strong Reformed tradition. Here, a Lutheran and Reformed union was established in 1818 which was much more successful than the Prussian one. The two churches were able to reach agreement on a joint confession, so that a real union was achieved, not merely the establishment of a joint administration of Lutheran and Reformed (and Uniate) congregations, as was the case in Prussia. Church development in the Palatinate was quite different and separate from the church of the Bavarian homeland. This, too, is an example of the complexity of the situation. 'German' church history is in reality the history of a great number of different states (and territories within them which have their own individual circumstances).

Despite the existence of synods, in Bavaria as well as in the other German countries the consistories were the most important constitutional institutions of the Protestant churches. In Bavaria, as in the other monarchies, the king was not willing to abandon his power over the church and give it autonomy. The consistories had an ambivalent position in this constitutional system. They were to a certain extent able to gain considerable independence of the state. On the other hand, they were still the authorities through which the king ruled over the churches. They were symbols of the twofold position of the monarchs as rulers of the state and of the Protestant Church.

Revolution 1848-1849 and its Aftermath

Revolution and Church Politics

The European revolutions of 1848-1849 could not avoid considering matters of church politics. "Religious conflicts and conflicts with the state [...] overlapped and fed on each other."[3] Religious controversies were politicised. The importance of religion in this context arose from the fact that not only Jews but also many Christian religious denominations or groups still lacked official recognition in many European and also German states. Their members had to face discrimination and disadvantages in everyday life. It was also due, however, to a general rise not only in religious feeling but also in competition between the major churches. This competition also involved various other religious groups and denominations, particularly in Germany with its multi-confessional religious landscape. Robert Prutz, one of Hegel's followers, wrote in 1846 that Germany was like a grand church council. Pastors were its public heroes and controversies in theology were the pressing questions of the time and the nation.[4]

In Germany churches and religious groups were affected by the revolution particularly in four different ways: firstly, the broad discussion in the revolutionary parliament in the Frankfurt Paulskirche on the fundamental right of religious freedom; secondly, the issue, one both for parliament and the public, of the separation of church and state and the inner constitution of churches and denominations; thirdly, the questions of schooling and education to which that issue was closely linked; finally, the rise of religious associations and denominationally-orientated political parties. Protestant pastors as well as Catholic priests were frequently amongst the political activists of the revolution. The revolutionary parliament intended to regulate the first three of these points in the paragraphs 144-151 of the Frankfurt constitution. Although the revolution failed and the constitution was never put into effect, some of these regulations found their way into constitutions or similar legal regulations of individual German states where these topics continued to be discussed. In the context of this volume, the first two of these fields are of particular relevance, the others will be dealt with in those which are to follow.

168

---

[3] Sperber, *The European Revolutions*, 52.   [4] Wehler, *Deutsche Gesellschaftsgeschichte*, II, 467.

Religious Freedom: an Ambiguous but Fundamental Right?

Even though constitutional developments of the first decades of the nineteenth century had furthered religious toleration in Germany, the legal position of the Jewish population in particular stayed insecure in many German states. Some states continued to deny the Jewish population citizenship and excluded them particularly from any jobs within the extensive system of their civil service. Anti-Jewish sentiments and actions also grew in several parts of the confederation of German states during the first half of the nineteenth century. Many Jews converted to Christian denominations in order to gain full citizenship and access to higher academic or other positions. Therefore, the granting of freedom of religious belief as a fundamental right was particularly vital for the Jewish population who in their majority supported the revolution. However, interest in this topic was by no means restricted to Jews. There were also Christian groups like the Mennonites and other denominations or 'sects' which were either still subject to, or had only recently escaped, discrimination, and they also had their representatives in the Paulskirche. In addition, even the major Christian churches had various conflicts with the secular authorities in those German states where they constituted a religious minority. In 1839, for example, a famous conflict started between the Protestant churches and the state in Bavaria, because Protestant soldiers were forced to kneel down in public like Catholics when they encountered a Catholic procession at Corpus Christi and other religious festivals. Cases like this demonstrate that even though there was general recognition of the major churches, there was still a tendency within several states to maintain something like the idea of a privileged established church within their territory and inhibit the religious freedom of members of other churches.

Religious freedom is one of the most essential rights in western constitutionalism. However, the members of the Paulskirche still found it difficult to guarantee complete religious freedom, which contained not only so-called 'negative' religious freedom, i.e. the right to follow one's own belief and conscience (*Glaubens- und Gewissensfreiheit*) in private as well as in public, but also the 'positive' right to form new religious associations without the consent of any state institution. Several Protestant as well as Catholic members of parliament feared that this might open the gates too far. Permitting full religious diversity might eventually result in a spread of secularism. However, there was intense public interest, and parliament received numerous petitions on this matter. Several members of parliament belonging to smaller religious denominations or sects fought successfully for this right. Thus parliament eventually decided in favour of a constitutional right to complete religious freedom. All churches and religious associations (*Religionsgemeinschaften*) were to be equal and free from the state and be able to administer their affairs for themselves. New religious associations could be founded without any state approval. Like every other association, however, churches and other religious associations were bound by the laws of the secular state.

J. Ventadour, A procession of delegates to the
German pre-parliament moves toward St Paul's
Church in Frankfurt on 30 March 1848, *lithograph,*
1848.
[© bpk: no 00023090 / Dietmar Katz]

Plotting the Future: Constitutional Solutions

When the Catholic member of the Frankfurt Parliament, Peter Ernst von Lasaulx, joined the debate on religious freedom in the Paulskirche, he told his colleagues that their "decision on the freedom of the church will [...] decide on Germany's future" as it would prove whether they had a sincere and vigorous trust in the healing powers of truth and freedom.[5] However, Lasaulx was not a radical democrat who wanted to dissolve the bond between the Catholic Church and the state entirely. What he and many other moderate Catholics and Protestants worked towards was the right of the churches to control their own affairs. They did not, however, support the idea of a

---

[5] Huber and Huber, *Staat und Kirche*, II, 3.

secular state. They considered that Christian monarchs and particularly church control over at least primary schools constituted a guarantee which maintained the Christian character of society. Thus the question of the constitution of the major Christian churches comprised two different aspects: their relationship with the state and their internal organisation.

The Frankfurt Parliament touched on the problem of the internal organisation of the churches at various points, but left it eventually to the individual churches and religious organisations to determine their internal affairs. Thus the democratisation of churches, which was an important issue, particularly for Protestants, had to be resolved in another way and was transferred to the level of the individual states and churches. However, the Frankfurt constitution did disestablish all churches. Quite how far the independence of the churches and religious associations was to go was nevertheless highly disputed in the parliamentary commission, as well as in the plenary debates. Whereas most radical democrats supported complete separation of church and state, with all its consequences, many Catholic members across the political spectrum preferred what they called independence of the church from the state. Democrats as well as many moderate liberals insisted that this had also to entail the independence of the state from the church, defining, of course, the area of state competences in a much broader way than the Catholics. Other, mostly Protestant and Catholic dissident members, did not want to loosen the close relationship between the two. Some even favoured keeping state control over the churches in order to avoid internal religious conflicts or even to protect the people - as the prominent German-Catholic member, Franz Jacob Wigard, argued in these debates - from Catholic clerical power which offered German citizens not religious freedom, but "the bonds of serfdom and suppression through its hierarchy".[6] A compromise was finally hammered out in the wording of paragraph 147 which stipulated that every religious association (*Religionsgesellschaft*) had to order and administer its own affairs independently, but would remain subject to general state laws in doing so. It further regulated that no religious association was to be 'established' or privileged by the state.

On the one hand, this paragraph was a victory for the liberals over the 'etatists'. On the other hand, however, it left the exact details of church independence open. Thus it remains unclear what precisely this paragraph would have entailed had the constitution been implemented. As the vision on the far left to turn the German states into democratic republics had no majority in the revolutionary parliament, the consequences probably would not have been radical. However, many liberal and Catholic members of parliament, and also many of the numerous petitions, wanted the state not only to refrain from interfering with matters of doctrine, but also to treat religious associations including the old churches like any other association and leave the appointment of staff and the administering of their financial affairs entirely to them. Even very

171

---

[6] Scholler, *Die Grundrechtsdiskussion in der Pauls-kirche*, 181.

conservative Catholics like Joseph Maria von Radowitz, who was also very close to the Prussian monarch, argued in parliament in that direction. Taken literally, this would have meant that German monarchs could have no longer interfered with the appointment of Catholic bishops (and there would have been no need for regulating these controversial matters by means of concordats) nor could they have prevented the introduction of democratically-elected synods in Protestant churches. In the understanding of some members of parliament, the independence of the churches also entailed the abandonment of patronage rights possessed at the local level by the nobility and town magistrates. As there was quite wide support both inside and outside parliament for reforms along these lines, pressure for far reaching reforms in the individual German states would have been considerable.

Even though there was no explicit mentioning of these matters in the constitution, in the long run the separation of church and state, and particularly the recognition of the equal legal status of all religious associations, would have had to result in the difficult disentanglement of church and state property. Only a small number of members of parliament also found the direct or indirect support of the state for theological faculties problematic. However, doubts about this could not only be found on the left, but also on the right, because people felt that the representatives of a secular state could not be trusted with religious matters. "If baptised as well as un-baptised, if bricklayers and plumbers can become ministers", argued Johann Nepomuk Sepp, a Bavarian member of parliament from the national-liberal *Casino* party, in the Paulskirche, "then no-one can any longer with any right insist on the state having the right to influence the distribution of church prebendaries or the appointment of professors to theological faculties".[7]

Whereas the realisation of such presumptive consequences remained open to further debates at state level, the constitution of the Paulskirche made it clear that the churches would have to give up their right to supervise primary schools and to function as registrars for marriages (§§ 150-153). Apart from religious instruction, the entire system of schooling and education was to be put under state supervision, and church weddings could be only performed after marriage in a civil registry office.

The failure of the revolution meant that these regulations were not put into practice at the time. However, as all church matters were still the prerogative of the individual states of the German Confederation (*Deutscher Bund*), discussions continued on that level. In fact, many of the Frankfurt regulations found their way into the constitutional law of the states, and later into that of the German Empire which introduced, for example, compulsory civil marriages in 1875. The Prussian constitution of 1850 provides an interesting example of this process.

---

[7] Scholler, *Die Grundrechtsdiskussion in der Paulskirche*, 173.

Conservative Change: the 1850 Prussian Constitution and the Churches

During the revolutionary days of March 1848 the Prussian king, Friedrich Wilhelm IV, was forced to summon a Prussian National Assembly on the basis of general elections. One of the main ambitions of the revolutionaries was to have their own constitutional bill passed by parliament rather than accept a draft bill which came from the king and the moderate liberals of his newly appointed ministry. By July parliament was able to present a first draft which also contained detailed regulations concerning the relationship between the state and the churches. The king refused to sign this bill in principle because it was a revolutionary document. However, despite having actively helped to crush the revolution by military force in Prussia and elsewhere, Friedrich Wilhelm IV nevertheless accepted the need for some constitutional regulations. In December 1848 he 'granted' a constitution which was not passed by parliament. It was amended in 1850 and from then on served as the legal framework for the monarchy and also for the church-state relationship in Prussia until the 1918 revolution.

Religious questions had become a very sensitive matter in Germany, particularly in Prussia. There had been fierce inner-protestant debates in the decades leading up to the revolution in which the Prussian kings and their governments clearly took sides. In addition to (but not entirely independent of) the criticism of the Prussian church constitution, there was also criticism of the state-enforced union, which has been referred to earlier, of the Reformed and Lutheran Church of 1817. Opposition was particularly strong amongst Prussian Lutherans, some of whom left the new *Evangelische Kirche in Preußen* and in 1830 formed the *Evangelisch-Lutherische Kirche in Preußen*. The Prussian government did not want to tolerate this and several Lutheran theologians were in fact imprisoned. When in 1840 Friedrich Wilhelm IV came to the throne (he had himself married a Catholic Bavarian princess who only later in life converted to the traditional Reformed faith of the Hohenzollern) he ended these quarrels and tolerated the so-called *Alt-Lutheraner* (Old Lutherans) in 1841 and officially recognised them as an independent Protestant Church in Prussia in 1845. However, at the same time, as personally a conservative romantic, he tolerated the massive attacks which the conservative Protestant church newspaper, the *Evangelische Kirchenzeitung* and particularly its chief editor Ernst Wilhelm Hengstenberg, a Berlin Old Testament professor, launched against a group of rationalist-enlightened Protestant theologians, some of whom tended towards a form of enlightened deism. The political conflict escalated, the *Lichtfreunde* (Friends of Light) as they were ironically called by their enemies, soon grew to a fully-fledged dissenting denomination with approximately 150,000 followers. Their public meetings were suppressed in Prussia in 1845 and Protestant pastors publicly adhering to the *Lichtfreunde* were threatened with dismissal. In 1848 the *Lichtfreunde* were mostly to be found amongst the political activists on the democratic left.

The 1840s were a time when religious strife in Prussia was a serious public topic and it was quite clear that the monarch was not neutral and did not intend to give up his involvement in Protestant church matters. The enlightened General Law Code of 1794 had granted all Prussian subjects the individual right of religious freedom. State intervention into what people believed and how and where they practiced their religious beliefs was abolished. However, this did not mean that the Prussian state became neutral with regard to any kind of religious organisation and that anyone could form religious associations or churches free of any state intervention. Corporative rights of religious freedom were not part of the Prussian General Law Code. Forming religious groups still required registering with, and admission by, the state authorities. Thus, in 1794 the problem of corporate religious rights was far from being solved in Prussia, and it was precisely this side of religious freedom which in 1848 was at the core not only of the debate in the Frankfurt Parliament but also in the Prussian National Assembly. The contemporary religious quarrels of the 1840s seemed to render a solution of this topic particularly important.

The king was conservative. In religious matters, however, he was not a hardliner in the sense of trying to enforce religious unity at all costs. His own personal experience of living in a mixed marriage certainly played some role in this. The 1850 constitution not only guaranteed the freedom of individual religious belief, but also introduced some important restrictions concerning the state's role in church affairs. It stipulated that the Protestant and Catholic Churches, as well as any other religious association (*Religionsgesellschaft*), should be responsible for the ordering and administration of their own affairs and should be allowed to keep or continue using the buildings, foundations and other funds dedicated to their ecclesiastical, educational or charitable work and purposes. The constitution also guaranteed that the Prussian state would not interfere with the communication between religious bodies and their ecclesiastical superiors, nor would internal ecclesiastical announcements be subjected to any other control and restriction than what was usual for public announcements in general. The constitution abolished any right of the state to get involved in making ecclesiastical appointments. Local rights of patronage in the matter of appointments still continued for the time being. They were to be dealt with in further legislation (which never in fact came).

These regulations were of particular importance for the Catholic Church. They finally gave its bishops the constitutional right to deal directly with the Vatican without having to go via the Berlin ministry, and the church was also granted almost full control of its internal affairs. The same was only nominally true for the Protestant Church, as the king continued to be its head. Even though matters of church administration now passed from the Prussian *Kultusministerium* to the *Evangelischer Oberkirchenrat* (Protestant Consistory), the king as *summus episcopus* still had the right to appoint its members. Thus matters of church and state were formally and institutionally separated, but for Protestants the links between the two remained strong.

There were two additional points in which the 1850 Prussian constitution clearly fell short in comparison with what the Frankfurt Parliament would have enforced. Both stayed very much contested areas for the next decades. The first point was the introduction of civil marriage. Here the king, in his 1848 constitution, had originally followed the liberal lines of his own ministers and the Frankfurt Parliament and required that a civil marriage should precede a subsequent church ceremony. The Catholic Church, for whom marriage was a sacrament and not a civil contract, saw this as a major infringement of 'church territory'. Conservative Protestants did not like this regulation either as they feared it would lead to a decline in church weddings and further the general secularisation of society. However, it also touched on financial issues, since the fees for weddings and funerals formed a share of the income of the local parish clergy. After some pressure from both sides, the 1850 amendment of the constitution withdrew this paragraph and transferred the introduction of civil marriage to future special regulation. For the liberals, the introduction of civil marriage had been a major political objective. This amendment was therefore a major blow for them, and the issue remained on the political agenda for the next decades.

The other point where the 1850 amendment at least watered down a previously clear regulation was the field of church involvement in primary school education. Whereas the original constitution of 1848 took primary schools completely out of church hands and parish clergy were restricted to concerning themselves with religious education, the 1850 amendment stipulated that the local confessional situation had to be taken into account in decisions on school matters. This paragraph reopened the debate on confessional schools as well as on staff policies (e.g. not sending Protestant teachers to primary schools in Catholic areas).

Liberal as it was in some respects, the 1850 constitution still can be seen as a document by means of which the monarch primarily reduced tensions with ultramontane Catholicism in his Rhenish territories, and, at the same time, managed not to give away too much of his power over the Protestant churches. He also kept control over the formation of new religious associations. This term was interesting in itself. Invented by the jurist who drew up the General Law Code of 1794, it avoided the term 'church' for any religious organisation other than the Protestant and Catholic Churches, and put all the others under the category of a civil association. This provided the state with several possibilities of exercising organisational control. Religious associations could only be raised to the same legal status as the old churches by being granted the rights of a public corporation. What exactly this entailed was left open. However, as far as the Jewish religion was concerned, Art. 14 of the constitution made clear that certain state institutions were Christian by definition and that access to them had to be restricted to Christians.

Culture Wars and Accommodations: the Final Phase

Protestants: Some Ambivalent Autonomy

Despite the conservative tendencies of the constitution, a reform of the church authorities brought a step forward towards autonomy for the Protestant Church. On 28 January 1848 the institution of an 'Upper Consistory' was ordered, to which the control of the internal affairs of the Protestant churches would be transferred. Such matters would then therefore have been re-transferred from the state ministry to a church authority. However, the Upper Consistory was dissolved in the course of the *Paulskirchen-Revolution* on 15 April 1848, without having had any influence and after only one session of its members. As mentioned above, after the failure of the constitutional movement in Germany, however, in 1850 the *Evangelischer Oberkirchenrat* was instituted by a royal decree as an autonomous church authority, charged with church government. According to this decree, it was also asked to initiate - in cooperation with the state ministry - the necessary steps towards reforming local congregations and setting up an autonomous Protestant Church constitution. These attempts failed, however, after a short time, largely because the provision of synods constituted a representative element unacceptable to the Crown.

It was not until twenty-four years later, under the reign of King Wilhelm I that a constitution for the local congregations, districts and provinces within the Prussian realm came into force (September 1873). In 1876, after a session of an extraordinary synod held in 1875, an order establishing synods for the eight older provinces of the monarchy (excluding the churches of the territories which had been annexed by Prussia in the 1860s - Hanover for example) was enacted. This typical compromise between the representative principle and the monarch's rule over the church by the consistory, was put into force for the whole (older) Prussian state. Rule by the monarch remained unaltered until the monarchy itself came to an end. The monarch was owner of the *iura circa sacra* which he executed through the state authorities - especially the *Kultusministerium*. Also, however, because of the *iura in sacra*, he exercised power over internal church matters through the *Evangelischer Oberkirchenrat*.

The picture, however, could differ from state to state. In particular instances, as in Oldenburg, for a few years the church gained complete autonomy with the synod as its governing institution. In Mecklenburg, on the other hand, until 1918, the church was governed on the basis of a church order dating from the sixteenth century. It had no synods or consistories of the modern type. All in all, however, the Prussian and Bavarian models, with both the synod and the consistory as church organs, with increasing independence of the consistory from the states' ministries, typified the constitutional arrangements of the German Protestant churches in the late nineteenth century.

National Unity and Protestant Unity

How to achieve national unity was one of the great issues of German history of the nineteenth century. It was paralleled, in church matters, by the attempt to achieve Protestant unity. And just as national unity was not the aim of the monarchs, but of the democratic movement, the question of church unity was raised by lay movements, not by the monarchs as *summi episcopi* of the Protestant churches. Even today, the Protestant churches in Germany are not united as one organisation. The question of unity was the main issue of the first *Deutscher Evangelischer Kirchentag* in 1848, a meeting of church members from all parts of Germany, organised not by the church authorities or clergy, but by committed laity. Their appeal for unity, however, was not successful, but four years later a first step to unity was taken by the church authorities in establishing the *Konferenz Evangelischer Kirchenregierungen* (Conference of Protestant Church Governments) or *Eisenacher Konferenz* in 1903 as it was generally referred to. This was, however, only a kind of regularly held meeting of the church authorities to discuss church matters and coordinate their policies and had no constitutional status within church organisation. A step forward towards a single organisational roof for German Protestantism was the *Deutscher Evangelische Kirchenausschuss* (German Protestant Church Committee) which was instituted by the above-mentioned *Eisenacher Konferenz*. The committee was a permanent body of all *Landeskirchen* within the German Empire. It was the first serious attempt to form a single organisational framework which included all of them. The next step was the foundation of the *Deutscher Evangelische Kirchenbund* (German Federation of Protestant Churches) in 1922 - after the period which is covered by this article.

State and Catholic Church: the Kulturkampf

177

The political restoration after the defeat of Napoleon and the re-structuring of Europe at the Congress of Vienna did not - apart from the restoration of the Papal States - bring about any restitution of secularised church property either in Germany, France or Italy. Nonetheless, during the early nineteenth century there was a remarkable increase in the attractiveness and spiritual power of the Catholic Church, especially of the Papacy. As early as the first half of the nineteenth century in Germany, the church's new-found self-confidence led to numerous disputes, especially with the Prussian state. The Revolution of 1848 had strengthened Catholicism to some degree - the disputes over state control of schools and the ban on the Jesuit order had led to Catholicism becoming politically organised. Starting with the *Katholischer Klub* (Catholic Club) of Catholic deputies, then moving on to the foundation of a *Katholische Fraktion* (Catholic Group) in the Prussian House of Deputies, a party was eventually founded in 1852, when 48 Catholic deputies formed the *Fraktion des Zentrums* (Centre Group). After the founding of the Empire this then became the *Deutsche Zentrumspartei* (German Centre Party), whose members stood for election to the Reichstag.

In the second half of the nineteenth century the Catholics' main dispute with the state was the so-called *Kulturkampf*. There are two definitions of this term, the broad and the narrow. The broader definition mainly refers to the clash between the Catholic Church, or indeed the churches *per se*, and the spirit of liberalism and nationalism embodied in the new European national state. During the course of his long pontificate, 1846-1878, Pius IX had been transformed from the liberals' great hope during the 1848 revolution into an opponent of reforms and the Italian national state. Two contentious steps taken by the Vatican contributed to the polarisation of opinion: the 1854 dogma of Mary's immaculate conception, the 1864 condemnation in the *Syllabus*

Errorum (Syllabus of Errors) of so much that liberal opinion held dear, a stance which appeared to range him against the entire modern bourgeois culture.[8] Finally, marking the zenith of the pope's ultramontane policy, in 1870, at the First Vatican Council, the doctrines of papal supremacy and papal infallibility in doctrinal decisions delivered *ex cathedra*, were proclaimed in the *constitutio de ecclesia*. Accordingly, in questions of belief and practice, the pope, in exercising his supreme authority, was infallible. For proponents of the broader definition, the *Kulturkampf* was, as the Catholic historian Josef Becker put it, the result of the confluence of various emancipation movements. It was to some extent a conflict of modernisation, in which Christian values had staked their claim to participate in formulating the state's political demands and objectives in the face of liberal views. In his view, the *Kulturkampf* was not, therefore, a purely Catholic or a purely German phenomenon. According to the narrower definition, however - the one generally preferred by Protestant historians - the *Kulturkampf* was German Catholicism, as represented here by the Centre, in conflict with the Protestant Prussian state and its Minister-President, the first German imperial chancellor, Otto von Bismarck.

There was a strong wave of protest against the resolutions of the First Vatican Council in all European countries. Ecclesiastically, it caused some Catholics to leave and form what became the Old Catholic Church. Politically, the German state conducted a *Kulturkampf*, primarily against political Catholicism. For Bismarck, organised Catholicism evoked the memory of the disputes with the Southern German states over a *kleindeutsche* solution. He saw in organised Catholicism a potential danger to the Reich, and in addition he regarded the non-confessional status of the state as a precondition for gaining the support of the liberals and for integrating the various parts of the country with their different confessions. The specifically Prussian-German problems during the period of the Reich's foundation thus also led to a more intense version of the *Kulturkampf* in Germany than elsewhere, a fact which, to some extent, justifies a narrower interpretation of the phenomenon.

The most important legal restrictions on the church's power (which naturally applied to the Protestants as well), were to be found in the so-called *Kanzelparagraph*. This decreed that any statements made by clergy from the pulpit on matters of state likely to threaten public order were punishable by up to two years in prison. This was followed in 1872 by the abolition of school supervision by the clergy and a new ban on the Jesuit order. In 1873 laws like the *Kulturparagraph* were introduced in Prussia which stipulated that no parish priest was to be instated who had not passed the *Abitur* (leaving examination) at a German *Gymnasium* (grammar school), studied at a German university and passed a general state examination in philosophy, history and literature. In 1874 the civil marriage law was passed; in 1875 the Catholic orders, with the exception of the nursing orders, were abolished. In order to enforce the Catholic Church's recognition of the new German Empire and its laws concerning the churches

---

[8] Huber and Huber, *Staat und Kirche*, II, 395-427.

FRONTIÈRE BELGE

Bismark expulsant les jésuites.

Victor Lemaître, Bismarck drives away the Jesuits,
anticlerical cartoon on the Kulturkampf, *published
in* Le Rasoir, *8 September 1872.*
[Mons, Mundaneum]

and religious matters Bismarck stopped - for Prussia - all state subsidies to the Catholic
Church. Only when bishops and parish priests signed a letter of recognition would
they be entitled to their former salaries or subsidies towards their bishoprics. This law
became known as *Brotkorbgesetz* (bread basket law) as it tried to increase pressure
on the Catholic clergy by taking away their personal income and means of subsistence.

The disputes over these laws dragged on throughout the whole of the 1870s. The bishops of Münster and Paderborn, in particular, refused the *Kulturexamen* for their seminaries and appointed priests without notifying Prussian officials. The consequences were harsh. The Prussian government stopped all state subsidies, closed Catholic institutions, even confiscated the personal property of bishops and finally imprisoned them. However, this only resulted in massive popular support for the Catholic Church in these regions and in anti-Prussian and anti-Protestant sentiment at all levels of society. It also increased the political organisation of German Catholicism. Catholic associations and Catholic newspapers effectively organised resistance and Catholic solidarity. When the Prussian authorities, for example, auctioned publicly the confiscated property of the bishop of Paderborn, devout Catholics tried to buy it and return it to him. The political organisation of Catholics round the German Centre Party (*Deutsche Zentrumspartei*) also increased rapidly. In the mid 1870s, at the height of the *Kulturkampf*, the Centre Party received 80 percent of all Catholic votes.

Under the new pope, Leo XIII, the Holy See took up negotiations with Bismarck. The relationship gradually eased and some of these laws were repealed or mitigated. The only ones to remain were the civil marriage law, state control of schools, and the *Kanzelparagraph*, which was only repealed in the Federal Republic in 1953. All in all, however, the end of the *Kulturkampf* marked a victory for ultramontane Catholicism, which indeed emerged stronger from this conflict both organisationally and theologically. The new pope cautiously opened the eyes of the Catholic Church to an encounter with modern culture and science. His most important achievement was the encyclical of 1891, *Rerum Novarum*, in which he laid the foundation stone for Catholic social doctrine.

Many Protestants saw Bismarck's rapprochement with the Catholic Church indeed as a defeat for Protestantism in Germany and stressed the need for more collaboration between the different Protestant denominations and a stronger organisational framework for the 27 territorial Protestant churches. The most important initiative in this context was the foundation of a Protestant Alliance (*Evangelischer Bund*) in 1887, which set out to curb the "power of Romanism"[9] not only by promoting Protestant unity, but also by actively fighting Catholicism, as well as modern religious indifference, through political action and an active media policy. On the eve of the First World War this association counted over half a million members. This shows that despite the end of open government action against the Catholic Church religious tension continued. It was fostered at the turn of the century by new attacks by the Holy See on historical criticism of biblical texts and any accommodation of Catholicism to modern philosophy, sociology or literature. This was announced by Pope Pius X in a new encyclical *Pascendi dominici gregis*, and was followed in 1910 by a policy which required Catholic priests to take an oath against all forms of modernism. When it was openly extended to professors of Catholic theology and teachers of Catholic religion at state schools,

---

[9] Huber and Huber, *Staat und Kirche*, III, 541.

this anti-modernist oath resulted in new conflicts between the state and the Catholic Church. It also sparked off another intense political and public debate. It coincided with another fierce political discussion on whether the law from 1872 banning the Jesuit order from Germany should be annulled. This was finally agreed by the Reichstag in 1914. However, the decision was postponed by the *Bundesrat* (Upper House) until 1917. When it was finally passed as part of Wilhelm II's policy of maintaining public unity during the war, this decision was fiercely opposed by the Protestant Alliance. Thus religious conflict and tension prevailed and perhaps even increased after the end of the *Kulturkampf*, as it was now less the state, but independent religious associations which continued the struggle about public influence and cultural hegemony.

Money Matters

State, Church and Finance

No understanding of the dynamics of the state-church relationship in this period is complete without an emphasis on the complex funding issues which lay at its heart. The sections that follow indicate some of its dimensions and again, by highlighting different solutions, or attempted solutions, stress once again that there was no all-German outcome. It is a very complex issue because ecclesiastical finances comprised very varied types of income which the churches had been able to acquire over time and which, from the late eighteenth century, came increasingly under pressure from different sources - economic, social and political. Sometimes debates on the ways church expenditures should be met were part of the wider problems of the transition from feudal duties to modern taxation and were intertwined with general political issues of the time. Sometimes, however, they touched on very specific problems which related solely to either Catholics or Protestants or were of regional or even local relevance only. There are, even so, also some general trends in this field which can be discerned. A major problem for the Catholic Church in Germany was the massive secularisation of its property. It started as early as the late eighteenth century when Emperor Joseph II made the secularisation of church property part of his modernising programme for his Habsburg territories; following the example of the French Revolution it also became an important tool in the context of Napoleon's re-shaping of Germany; finally, it was taken up again by the German princes in the context of their land-bartering at the Congress of Vienna. Its consequences influence the fiscal relationship between the Catholic Church and the state in Germany even to the present day. Independent of this specifically Catholic problem there was, right through the nineteenth century, a growing dissatisfaction on all sides with the traditional ways of financing the churches. Rapid urbanisation, for example, rendered a system based on agricultural dues dysfunctional when it came to endowing new churches and parishes in industrial areas. Growing religious pluralism and religious freedom, together with increasing mobility, led to great injustice and inequality in the way individuals contributed to church finances. The growth of religious diasporas meant that the traditional fusion of secular and religious parishes was perceived as discriminatory and unjust by many citizens. Religious minorities had to contribute, via their local taxes, to the upkeep of church buildings and other expenditures of the religious majority (and sometimes vice versa). Furthermore, in the last quarter of the nineteenth century political decisions like the introduction of obligatory civil marriage ceremonies in the new German Reich in 1875 resulted in the fear of a decline in church weddings, primarily for financial reasons, particularly in urban working class areas. The churches, therefore, abolished fees for church weddings and as a result clergy lost part of their traditional income and needed to be compensated.

Such different types of political and economic processes and changes compelled the churches to find additional sources of income to maintain their buildings, their services, and their staff. Mostly they turned to the state which had stripped them of their assets and demanded compensation. However, the outcome of such negotiations was rarely fully successful and sufficient. The states themselves were notoriously short of money and unable to meet the demands of the churches. Additional fundraising from church members, first on an irregular and local, then on a continuing and general basis, became inevitable. This was true for all German states which over the course of the nineteenth century all gradually introduced an additional income-related church tax.

Finance: a Tangled Inheritance

Traditionally the churches derived most of their income from five different sources. Firstly, the most important part of the income of the individual parish came from dues connected with land which belonged to the church or where the church had at least the right to ask for these dues. Around 1800 in Bavaria nearly a quarter of the farmsteads belonged in one way or the other to church institutions. Tithes which partly (traditionally a third) went towards the financing of the parish priest had often been transferred to the patron of the church (*Laienzehnt*), however, they partly still contributed to the financing of the parish. Secondly, monasteries and several other ecclesiastical institutions tended to create an important part of their income through their own agricultural or other commercial enterprises, such as breweries, vineyards or pharmacies. They normally had large farms which they worked themselves in addition to those farms and villages with which they were endowed and where they were entitled to collect the tithe. Rural parish priests - Protestants and Catholics alike - were also frequently endowed with their own fields which they could either let or work themselves. Thirdly, a minor source of income came from fees for specific services rendered by the priest to the parish, particularly for marriages and burials (*Stolgebühren*), reading special masses, ringing the bells on specific occasions, or for providing pews. These fees mainly contributed towards the income of the parish priest and other staff. Fourthly, a major source, particularly for the charitable work of a parish, came from pious foundations. Finally, there were the offerings collected during services.

Georg Knorr, Collection after the Mass, *oil on
canvas, 1881.*
[© bpk: no 20027895]

At the end of the eighteenth century this system of financing the different levels
of the ecclesiastical hierarchy and to meet different types of expenditure was still in
use in both the Catholic and the Protestant Churches. The Reformation had not altered
the basic principles of this system of church financing. On the level of a parish, the
various permanent sources from which the priest derived the main part of his income
constituted his benefice (*Pfründe*). It comprised the vicarage where he could live for
free, fields which he could either work or let, tithes or other duties and possibly, in
some parts, even corvée labour from farmsteads belonging to the parish. In Prussia, for
example, the General Law Code of 1794 dealt in detail with the collecting of the tithes
as potential parts of the income of Protestant pastors as well as Catholic priests. Even
in mid-nineteenth-century Prussia, between 25% and 60% of the income of the rural
clergy consisted of agricultural goods. The priest with the highest such share was the
most secure since he otherwise only received cash for irregular duties and subsidies
from the secular parish, both of which were likely to be modest.

However, in Württemberg and some other Protestant territories of the Empire
governments had already centralised the collection of church revenues during the

Reformation period and installed a separate financial administration for church finances as part of the central government. This was primarily a consequence of the secularisation of monasteries. As a result, the new Protestant pastors had to be paid by the respective government institutions and they could be grouped into 'wage brackets' according to criteria which differed from those relating to the original wealth or poverty of their benefice and parish, now with reference to their expertise, age and length of service.

Even though this made the Protestant Church in Württemberg part of the state and turned its clergy effectively into civil servants, at least the salary system had its advantages over the inequalities, inherited from the past, between the endowments of different parishes. Reforms along these lines were, therefore, also tried elsewhere during the eighteenth century, e.g. in the margravate of Baden. However, even in the reform-oriented 'absolutist' state of Baden legal problems proved to be too difficult to solve through normal political processes. During the eighteenth century attempts at substantial reforms failed not only in Baden but also elsewhere. The most pressing problem, the increasing poverty of some rural priests and pastors and the injustice of sometimes vast discrepancies between clerical incomes, could only be provisionally alleviated in Baden by creating a small state fund for the support of impoverished clergy.

Finance: South German Solutions

In 1806, the newly created king of Württemberg, Friedrich I, abolished the separate administration of church property and integrated all church funds into the general government finances. Like Catholic priests in France, Württemberg's Protestant pastors, as well as Catholic priests, became state employees, and former church property was now to be used by the state for the financing of schools, hospitals and poor relief. Although these had been traditional fields of activity for the Protestant as well as the Catholic Church, they were now taken out of their hands. It was difficult to control whether all income derived from former ecclesiastical property was exclusively used to finance such former church responsibilities or whether it went into other sectors of public expenditure. Centralised church funds have always been in danger of being raided by governments in need of money, and Württemberg was no exception to this.

Friedrich's policy of secularisation and centralisation of church funds followed through what had been started, as has been earlier explained, by the 1803 *Reichsdeputationshauptschluss*. Württemberg like Baden, Bavaria and other member states of the Empire gained new territories which had to be incorporated into the existing state and church structures. This presented the monarchs with an opportunity to carry out general reforms which they frequently had been thinking about or even attempted for some time. However, in Württemberg these centralising reforms were immensely unpopular and met with fierce resistance from the Protestant as well as the Catholic side. Friedrich's successor, King Wilhelm I, was forced to reverse them. Thus, the 1819

Württemberg constitution ruled that the property of the former dukedom's Protestant Church had to be restored, and that the new Catholic Church was to receive an independent church fund to enable it to run its parishes and in particular its seminary. The parliamentary commission given the task failed to sort out, for both Catholic and Protestant Churches, what was state and what was church property. No final agreement could be reached, and the problem remained unsolved until the end of the monarchy.

In Württemberg, therefore, right through the nineteenth century, the Protestant as well as the Catholic Churches depended on regular state subsidies to run their parishes and administration. This was particularly important for salaries and costs that went beyond the responsibilities of the individual parishes. The Catholic Church succeeded in the 1820s in Württemberg in securing state guarantees for the financing of its newly established bishopric of Rottenburg which included salaries for the Catholic priests and the bishop himself as well as money for the seminary. For all other parish expenditures, the local parishes had to provide the necessary funds themselves. These could come from religious foundations, local donations or other sources of local income. In 1887 secular and religious parishes, which were basically merged in Württemberg, were finally separated. However, neither was former church property fully returned to the churches nor were they fully compensated for their losses. Instead the local churches were allowed to supplement their insufficient funds by levying taxes at a parish level. Such taxes had to be approved by the state, and were not to exceed a maximum of ten percent of what parish members had to pay in state taxes.

185

It was only after the First World War that a more comprehensive solution was in sight. Within the framework of the constitution of the Weimar Republic the individual German states were legally bound to solve the problem of separating church and state property and compensate the churches for the loss of property incurred through secularisation at the turn of the nineteenth century. However, owing to the economic strains of the time this proved again to be a matter too complex to be resolved in a comprehensive way. The solution finally established in the 1924 Württemberg law on state-church relations was one which at least enabled the churches to act and plan more independently from the state. Apart from being given the property rights to those former ecclesiastical buildings which were still used by the churches, they were also granted the right to collect taxes from their members, a solution which continues to the present day.

In another South German territory, the former margravate and newly (1806) created grand duchy of Baden, the discussions of the first half of the century resulted in the 1860s and 1870s in reforms which replaced, in stages, the former unequal system of payment of the clergy with one whose income brackets were primarily age-related. Salaries became independent of the specific endowments of individual churches or parishes, and the horizontal transfer of funds between them was administered by a newly established central fund (*Zentralpfarrkasse*). However, even then, the funds were not sufficient to guarantee a minimal income for all clergy and needed further subsidies by the state. As in Württemberg this shortage of church funds led to discussion of a regular taxation of church members. In 1888 and 1892 Baden introduced a system of local taxation of church members which catered first for local and then also for the central financial needs of the churches. These regulations applied to both the Catholic and the Protestant Churches, but as in Württemberg it did not mean that the churches were fully independent. The churches themselves did not want full independence. As long as former church property and resources were not returned or fully compensated for, they needed to be able to claim regular financial contributions from the state. Thus in Baden, too, the state continues to pay its share (the so-called *Staatsleistungen*) to the running costs of the churches up to the present day.

Finance: Prussian Solutions

In most of the old and new (Rhenish) Prussian territories, church funding was similarly precarious. More than other German states, Prussia had become multi-confessional as a consequence of its territorial gains through the Silesian wars, the divisions of Poland, and as a result of the Congress of Vienna. In both the east and the west Prussia had gained large numbers of new Catholic citizens, particularly in Upper Silesia and the former Polish territories as well as the Rhenish prince-bishoprics of Cologne, Trier, Münster and Paderborn. As elsewhere in the *Deutscher Bund*, the Catholic Church lost most of its former possessions, its buildings as well as its landed property and other sources of income, to the Prussian state. In Silesia and the former Polish territories this was partly a consequence of the bankruptcy of the Prussian state and its massive financial obligations towards France after the peace treaty of Tilsit (1807) and the following Paris convention (1808). In the western provinces left of the Rhine church property had already been secularised by France. Catholic and Protestant clergy had been turned into state employees. After taking over these territories, Prussia also had to meet these financial obligations towards the churches. Thus, there was a need for reorganising the material basis of the Catholic as well as at least of some of the regional Protestant churches.

As far as the Catholic bishoprics were concerned, the state contributions towards the running of the dioceses (particularly the incomes of bishops and other dignitaries), cathedrals and the seminaries were regulated in the 1821 bull of circumscription *De salute animarum*. Although it was also stipulated in this bull that by 1833 the Prussian state had to return enough land to these dioceses to provide them with an equivalent independent income, this never happened. Instead, the Prussian state continued to pay the salaries and administrative costs of the Catholic dioceses right through the nineteenth century.

Even more money had to be allocated by the state for subsidies to the incomes of parish priests and pastors. Particularly in many rural areas, most Protestant as well Catholic clergy suffered increasingly from extremely low incomes. As in other parts of the country this was aggravated in the mid-nineteenth century by the bad harvests and the general economic crisis. It was also the case, however, that in the main Prussian lands many parishes were dependant for additional funding on the local nobility

186

who held the patronage of the churches. These families of lower nobility, however, also faced declining incomes in times of crisis and were unwilling to grant substantial support on a continuous basis. Thus, at least in the case of the Protestant clergy, their social status as part of the learned academic elite of the country was endangered as they were hardly able to send even one of their sons to university. After the Prussian Protestant pastors had proved particularly loyal during the revolutionary years of 1848-1849, their protest against the continuing deterioration of their economic position grew louder, and they demanded more state subsidies and an income equivalent to that of other academic professions like grammar school teachers or doctors. Some state subsidies for clergy salaries existed also in Prussia, however only on a small scale, and they were by no means enough to alleviate the problems in an effective way.

It was only after the foundation of the new German Empire when the Prussian state was in good economic shape for some years and when the salaries of civil servants were raised considerably that, after some campaigning, the minimal salaries of the Protestant clergy were also raised and guaranteed through state subsidies. At the same time, at least for those parishes where the monarch possessed the patronage rights, a system of age-related payment was introduced similar to that in Baden, stretching from 1,800 Marks (in Baden it was only 1,600 Marks in 1876) per year minimum to 3,600 Marks (in Baden 3,400) maximum in the 1870s. Only in well-endowed parishes with other patronage rights could even long-serving clergy earn more than that. Grammar school teachers by comparison could reach at the same time a final yearly salary of 4,500 Marks, whereas judges were already entitled to this kind of income after a few years of service. Throughout the nineteenth century the discrepancies between clerical and other academic income scales remained substantial. It was only at the end of the century, in 1898, that the whole salary system of the Catholic and Protestant clergy in Prussia was put on a new legal basis. Five wage brackets were introduced related to age and years of service and guaranteed by the state. The former government 'endowment fund for the improvement of the material condition of the clergy' which subsidised individual priests and pastors on an irregular basis was dissolved and the churches now obtained a legal right to a fixed yearly sum (about 6.5 million Marks for Protestant and 3.5 million Marks for Catholic parishes which were unable to meet their financial obligations) which they had the right to allocate themselves. However, clerical salaries were not the only sector where rising expenditures had to be met by the churches. Thus, in Prussia the need to increase the regular income of the churches also led to the introduction of church taxes.

Finance: Church Taxes

As early as the late 1820s in some states of the German Federation the need to meet the rising costs of the churches had resulted not only in state subsidies but also in the additional taxation of its members. It started in smaller North German Protestant states. In 1827 Duke Leopold II of Lippe introduced the possibility of additional church

187

taxes in his small territory. In 1831 the duchy of Oldenburg followed with similar regulations, as did the eastern German duchy of Sachsen-Altenburg and the kingdom of
Sachsen in 1837 and 1837. These were separate legal regulations which allowed individual parishes to tax all their members, not on a permanent basis, but for specific
purposes. As early as 1852 the duchy of Oldenburg, as has been noted earlier, which
was the only German territory to have adopted the ecclesiastical regulations in the
revolutionary 1848 constitution almost verbatim, introduced the constitutional right
of the churches to tax their members and administer their finances independently. In
all other states, the taxation of church members remained under much tighter control
of the secular authorities. Prussia and Hesse in 1875, Württemberg in 1887, Baden in
1888 and Bavaria in 1908 granted the traditional churches and other religious associations recognised as public corporations the right to occasional taxation. However,
there were clear state restrictions concerning the level of taxation and the state had the
right to decide whether it was necessary at all.

It was only at the beginning of the twentieth century, in 1905 and 1906, that
Prussia granted its churches a more comprehensive right to levy taxes not only for local
purposes, but also for Catholic diocesan or Protestant *Parochialverbände* (parochial
unions) general purposes, on a regular basis. But this was still supervised by the state
authorities. For the Catholic Church this was a compromise, since it meant possible
interference by the state in church matters, and compelled it to recognise the local
church councils - which it found alien - responsible for administering local taxation
created by the Prussian government. In the end, however, after years of opposition, the
Catholic bishops accepted the regulation of 1905 and 1906 as they gave the churches a
much better financial basis. The Weimar Republic finally incorporated the right of all
religious associations recognised as public corporations to tax their members according to the specific tax regulations of the individual states (*Länder*). This paragraph of
the Weimar constitution (§137) was adopted into the basic law of the Federal Republic
and is still valid today.

Disputed Territory: the State, the Churches and Welfare

Right through the nineteenth century, public debates on reform in state, church and
society were dominated by problems which since the 1830s were summarised by the
term 'the social question'. The full complexity of that question will be dealt with in
another volume in this series but some treatment cannot be omitted here. At first this
term related to the increasing pauperism of the rural and urban lower classes, later it
became a synonym for the poverty and insecurity of the new industrial working classes.
Even though the care of the ill and poor had always been subject of ecclesiastical activities, the legal framework of church involvement in this field changed considerably over
the century. These changes were most marked for the Catholic Church.

The need for reform of poor relief was debated in Protestant as well as in Catholic territories as early as the fifteenth century. In most Protestant territories the tradi-

tional Christian charity through individual alms and relief organised by the churches and monasteries had been replaced after the secularisation of the monasteries in the course of the Reformation by a more systematic and rigid system of relief handed out and supervised by the secular authorities of the towns and rural parishes. In Germany this shift in responsibility for relief of the poor away from the individuals and the churches to the secular authorities was termed 'communalization' (*Kommunialisierung*) of relief. In many Catholic areas reforms were not quite as comprehensive. Particularly, monasteries continued to play a vital role within the system of Catholic poor relief right through to the end of the Holy Roman Empire. Even though poor relief was reformed in many Catholic territories during the seventeenth and eighteenth centuries along the same lines as in Protestant ones (even in the Catholic prince-bishoprics giving alms to beggars became a punishable offence!), the secularisation of most monasteries, of large parts of the wealth and charitable foundations of the Catholic Church, meant that new arrangements had to be made not only to help people in need, but also to fulfil one's Christian obligations towards individual charity.

In Germany the first comprehensive legal regulation of poor relief and particularly the role of the state can be found in the Prussian General Code of Law of 1794. It acknowledged the obligation of the state to cater for those citizens who could not support themselves and for whose maintenance no other person or institution could be made responsible. This was an important step towards the principle of the modern welfare state. However, the main responsibility and onus of poor relief stayed with the parishes where the individual paupers were living. State expenditure for the poor, therefore, remained negligible in Prussia as well as in other territories right through the nineteenth century. Catholic charitable funds were incorporated mostly into the local funds for poor relief controlled by the secular parishes. This was started by the French government which set up secular *bureaux de bienfaisance* (welfare offices) in the occupied parts of Germany left of the Rhine during the French Revolution. The French system was later more or less taken over by Prussia when it acquired these territories after 1815 and also copied by other German states. The Catholic Church not only resented this expropriation of ecclesiastical funds, but also the loss of a crucial field of Christian activity. It added to the severe tensions with the Prussian state in the first half of the century.

However, it soon became clear that the capacities of many of the secular parishes were overstretched and unable to cope with mass poverty during the early nineteenth century and the problems caused by modern cyclical crises of unemployment. Private charity was needed after all to supplement the deficient local means, and also to care for very specific needs, for example of young people, released prisoners, alcoholics, single mothers, the homeless or the unemployed who were hardly catered for by public relief. Some of these social tasks were taken over by organisations within the churches. As social problems and tensions grew with increasing pauperism in the first half of the century and the rapid advance of urbanisation in the second half, new forms of organising Christian charity evolved. These gave them also a new position within the state administration, and they also changed the relation between church and state in this field.

The main organisational framework of Catholic as well as Protestant charity in the nineteenth century consisted of private voluntary associations organised by church members (*Vereine*). As registered organisations they were governed by public law and were legally independent of the churches. Such local charitable associations sprang up everywhere in Germany during the first half of the nineteenth century. The driving forces behind them were usually religiously motivated men and women. In Protestant areas, it was mostly members of evangelical circles who were most active in this field. In Stuttgart, the capital of Württemberg, a first *Privat-Gesellschaft freiwilliger Armen-Freunde* (Private Association of Voluntary Friends of the Poor) was founded in 1805 under the initiative of a pietist local merchant. It served as a model for others and became in 1817 part of a newly established *Allgemeiner Wohltätigkeitsverein* (General Charity Association) in Württemberg, an umbrella organisation initiated and partly endowed by the queen. It comprised, coordinated and supported Protestant as well as Catholic local initiatives, and though legally a private association, the *Wohltätigkeits-verein* soon gained semi-official status within the system of poor relief.

Religiously motivated charity of Protestants and Catholics alike as well as state support were major driving forces behind the Württemberg *Wohltätigkeitsverein*. During the course of the nineteenth century, however, such multi-confessional initiatives as the *Wohltätigkeitsverein* gave way to more confession-bound umbrella organisations. This was also a sign and outcome of the increasing competition and tension between the Catholic and Protestant Churches. At the same time, these charitable initiatives served as a field where Protestants and Catholics could combine on a larger, supra-territorial level.

The first organisation of this kind which originated in the middle of the nine-teenth century was the Protestant *Gesamtverein für Innere Mission* (General Associa-tion for the Inner Mission) which was initiated in 1850 by the Hamburg theologian and evangelical philanthropist Johann Heinrich Wichern, who not only tried to fight pover-ty and destitution, particularly of children, but also all revolutionary tendencies by combining charity with evangelising the urban poor. The Inner Mission was supposed to remedy the failure of the Protestant churches to reach and help the poor. Organisa-tionally, however, it was independent of them (as remained the case with its succes-sor the *Diakonie* until after the Second World War). It is interesting to note, however, that the independence of the church did not mean that these organisations kept at a distance from the state. They often had closer links with reform-oriented members of the state administration than with conservative Protestant consistories which were frequently suspicious of their evangelical fervour. Wichern, for example, became advi-sor to the Prussian king, Friedrich Wilhelm IV, on prison reform in 1842 and quickly moved up within the Prussian welfare administration.

Religious Minorities: Parity, to a Degree

As in most European states, the spread of religious pluralism was a characteristic feature of Germany's religious development during the nineteenth century. This was partly due to internal divisions, particularly within the Protestant churches, which resulted in the formation of Protestant sects and free churches, partly a result of increasing transatlantic connections through migration and the influx of the great variety of American Protestantism. However, growing pluralism was not an exclusively Protestant phenomenon. The Catholic Church also had its dissenting groups in Germany during the nineteenth century, particularly the German Catholics (*Deutschkatholiken*) in the 1840s and the Old Catholics (*Altkatholiken*) who left the church as a consequence of various controversial dogmas, particularly the dogma of papal infallibility of 1870. To a certain extent also, the considerable increase in Catholic orders, congregations and brotherhoods during the nineteenth century can be seen not only as a sign of a vibrant Catholic religiosity, but also of a rising tendency towards religious pluralism, albeit within the framework of the Catholic Church.

However, the question of the legal status of these more or less independent religious groupings or new denominations and of the political and legal discrimination faced by their members was a problem which (apart from the Old and German Catholics) affected predominantly the Protestant sects and free churches. In the course of the early-nineteenth-century awakening movement (which also affected the Catholic Church) several pietist preachers found enthusiastic followers who formed groups sometimes of only regional character, but sometimes also with a wider impact which succeeded in establishing themselves as independent religious groups or free churches, for example Count Zinzendorf's eighteenth-century foundation of the Moravian Brethren, the *Herrnhuter Brüdergemeine*, which quickly established itself as a global free church, the *Evangelische Brüdergemeinde Korntal* which was primarily inspired by Württemberg farmer-theologian Michael Hahn and still is at least of regional importance in South West Germany, or the *Evangelische Gesellschaft für Deutschland* initiated by the Lutheran pastor Ludwig Feldner from Elberfeld in 1848 (which also still operates as an independent religious association). In addition several new Protestant denominations which originated in Britain or the United States also found followers in Germany. Since the 1830s, Methodist preachers toured Germany and were particularly successful in Württemberg, Saxony and Bremen; in the 1840s the Baptist Johann Gerhard Oncken, who had been converted in Britain, started his mission in Germany; in the late 1870s organised mission by Adventists from the United States commenced; other Protestant groups of Anglo-Saxon origin, which established themselves as permanent religious communities in Germany include Irvingites, Darbyists, Anglicans and Quakers.

The formation of new religious groups inside or outside the established churches is as old as Christianity, but so is the fight of the Catholic Church and later also of all established Protestant churches against any kind of public heresy and against organised sects which split off and offered competition in an expanding religious market. This is not only true for the early modern period, but continued well into the nineteenth

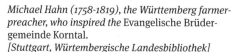

Michael Hahn (1758-1819), the Württemberg farmer-preacher, who inspired the Evangelische Brüder-gemeinde Korntal.
[Stuttgart, Würtembergische Landesbibliothek]

Johann Gerhard Oncken (1800-1884), a pioneer German Baptist preacher, also known as the 'Father of Continental Baptists'.
[Hamburg, Johan-Gerhard-Onckenkirche]

century. Before the nineteenth century, therefore, it had normally been the states and their rulers who, mostly for economic reasons, had decided to invite religious minorities which were prosecuted elsewhere to settle in their territory. They were particularly privileged by the grant of religious toleration and were often awarded specific economic advantages. Mennonites received such royal privileges in eighteenth-century Prussia, Poland and Russia; the Calvinist French Huguenots were granted exile in Prussia (and other states) after 1698 - much to the displeasure of the Lutheran population and particularly its clergy; the Waldensians from Piedmont were allowed to settle and form a separate religious minority in Lutheran Württemberg.

However, the same Protestant states which granted exile to old religious minorities which had mostly originated during the Reformation period or to victims of Catholic religious intolerance within or outside the Reich could be highly suspicious of and intolerant towards new separatist groups which tried to emancipate themselves from the established Lutheran or Reformed Churches in their own territories. Count Zinzendorf was compelled to leave Saxony in 1736. In the electorate of Hanover, Moravians and all of Zinzendorf's writings were also prohibited from 1748. In Württemberg all pietists were put under the strict supervision of the local clergy and the state in 1743. Right through to the end of the eighteenth century and partly well into the nineteenth century radical pietist groups were viewed with suspicion, and many of them faced legal trials and imprisonment, particularly if their religious rules brought them into conflict with the laws of state.

The legal basis of this religious discrimination was the fact that according to imperial law only the three established churches had to be tolerated. As mentioned earlier, this predominance of three or, since the unions of Lutheran and Reformed Protestants in Prussia and Baden, four established churches prevailed right through the nineteenth century. Neither the 1815 Act of the German Confederation nor the constitution of the new German Reich of 1871 introduced a general license to form religious associations or churches independent of state approval and control. Constitutions of individual territories mostly restricted full recognition of such religious associations. The Saxon constitution of 1831 guaranteed the inhabitants complete freedom of conscience but restricted the political and social rights of citizens in the kingdom to members of the established churches. All members of other religious associations could share those rights only if, and to the extent that, they were explicitly granted them by special legislation. The Hanover constitution of 1840 stated that if the king admitted Christian sects in his territory they were entitled to the social and economic rights of citizens but political rights had to be granted separately (as was also the case in Saxony).

Thus, before 1848, discrimination against members of dissenting religious groups was still the rule in German territories, even though individual religious freedom was granted in all nineteenth-century constitutional regulations. Frequently, this went beyond exclusion from full social or political citizenship and turned into police prosecution of individuals and groups. Foreign religious groups seeking adherents in German territories such as Methodists, Baptists or Adventists were controlled with particular suspicion. In the 1830s the Baptist missionary Johann Gerhard Oncken held public adult baptisms in Hamburg, Hanover and other regions. In Hamburg this resulted in prosecution and imprisonment because only pastors of the established churches were allowed to act as official registrars of baptisms, weddings and funerals. In Hanover, Oncken was also prosecuted by the police, and Prussia barred him entirely from entering the country. In most German states it lasted until the 1870s before discrimination ended and Baptists were able to achieve the status of an officially recognised religious association.

Legal discrimination of religious groups outside the established churches and of their members was supposed to come to an end in 1848. However, the revolution failed, and its regulations concerning religious minorities were only taken over by the constitutions of some German states. Oldenburg did so almost verbatim and, as has also been noted earlier, Prussia's constitution of 1850 stuck to substantial parts of the 1848 regulations, especially the fact religious denomination or belief was of no consequence for the exercise of the political and social rights of local and state citizenship. However, the constitution still differentiated between forms of religious associations. The Prussian General Law Code of 1794 had introduced this term *Religionsgesellschaft* (religious association) into German constitutional terminology. It differentiated between *Kirchengesellschaften* (church associations) which were officially recognised by the state and granted the rights of privileged public corporations. Other religious associations could acquire the status of tolerated private associations, but they faced several legal restrictions, particularly concerning the acquisition of property. They were also restricted in their access to public spaces, were not allowed to have religious processions or ring church bells for their services. The constitution of 1850 did not make such explicit differentiations, but still left it to the discretion of the state or the monarch to give religious associations the status of public corporations. Such status not only added the prestige of public recognition but also restricted possible state interference with their internal affairs and their daily activities by means of regulations which applied to private associations (and particularly through police regulations regarding public meetings and public order).

Other German states had similar regulations and frequently used the possibilities to control or even hinder the free exercise of religious activities by dissident groups. The suppression of Baptist activities was only one example. Even though the last decades of the nineteenth century saw a general liberalisation of state supervision in these matters, there was still a clear hierarchy of religious associations. Among the tolerated religious associations without corporation rights were in Prussia the German Catholics and most Anglo-Saxon groups like Methodists, Quakers, Irvingites and Anglicans. Moravians (*Herrnhuter*), Old Lutherans, Mennonites and particularly Jews, however, were accepted as public corporations.

It was only after the First World War that a new start seemed not only possible but necessary. The Weimar constitution, as has been noted, abolished all established churches and also removed all restrictions on forming religious associations. However, it still kept the notion of the old churches and some other religious associations as being public corporations, whereas some others were not. All religious associations could apply to be granted this status. According to the Weimar constitution, this status had to be conferred if the constitution and the number of its members seemed to guarantee that such religious associations were likely to be a permanent legal body. But these were not very clear criteria, and even though there was parity between all religious associations in principle, there were still differences. The Weimar constitution continued a system of 'graded parity' which still privileged the former established churches.

Keeping it all Together: Monarchs as Linchpins

The Prussian constitution of 1850 granted the freedom of religious belief and associations, but protected at the same time the Christian character of certain state institutions (Art. 14). This article was inserted into the revised constitution on the initiative of conservative members of the Upper House, particularly the Berlin professor in philosophy of law (including state and church law), Friedrich Julius Stahl. Influenced by the early-nineteenth-century Lutheran 'Awakening' at Erlangen university, Stahl was a fierce opponent of any form of rationalist enlightenment and particularly of its political manifestation in the French Revolution. He fought not only for the preservation of the 'natural' order of the hierarchical monarchical state, but also for its Christian

194

character. His book *The Christian State*, published in 1845, became a household text of nineteenth-century German conservatism, particularly in Prussia, where conservatism had strong links to Lutheran pietism. Stahl, himself a converted Jew, did not object on principle to the liberal demands that the state should grant full citizenship to people who did not adhere to its recognised form of public worship. In his view this did not necessarily bring the Christian state into question as long as its institutions could retain their Christian character. What was essential, therefore, and had to be defended by the churches was, for example, that oaths were still taken in the name of the Christian God, not of an abstract deity; that church weddings were allowed to constitute a legal marriage; that religious education was still part of primary school teaching and that one of the Christian churches was recognised and protected as a 'national' form of public worship.

This Christian character of state institutions was above all symbolised in the office and person of the Christian monarch. This was not only the perception of Protestants who were accustomed to the close link between church and state, but also of Catholics. Since Carolingian times European ruling families and monarchs had legitimised their claim to the throne by employing the divine will and the grace of God as the prime source of their entitlement to this position. After having been questioned by enlightened contractual theories of state power, nineteenth-century political romanticism saw a revival of medieval concepts of the divine right of kings and the religious quality of monarchs in both, Protestant and Catholic political theory and particularly monarchical self-representation. During the early decades of the nineteenth century conservative political theory tended to blend particularly well with the opposition of the Catholic Church not only to the French Revolution, but also to the fundamental changes connected with the dissolution of the Holy Roman Empire. Conservative romantics who looked back longingly to the 'Reich' praised the Catholic Church as a guarantor of stability and Christianity in Europe. In their view, state and church needed to be closely linked and were so in the context of the feudal structure of the medieval Reich. As a consequence, several prominent conservative intellectuals of the early nineteenth century converted to Catholicism such as the philosopher and political scientist Adam Heinrich Müller, son of a Protestant Prussian civil servant, the poet and literary critic Friedrich Schlegel, son of a Hanoverian Lutheran pastor, or the prominent Swiss professor of constitutional law, Carl Ludwig von Haller. At the same time they were attracted by the imperial court in Vienna as well as its arch-conservative first minister, Count Metternich, and his intellectual aide, Friedrich von Gentz.

Adam Heinrich Müller put particular emphasis on the fact that religion was the foundation of all true and persistent law and thus also of social cohesion in society. He doubted that regulations and laws solely based on contract or the arbitrary decision of a territorial lord could be of lasting quality. They were always open to dispute and could be questioned by competing individual or collective wills. Thus, religion and religious rules were needed to provide basic principles also for secular law and as guarantors of social stability. However, in order to be able to provide such a basis, religious rules and institutions had to be authoritative and remain unquestioned. The Protestant Reformation was, therefore, regarded by Müller as the first step of decline into that disorder in church and state which for him was so characteristic of the modern age, and against which he and other conservatives fought. In both church and state, legitimate power had to be concentrated in one person, and legitimate reform could also only be initiated by those in power. As soon as individuals or, as Müller termed it, 'the so-called people' started taking the initiative for change, anarchy would be the result. Müller and his conservative circle defended monarchical as well as papal power and longed for a close connection between the two, with the unity of the church restored under the rule of Rome.

Based though they were on different theological arguments, many Lutheran pietists also defended the divine right of kings and their position as heads of the church during and after the revolution of 1848. For them, the notion that kings derived the legitimacy of their offices from God was closely linked to their anti-enlightenment perception of the Christian God as one who actively shaped the history of individuals as well as of nations. All human history was seen as part of God's all-encompassing salvific history. God's judgement would come, and it had to be feared by those who denied his power and presence in history. Real sovereignty, therefore, rested in God, and not in the people. God was king, the monarchs his representatives. Any form of democratic revolution was also a rebellion against God and the divine order of society.

This longing for God's active participation in history and the notion of the divinely ordained quality of kingship were widespread in the nineteenth century and went beyond narrow circles of Lutheran pietists or other brands of evangelicalism. They were also eagerly accepted by the monarchs themselves, both Protestant and Catholic. The prime examples of such religious self-fashioning of monarchical power in the nineteenth century were the Protestant Friedrich Wilhelm IV of Prussia, the Catholic Ludwig II of Bavaria, and finally the last emperor of the new German Reich, Wilhelm II. Friedrich Wilhelm IV came to power in 1840, and during the first years of his reign he was the hope of Prussian reform-oriented liberals. However, he was deeply captivated by romantic concepts of medieval kingship and the vanished Holy Roman Empire. This found its expression in his enthusiasm for Gothic architecture and monuments and medieval knighthood. Friedrich Wilhelm combined this, however, with a modern religious fellow-feeling with Prussia's Lutheran pietists whose notion of the religious character of kingship he took up, together with von Stahl's concept of a Christian state. A few decades later, the Catholic king Ludwig II of Bavaria developed similar dreams of the religious quality and divine rights of kings, also combining it with specific enthusiasm for medieval architecture and culture. The throne room for his new castle Neuschwanstein - which was built during the 1870s and 1880s - was designed in the form of a Byzantine cathedral, moving the king into a god-like position.

However, whereas Friedrich Wilhelm's religious concept of kingship was still compatible with pietist and - to a certain extent - with general conservative ideas about the foundation and the role of monarchical power, this was hardly the case with Ludwig. Not only was the symbolism of his dream world too far removed from the realities of the late-nineteenth-century Bavarian constitutional monarchy, but the king himself was also in conflict with the Catholic Church, which reduced his credibility as a head of the church in Bavaria as well as a king by divine right. Ludwig did not accept the dogma of infallibility of the pope, and he refused to have it publicised in Bavaria. He supported the Catholic theologian Ignaz von Döllinger, who turned from an ultramontane follower into an opponent of Rome. In questions of constitutional politics in which Döllinger, a former member of the Paulskirche parliament, supported the separation of church and state, Ludwig was, however, of different opinion. He continued to see himself as the head of church in his territory.

In a similar way, Emperor Wilhelm II kept stressing the divine right of kings and the fact that he was as an instrument of the Lord and felt only responsible to Him. Wilhelm, too, combined this conviction with a romantic glorification of the medieval Reich and its emperors and a particular liking for the Byzantine empire. Like his great-uncle, Friedrich Wilhelm IV, he too had churches built in Romanesque or Gothic style such as the Emperor Wilhelm Memorial Church in Berlin, dedicated to his grandfather, the first *Kaiser* of the new German Empire. Here the new imperial dynasty was depicted in large mosaics in Byzantine style, removing them from the common world into a religious heavenly sphere. An important part of Wilhelm's attempts to establish a new quasi-religious public position for the emperor was his journey to the Holy Land in 1898. There he took part in the dedication of the Protestant Church of the Redeemer in Jerusalem. He was accompanied by the empress and travelled with an enormous entourage to make sure this modern crusade gained enough public interest. Wilhelm was the first German emperor since Friedrich II to travel to Palestine. He made sure that these historic connections were adequately noticed and reported.

197

Public response, however, to these forms of monarchical self-representation was usually very mixed. Wilhelm II and the dream world of Ludwig II of Bavaria in particular were often publicly ridiculed. The exotic historicism of these monarchs, linking their office to medieval Western or Byzantine emperors through art and invented ceremonial traditions, could hardly cover up the fact that their power was limited by constitutions. Pressure for democratising state, church and society was increasing. It is nevertheless important to see that some notion of a religious quality and foundation of their office was adhered to by the German kings themselves and by parts of the conservative public right to the end of the monarchies at the close of the First World War. This also influenced the relationship between the monarchs and the churches. Insisting on their position particularly as heads of the Protestant churches was not only part of a strategy of embedding their claims to powerful monarchical rule into long historical traditions and thereby adding to its legitimacy. Being Christian kings was also part of their traditional upbringing and self-understanding. In territories like Prussia, with multiple Protestant churches, it was also a means of keeping Protestantism together. For Wilhelm II, this was one of the main reasons for his insisting on his prerogative as supreme head of the churches.

At the same time, however, Wilhelm II and his advisors were interested in strengthening Protestantism to enable it to "fight successfully against Rome and the

198

Emperor Wilhelm II and Empress Augusta Victoria
visiting Jerusalem after the inauguration of the
Protestant Church of the Redeemer on Reformation
Day (31 October) 1898, *photograph*.
*[Washington, Library of Congress: LC-M36- 13726
[P&P]]*

sinister powers of infidelity and sedition".[10] The spirit of the *Kulturkampf* still persisted, not only in the heads of members of the Protestant consistories, but also in that of the emperor. The Catholic Church and the new enemy, social democracy, were equally evil forces and targets of Wilhelm's religious activities and the leadership he was prepared to provide for Protestantism in the Reich. The *Kulturkampf*, however, had not only weakened the public acceptance of such concepts, but also the position of the monarch as a religious leader in general. The new strength of Catholicism together with the progress of Jewish emancipation and the general increase in religious pluralism in the *Kaiserreich* rendered such a close and partisan relationship between monarch and any one of the churches not only dysfunctional for the social integration of the state, but also for the development of the churches. Even in traditionally conservative pious circles in Prussia, criticism of this state-centred ecclesiastical structure of the Protestant churches grew. Some major reforms in the constitutional regulations for the churches had been initiated during the second half of the nineteenth century, but it was clear that the new Weimar constitution had to provide a clear framework for the long process of disentanglement of state and church in Germany.

The Weimar Constitution: New Epoch, New Principles

Neither on the Catholic nor on the Protestant side did the *Kulturkampf* in the end lead to any substantial changes in the legal framework of the relationship between the church and the state. It was only Germany's military defeat in the First World War which led to the democratic constitution of the ensuing 'Weimar' republic (its constitution was discussed at Weimar, hence the label). The resignation of the monarchs - the German emperor and the kings and princes of the German states - also put an end to state rule over the Protestant churches. As the most important rules concerning religion were included in the Weimar constitution (*Weimarer Reichsverfassung*) of 1919, we can at last speak of a uniform law which sets out the state-church relationship in Germany as a whole. By Article 135, full freedom of religion was guaranteed by the Reich and, by Article 137 sect. 1, the separation of state and church was laid down. The churches were given the right to govern their own affairs within the common limits of law by Article 137 sect. 3. Together with the equality afforded all religions, these are the core principles of German state church law until today, as the main articles of the Weimar constitution on the relationship between state and church were taken over by the German Basic Law in 1949 und so are still in force.

The call to keep the churches totally out of the public sphere, which was made by some leftist politicians in the course of discussion of the Weimar constitution, had no success. The *Weimarer Reichsverfassung* is a compromise between a strict separation of state and churches and the German tradition which has been outlined in this chapter.

---

[10] Huber and Huber, *Staat und Kirche*, III, 544, n. 9.

It embodies the so-called *Weimarer Kulturkompromiß* (Weimar cultural compromise). Some of its characteristics can be found in the status of the churches as public corporations, in the opportunity for religious activities and spiritual welfare in public institutions and the army, and in the guarantee of religious instruction in state schools. All this makes clear that the separation of state and church was not meant as a measure against the churches but rather in favour of their freedom, even in the public sphere.

These elements show that the Weimar constitution did not mean a complete breach in the traditional state-church relationship, but it did mean a new epoch and new principles. With the ending of state rule over the Protestant churches, they were given autonomy which the Catholic Church had achieved earlier (since the end of the *Kulturkampf*). Now the Protestant churches were in the position to establish their own autonomous ecclesiastical law and organisation. For them, the end of the monarchy brought with it the end of a tradition, lasting four hundred years, of a close relationship with the state. Until then, the distinction between political and legal reform on the one hand, and internal ecclesiastical reform on the other, the division which lies behind the first two volumes in this series has in fact hardly had any significance for the Protestant churches in Germany.

Bibliography

Barclay, David E. *Frederick William IV and the Prussian Monarchy 1840-1861*. Oxford, 1995.

Baumeister, Martin. *Parität und katholische Inferiorität. Untersuchung zur Stellung des Katholizismus im Deutschen Kaiserreich*. Paderborn et al., 1987.

Besier, Gerhard. *Religion - Nation - Kultur. Die Geschichte der Kirchen in den gesellschaftlichen Umbrüchen des 19. Jahrhunderts*. Neukirchen-Vluyn, 1992.

Benner, Thomas. *Die Strahlen der Krone. Die religiöse Dimension des Kaisertums unter Wilhelm II. vor dem Hintergrund der Orientreise 1898*. Marburg, 2001.

Betz, Hans Dieter et al., eds. *Religion Past and Present. Encyclopedia of Theology and Religion*. Tübingen, 2006-2013, 14 vols.

Blaschke, Olaf, ed. *Konfessionen im Konflikt. Deutschland zwischen 1800 und 1970. Ein zweites konfessionelles Zeitalter*. Göttingen, 2002.

Clark, Christopher. *The Politics of Conversion: Missionary Protestantism and the Jews in Prussia 1728-1941*. Oxford, 1995.

Diephouse, David J. *Pastors and Pluralism in Württemberg 1918-1933*. Princeton, 1987.

Dietrich, Stefan J. *Christentum und Revolution. Die christlichen Kirchen in Württemberg, 1848-1852*. Paderborn et al., 1996.

Friedrich, Martin. *Kirche im gesellschaftlichen Umbruch*. Stuttgart, 2006.

Gatz, Erwin, ed. *Geschichte des kirchlichen Lebens in den deutschsprachigen Ländern seit dem Ende des 18. Jahrhunderts - Die katholische Kirche. 6: Die Kirchenfinanzen*. Freiburg et al., 2000.

Goeters, Johann F. and Mau, Rudolf, eds. *Die Geschichte der Evangelischen Kirche der Union*. Vol. 1. Leipzig, 1992.

Hasenclever, Catharina. *Gotisches Mittelalter und Gottesgnadentum in den Zeichnungen Friedrich Wilhelms IV: Herrschaftslegitimierung zwischen Revolution und Restauration*. Berlin, 2005.

Hauschild, Wolf-Dieter. *Lehrbuch der Kirchen- und Dogmengeschichte*. Gütersloh, 2005-2007, 2 vols.

Huber, Ernst Rudolf. *Deutsche Verfassungsgeschichte seit 1789*. Stuttgart, 1957, 7 vols.

Huber, Ernst Rudolf and Huber, Wolfgang. *Staat und Kirche im 19. und 20. Jahrhundert*. Berlin, 1973-1988, 4 vols.

Hürten, Heinz. *Kurze Geschichte des deutschen Katholizismus, 1800-1960*. Mainz, 1986.

Janz, Oliver. *Bürger besonderer Art. Evangelische Pfarrer in Preußen, 1850-1914*. Berlin-New York, 1994.

Jedin, Hubert and Repgen, Konrad, eds. *Handbuch der Kirchengeschichte*. Freiburg, 1962, 7 vols.

Kim, Sun-Ryol. *Die Vorgeschichte der Trennung von Staat und Kirche in der Weimarer Republik. Eine Untersuchung über das Verhältnis von Staat und Kirche in Preußen seit der Reichsgründung von 1871*. Hamburg, 1996.

Körner, Michael. *Staat und Kirche in Bayern, 1886-1918*. Mainz, 1977.

Kroll, Frank-Lothar. *Friedrich Wilhelm IV. und das Staatsdenken der deutschen Romantik*. Berlin, 1990.

Kroll, Frank-Lothar. "Herrschaftslegitimierung durch Traditionsschöpfung. Der Beitrag der Hohenzollern zur Mittelalter-Rezeption im 19. Jahrhundert". *Historische Zeitschrift*, 274 (2002), 61-85.

Kuhlemann, Frank-Michael. *Bürgerlichkeit und Religion. Zur Sozial- und Mentalitätsgeschichte der evangelischen Pfarrer in Baden, 1860-1914*. Göttingen, 2002.

Langewiesche, Dieter. "Die Anfänge der deutschen Parteien. Partei, Fraktion und Verein in der Revolution von 1848/49". *Geschichte und Gesellschaft*, 4 (1978), 324-361.

Müller, Gerhard et al., eds. *Handbuch der Geschichte der evangelischen Kirche in Bayern*. St. Ottilien, 2000, 2 vols.

Lill, Rudolf, ed. *Der Kulturkampf*. Paderborn, 1997.

Link, Christoph. *Kirchliche Rechtsgeschichte.* Munich, 2009.

Mayeur, Jean-Marie et al., eds. *Die Geschichte des Christentums.* German vols. ed. by Norbert Brox et al. Freiburg, 1992-2004, 14 vols.

Nowak, Kurt. *Geschichte des Christentums in Deutschland.* Munich, 1995.

Nipperdey, Thomas. *Religion im Umbruch.* Munich, 1988.

Rau, Gerhard; Reuter, Hans-Richard and Schlaich, Klaus, eds. *Das Recht der Kirche.* Vol. 2. Gütersloh, 1995.

Schleiermacher, Friedrich Daniel Ernst. *Vorschlag zu einer neuen Verfaßung der protestantischen Kirche im preußischen Staate* (1808) in: Friedrich Daniel Schleiermacher. *Kritische Gesamtausgabe. Schriften und Entwürfe. 9: Kirchenpolitische Schriften.* Ed. Ernst Günter Meckenstock and Hans-Friedrich Traulsen. Berlin-New York, 2000, 3-18.

Scholler, Heinrich, ed. *Die Grundrechtsdiskussion in der Paulskirche. Eine Dokumentation.* Darmstadt, 1982.

Spangenberg, Marcus. *Der Thronsaal von Schloss Neuschwanstein. König Ludwig II. und sein Verständnis vom Gottesgnadentum.* Regensburg, 1999.

Sperber, Jonathan. *The European Revolutions 1848-1851.* Cambridge, 1994.

Strötz, Jürgen. *Der Katholizismus im deutschen Kaiserreich.* Hamburg, 2005, 2 vols.

Toews, John Edward. *Becoming Historical: Cultural Reformation and Public Memory in Early Nineteenth-Century Berlin.* Cambridge, 2004.

Wallmann, Johannes. *Kirchengeschichte Deutschlands seit der Reformation.* Tübingen, 2006.

Wehler, Hans Ulrich. *Deutsche Gesellschaftsgeschichte. 2: Von der Reformära bis zur politischen und industriellen 'Deutschen Doppelrevolution', 1815-1845/49.* Munich, 1990.

Wolf, Hubert, ed. *Ökumenische Kirchengeschichte. 3: Von der Französischen Revolution bis 1989.* Darmstadt, 2007.

THE NORDIC COUNTRIES

This section considers church reform in its legal and political aspects across Scandinavia/the Nordic region as a whole. It is obvious that it is in many respects a single story given the partially overlapping and certainly interlocking histories of Denmark, Norway and Sweden at this time. In the absence of an attempt at such a total history, as initially contemplated from another source, however, Liselotte Malmgart and Anders Jarlert have composed two parallel accounts of Denmark/Norway and Sweden respectively. They both dwell on the distinctiveness of three Protestant countries where religious bodies outside the state church were numerically very small. The ties between state and church remained close, even to the extent of questioning whether 'the church' existed in a form which could be detached from the state. Some ties loosened but not such as to bring about fundamental change. It is a 'conservative' picture which presents a striking contrast to the analysis which is made elsewhere in this volume.

State and Church
in Denmark and Norway

Liselotte Malmgart

Reformation and Absolutism

The relationship between state and church in the Scandinavian countries in the period covered by this volume remained profoundly influenced by two major developments: the sixteenth-century Lutheran Reformation and seventeenth-century absolutism. The account that follows identifies challenges and adaptations to these 'foundations' but the state-church relationship cannot be understood without some preliminary commentary which explains their significance.

After the Reformation, the Evangelical Lutheran Churches were established as state churches, resulting in a close cooperation between the monarchy and the ecclesiastical authorities, foremost the bishops, who in practice were senior civil servants. Despite similarities in the Nordic countries, their circumstances did not exactly correspond. In the eastern regions, Sweden and Finland, the Reformation was more gradually implemented and the Swedish Church was initially more autonomous than was the case in the western regions, Denmark and Norway, Iceland, Faroe Islands and the duchies of Schleswig and Holstein, all of which territories were at the time united under the Danish king. Here contacts with Wittenberg and elsewhere in Germany were closer and the first Danish Church Ordinance (*Kirkeordinansen*, 1537) was drafted by Luther's close associate, Johannes Bugenhagen. A modified edition was authorised for Norway in 1607. In the famous preface to the Church Ordinance, the king set out the view that two separate spheres or ordinances existed: in the one, the ordinance of God was responsible for the rightful proclaiming of the gospel in word and sacrament, but in the other, where its practical affairs were concerned, the king was responsible, aiming to serve God and facilitating the proclamation of His Word. In the preface the term 'church' is not used; the separation is not between 'church' as an institution and the Crown, but between God and the king. In the period 1536-1814, Norway was a part of the Danish monarchy and most church regulations were the same. The Norwegian Church was basically ruled from Copenhagen and all Norwegian clergy, until the University of Christiania (Oslo) was established in 1811, were educated at the University of Copenhagen.

Absolutism and the hereditary monarchy were introduced in 1660. Subsequently a new law, Lex Regia (*Kongeloven*, 1665), stated that the Danish king was supreme head both in church and state. It gave the king very wide powers, stating that he has "supreme power over the entire clergy and other civil servants from the highest to the lowest, supreme power to decide and arrange everything related to the church and public worship, and to order or forbid, when he considers it advisable, meetings, assemblies, and conventions on religious matters in accordance with the will of God and the Augsburg Confession".[1] Lex Regia endowed the Danish king with more power than any other monarch in Europe and was to remain the constitution until 1814 (Norway) and 1849 (Denmark). It thus remained as the basic regulation of the relationship between church and state well into the nineteenth century. The great law codes (*Danske Lov*, 1683 and *Norske Lov*, 1687) dealt in great detail with the everyday life of the church and church discipline. It placed the minister firmly in parish life, instructing the minister to live among the parishioners. Even if his vicarage should burn down, he could not live outside his parish without obtaining permission. This basic principle meant that, unlike what often happened elsewhere in Europe, the church did not experience the problem of the absentee incumbent. The law code helped to create uniformity as did the Danish Rite (*Danmarks og Norges Kirkeritual*, 1685) when it came to liturgy.

In the beginning of the eighteenth century pietism influenced the religious life of Denmark and Norway. King Christian VI (1699-1746) who acceded to the throne in 1730 was personally pious and supported the pietistic theology through legislation, most importantly in 1736 by introducing confirmation as a general obligation placed on all children. The clergy had to encourage the personal conversion (in the pietistic sense) of the young. The state was also aware however, of the danger of separatism inherent in a lay-dominated pietistic movement and tried to control it with the Conventicle Poster (*Konventikelplakaten*, 1741). This did not place a ban on all meetings, only those not approved by the local vicar (who did not have to attend the meetings himself) and to that degree can be seen even as encouraging the private piety of the laity outside the official state-controlled provision.[2] However, it did become an important tool in the suppression of revival movements in the beginning of the nineteenth century, for instance in the trial of the Norwegian lay preacher, Hans Nielsen Hauge (1771-1824), who was convicted in 1813 of ignoring this requirement.

206

---

[1] Translation of Lex Regia §VI in Hope, *German and Scandinavian Protestantism*, 79.

[2] Amundsen, *Norges religionshistorie*, 301.

Enlightened Legislation and Religious Debate

By the end of the eighteenth century, however, personal circumstances brought about a change in the exercise of power. King Christian VII (1766-1808) had become incapacitated and the absolutism he embodied turned into an absolutism of the central administration, one which has been described as "absolutism directed by public opinion" (*det opinionsstyrede enevælde*).[3] The basis of royal power was changing and a new generation of civil servants reformed the Danish state after 1770. The penal code in *Danske Lov*, based on the Ten Commandments, was altered to reflect a more enlightened age and in 1770 the number of religious holidays was reduced, based on both economic and moral grounds. The legislators had realised that even though the holidays were religiously-motivated, the common people had not used them to worship God, but to indulge in vice and enjoy idleness - so it would be beneficial to the country to use these days for work and profitable deeds.[4] However, the arguments were not based only on reason and the benefit to society, the court chaplain was also consulted and was able to assure that the Bible did not require more than one weekly holiday.

The strict regulations from the later part of the sixteenth century, which kept non-Lutherans from entering the kingdom (*Fremmedartiklerne*, 1569), were gradually lifted, as exemptions were granted for industrious foreign traders like the Moravians. In 1771 they were allowed to establish a colony in the north of Schleswig, called Christiansfeld. It also became a base for discreet missionary activity. Itinerant 'emissaries' paved the way for the revival in the early nineteenth century.

The Roman Catholic Church was not allowed in the realm after the Reformation, but the ban was gradually lifted as foreign diplomats were allowed to celebrate the mass (1671). Tacitly, a congregation was allowed to grow in Copenhagen, where a chapel was built in 1764 (replaced in 1842 by Sankt Ansgar, the present Catholic cathedral). For commercial reasons, the first Jews were also allowed to settle in Copenhagen in the 1670s and from 1684 allowed to meet for worship in private homes; a synagogue was built in 1833. This happened despite vigorous objections from the bishop in Copenhagen. Catholics and Jews were also allowed in Fredericia (South Jutland), founded in 1650 as a military stronghold (by the crossing to the island Funen). From 1682 it was a city with religious freedom, where Catholics, Reformed (Huguenots) and Jews were allowed to live. By 1720 a synagogue was built, assumed to be the first in the Nordic countries. Jews gained more rights in the end of the eighteenth century, for instance the right to university degrees (the 1780s). Their admission to membership of the guilds (1788) enabled Jewish boys to take an apprenticeship in order to "become useful citizens for the state". The culmination of these developments was the royal decree of 29 March 1814 (called *Frihedsbrevet*, the letter of freedom) which gave Jews equal citizenship. In fact, however, it was not so much freedom that was being emphasised in this letter as Jewish civic duty. In some ways, Jews were being asked to

---

[3] Bregnsbo, "Clerical attitudes", 4.   [4] Jensen, "Sekularisering af tiden?", 77-78.

subordinate their religious identity to their identity as Danish citizens.[5] The granting of citizenship to Jews can be seen as a first fracture in the linking of state and religion as non-Christians were now included in Danish society. Another fracture came in the first half of the nineteenth century with the question whether dissenting Danish citizens could be allowed to leave the state church, while remaining citizens, i.e. associated with the state.[6] Throughout the nineteenth century, there were more Jews in Denmark than Roman Catholics; by 1901 there were slightly more Catholics, probably because of the considerable number of conversions that occurred in the previous decade.[7]

A further factor in modifying attitudes towards foreign religions is to be found in the scientific enthusiasms of the late eighteenth century. In 1769 Europe was caught up in an astronomical craze caused by the passage of the planet Venus. The British king sent Captain Cook to Tahiti to observe it and the Danish king invited a Jesuit astronomer from Vienna to travel to the far north in Norway (Vardø) to observe the phenomenon. Pater Maximilian Hell managed to build an observatory and had during his journey contacts with several Lutherans ministers, among them the bishop of Trondheim who received the Jesuit in his recently founded Royal Norwegian Society of Sciences and Letters.[8]

Another manifestation of the enlightenment was the abolition of censorship for a short period (1770-1799). During the 1790s, several critics, inspired by modern philosophy and the French Revolution, attacked traditional Christianity and church life in public debate. Bishop Balle (1744-1816) in Copenhagen tried in dull prose and without success to prove the common sense of Christianity, but in the process became so disillusioned about the future of Christianity that he contemplated resigning his office.[9] Censorship was brought back in 1799 and was not officially lifted until the passing of the constitution in 1849. The theologian Grundtvig, for example, was censored in the period 1826-1837 and had to submit all his writings to the public censor before publication.

---

[5] Schwarz Lausten, *Oplysning i Kirke og Synagoge*, 133-136.
[6] The observation of these fractures has been made by Associate Professor Lene Kühle in an unpublished manuscript, based on her dissertation *Out of Many, One*.
[7] According to a survey of the 19th century (*Befolkningsforholdene i Danmark i det 19. Aarhundrede*, published by the National Bureau of Statistics 1905), the numbers were 1850: 724 Catholics, 3,941 Jews; 1890: 2,985 Catholics, 3,946 Jews and 1901: 5,373 Catholics, 3,476 Jews.
[8] Thuringer, "Jesuitter i Norge". The interesting travel diary of the two Jesuits was published in the Norwegian *Historisk Tidsskrift* 1895.
[9] Bregnsbo, "Præster under pres", 103.

The Danish Pastor between Church and State

Ministers were ordained to be servants of God, but were also servants of the king and carried out a number of public duties. They supervised the registration of the popula- tion in the church register (*kirkebøger*), introduced in 1646 as a tool for taxing and enlisting purposes. Further, the vicar announced new regulations and edicts from the pulpit. The church thus provided a direct channel from the sovereign to the population. He also played an important part in poor relief and the administration of local schools, since he was the designated chairman for the local poverty commission (1803) and the school board, when the law on compulsory school attendance was adopted in 1814. Being a government officer also meant that suspicious deaths had to be reported to the vicar, if the chief constable was not at hand (mentioned in Matzen and Timms book on Ecclesiastical Law from 1891, §68). As the nineteenth century progressed, the minister gradually lost this administrative role as local civil administration was reformed and democratised. After 1824 secular proclamations were supposed to be announced in the churchyard in the rural districts by the cantor and in the cities by the municipali- ties at town meetings. In the countryside, local councils (*sogneforstanderskab*) were established in 1842 and took responsibility for local affairs, but for a time the minister had a seat on the council (to 1867), for the first years (to 1855) even as the chairman.[10] Ministers retained their influence in the public schools longer, but their practical involvement gradually diminished and by the end of the century it was mainly limited to supervising religious education. The position of ministers in Norway diminished in a similar way after the passing of laws on local government (*formannskapslovene*) in 1837.[11] However, losing the administrative duties sparked a development which the Danish church historian P.G. Lindhardt has called "the spiritualisation of the clergy", meaning that ministers could now focus more on preaching and theological discus- sion.

Did these public duties inspire loyalty towards the absolute state? The histo- rian Michael Bregnsbo has examined sermons from the period 1775-1800 to determine which 'new ideas' were transmitted to the broad masses for whom sermons were a major source of information.[12] He has concluded that ministers did not speak up for democracy, but they did advocate "an absolutist form of government with acceptance of popular sovereignty"[13] and many considered the king to be a guarantor of stability. Generally they were in favour of freedom of opinion and public debate (not so much for the lower estates, though) and supported the agrarian reforms at the time which gave many peasants the opportunity to acquire the freehold on their farms.

209

---

[10] The term 'local council' will be used for the council responsible for public or municipal admin- istration (Danish: *sogneråd* or *byråd* and Norwe- gian: *kommunestyre*). The term 'parish council' will be used for the council responsible for local church affairs (Danish: *menighedsråd*, Norwegian: *menighetsråd*).

[11] Oftestad, *Den norske statsreligionen*, 103. The ministers' role in schools and poor relief will be further dealt with in volumes 3 and 4.
[12] Bregnsbo, "Clerical attitudes", 16.
[13] Ibid., 21.

The Constitution of Norway 1814

During the Napoleonic wars, Denmark-Norway entered into an alliance with France and after the defeat, the Danish king was forced, as we have noted, to cede Norway to Sweden. Sweden and Norway entered a personal union, in which Norway was permitted to maintain its own Parliament and possessed far-reaching independence in domestic policy; foreign policy, however, was dictated from Stockholm. In 1814, Norwegians convened at Eidsvoll and drafted their own constitution, at the time regarded as the most liberal in Europe, with a clear separation between the executive, legislative and judicial powers. In §2 it stated that "the Evangelical Lutheran religion remains the public religion of the State. Those inhabitants, who confess thereto, are bound to raise their children to the same. Jesuits and monastic orders are not permitted. Jews are still prohibited from entry to the Realm."[14] The word 'remains' underlined the traditional religion as a foundation for the new nation, now defining itself as a confessional state, dictating the confession not only of the head of state (§15), but also of all civil servants, including the cabinet (§93).[15] The constitution does not use the term 'church', implying that the church was a separate entity, but considers 'religion' to be a function of the state.

The king still had the central role in the leadership of the church, according to §16 he was to "ordain all public church services and public worship and all meetings and assemblies dealing with religious matters, and ensure that public teachers of religion follow the norms prescribed for them".[16] As a consequence, new liturgies and rituals have been issued as 'royal resolutions' (*kongelig resolutsjon*), coming directly from the king and his council. In this area, the constitution was modified in 1919 by the provision that only the members of the Council of State who professed the official religion of the state could take part in these decisions (§27, called Ecclesiastical Council of State, *kirkeligt statsråd*).

In the spirit of new freedom and modern liberal politics, several drafts for the constitution in 1814 did actually have a paragraph on religious freedom for all religious denominations, but in the final editing it was removed. The reason remains unclear, but perhaps it was just rushed through - and besides, it was not really a problem, since there were no other confessions or sizeable religious minorities in Norway to speak of.[17] However, the sentencing of Hans Nielsen Hauge the previous year was a presage that this situation was not to remain for long. The new state church was to be challenged

---

[14] "Den evangelisk-lutherske Religion forbliver Statens offentlige Religion. De Indvaanere, der bekjende sig til den, ere forpligtede til at oppdrage sine Børn i samme. Jesuitter og Munkeordener maae ikke taales. Jøder ere fremdels udelukkede fra Adgang til Riget."
[15] §93: "Til Embeder i Staten maa allene udnævnes de norske Borgere, som bekjende sig til den evangelisk-lutherske Religion."

[16] "Kongen anordner al offentlig Kirke- og Gudstjeneste, alle Møder og Forsamlinger om Religionssager, og paaseer, at Religionens offentlige Lærere følge de dem foreskrevne Normer."
[17] Molland, "Problemet religionsfrihed", 145; Hope, *German and Scandinavian Protestantism*, 333-334.

O. Wergeland, National Assembly at Eidsvoll in
1814, oil on canvas, 1885.
[Oslo, Stortinget, Stortingsarkivet]

211

by dissenters in the coming decades. The same year as Jews in Denmark gained their rights as citizens, they lost the right to enter Norway. They were allowed in Norway from 1851, but few immigrants came in the first decades and a Jewish congregation (*Det Mosaiske Trossamfund*) was not established until 1892 in Christiania. The ban on monks was lifted in 1897, but Jesuits were not legally allowed in Norway until 1956. However, the men at Eidsvoll had forgotten to think about nuns and the Sisters of Saint Joseph of Chambéry established the first community in Norway in 1865 (after an unsuccessful attempt by the Daughters of Mary in 1857). Formally, it was not until a change in the constitution in 1964 that the religious freedom applied to other than Christians and Jews.[18]

---

[18] Amundsen, *Norges religionshistorie*, 411.

Becoming Norwegian

However, even though the wording in §16 was close to Lex Regia, the king was no longer absolute and the constitution left the legislation concerning the church to the Norwegian Parliament (*Stortinget*). Some matters, however, such as the appointment of ministers, lay until 1884 with the Swedish Crown. The government appointed a Secretary for Church Affairs and the daily administration was in the hands of a department in Christiania (1818 named the 'Department for Church and Education', *Departmentet for Kirke- og Undervisningsvæsenet*).

There was little theological influence from the Swedish Church, an exception being the revival movement in the northern part of both countries, the Laestadius movement in the Sámi districts in the 1840s and 1850s. In some matters the influence from Denmark was still felt, for instance Norway did not get its own service book until 1889 when the Norwegian *Alterboken* (Ordinal) was issued.

The thoughts of the Danish theologian N.F.S. Grundtvig (1783-1872) also made an impact in Norway, especially after his only visit to Norway in 1851. The followers of Grundtvig "thought that nationality is an expression of the character of the people and that Christianity must be national in order to seize the average man and woman".[19] Their main influence was not in the church but on education with the founding of free folk high schools (*højskoler*) in the 1860s, where the rural youth was introduced to Norwegian history, myths and poetry to inspire a national awareness.

After 1870, the Grundtvigian notion of the importance of the mother tongue was also instrumental in nationalistic attempts to increase the use of 'Norwegian *Nynorsk*' (literally: New Norwegian) in the church. '*Nynorsk*' was developed in the nineteenth century as a new form of written Norwegian, based on dialects in opposition to the traditional use of 'Norwegian *Bokmål*' (literally: book language), which was closer to Danish. In 1892, the Secretary for Church Affairs and Grundtvigian theologian, V.A. Wexelsen (1849-1909), allowed congregations to use a hymnbook in *Nynorsk*, if they wanted to, and an ordinal was introduced in 1908.[20] Already in 1883, parliament granted money for a translation of the New Testament into *Nynorsk* (published 1889), but the whole Bible was not published in *Nynorsk* until 1921.

While the cultural nationalism marked a break with Denmark, a political nationalism developed in opposition to Sweden. It led to a dramatic constitutional battle in the 1880s resulting in the adoption of parliamentarism in 1884.[21] In this tense situation, the revivalist leader Gisle Johnson issued an appeal to the friends of Christianity (*Til Christendommens Venner i vort Land*, 1883) in which he warned that the ambitions

212

[19] Thorkildsen, "Church and Nation", 256.
[20] Id., "Da den norske kirke ble nasjonal", 411-414. The terms 'Norwegian Nynorsk' and 'Norwegian Bokmål' are the official terms used today (adopted 1929); until then the terms 'landsmål' and 'riksmål' were used.

[21] The adoption of parliamentarism in Norway in 1984 and in Denmark in 1901 removed the legal loophole which made it possible for the Crown to appoint a government which lacked a majority in the elected parliament.

of radical political forces were undermining Christianity as the foundation of society. The appeal, signed by 450 prominent men including all the bishops, underlined the conservative position of the revivalists and the ministers' scepticism about the national movement. In the words of Dag Thorkildsen, "this appeal scandalised the church for decades and made the gap between the church and the political democratic and national movement obvious."[22]

The union with Sweden was dissolved in 1905 and in November 1905 a national referendum was held to decide between a republican or monarchical form of state, formally a vote to accept as future king of Norway, the Danish prince Carl (son-in-law of the British king, Edward VII). In the 'Yes Campaign' a postcard with a portrait of the handsome prince was released with the text, "JA. Vox Populi - Vox Dei. (Folkets stemme - Guds Stemme)". God was now on the side of democracy and monarchy.

While the Norwegians were coming into their own, Danish nationalism manifested itself most clearly after the Second Schleswig War in 1864, when the land area of the Danish monarchy decreased by 40% and the population was reduced from 2.6 million to 1.6 million. In the now German territories, the free high schools and the churches played an important part in sustaining the Danish language and identity.

213

Norwegian Law for Dissenters 1845

In a testament for his followers published after his death in 1824, Hans Nielsen Hauge had urged them to stay in the state church and for the first decades afterwards the *haugianerne* were true to his wish. They had meetings, often led by elders or lay preachers, but they did not organise societies or associations with official membership until the 1850s and they still attended the state church for services and Eucharist.[23] Still, politicians with a positive attitude to the revival movement were the driving force behind the abolition of the Conventicle Poster. It was first suggested in 1836, but the king twice refused to sanction it before it was finally approved in 1842 (according to the constitution, the king could only veto a law twice, but not a third time). At the same, the king sanctioned congregations outside the established church. A group of Anglicans in Alta (1842) and Roman Catholics in Christiania (1843) were allowed to celebrate services in public (but no public processions allowed).

Another dissenting group gave a more direct impulse to legal changes, the Society of Friends or Quakers (*kvækerne*). Quaker ideas had been brought to Norway around 1814 by sailors, who had been prisoners of war in Britain during the recent wars. They were only a small group, but created conflicts because they refused to christen or confirm their children in the state church. The problem was solved with the Law

---

[22] Thorkildsen, "Church and Nation", 256. In other writings Johnson emphasised loyalty to the public authorities as expounded by Luther, not least on the part of ministers as servants of the (Swedish) Crown.

[23] Molland, *Norges Kirkehistorie*, I, 71, 88-89; Amundsen, *Norges religionshistorie*, 313-316.

for Dissenters 1845, which allowed Christians outside the state church (a term used for the first time) to practice their religion and to establish free congregations. The government still wanted some sort of control, so the dissenters were not allowed to hold their services behind closed doors (!) and their ministers or wardens had to swear to uphold the national laws. Among others, the Roman Catholics now established an official congregation, named after the medieval Norwegian royal saint, St Olav. In 1856 they consecrated their first church in Christiania with the same name. The number of people outside the state church were still quite small, the national census in 1866 only counted 0.3% of the population as not belonging to the state church.[24]

Initiated by Professor Gisle Johnson (1822-1894), the revival movements began to organise themselves in *indremisjonsforeninger* (societies for inner mission) in the 1850s and in 1868 a national organisation was established, *Lutherstiftelsen*. It is estimated that around 1900, 20% of the adult population belonged to a society for inner mission, but their members stayed within the state church and became a dominant influence. Some smaller groups left the state church and established *frikirker* (free churches), the first one being founded in 1856. Around 1900, however, their overall membership only amounted to 10% of that enrolled in the inner mission.[25] The national census from 1900 showed that only 2.3% of the 2,221,477 Norwegians were 'dissenters' outside the state church, including 1,969 Catholics, 642 Jews and 14,866 persons (0.67%) with no religious affiliation.[26] The Law for Dissenters was modified in 1891, giving the free churches more privileges, for example the authority to perform legally binding marriage ceremonies. Until that date, their members had to have registry-office weddings. In the period 1878-1894, the confessional restriction applied to civil servants was also gradually loosened, but before 1917 it was not possible for dissenters to teach in the public schools.[27] Today, only the professors at the Faculty of Theology at the University of Oslo have to be members of the Norwegian Church, but this law is expected to be changed in the near future.

The Constitution of Denmark 1849

The Danes were granted their free constitution in 1849, which ended the absolute monarchy and introduced a bicameral Parliament (the second chamber was abandoned 1953). The church was recognised in §3: "The Evangelical Lutheran Church of Denmark is the Danish Folk Church and, as such, is supported by the State."[28] How the government of the church should be organised, however, was left as an open question

---

[24] 5,105 people from a population of 1,701,756, but a possible other confession is not specified. *Resultaterne af Folketællingen i Norge i Januar 1866*, published by Departementet for Det Indre, 1868.
[25] Amundsen, *Norges religionshistorie*, 326-328, 337.

[26] *Folketællingen i Kongeriget Norge 3 December 1900*, published by Det statistiske Centralbureau 1904.
[27] NOU 2006:2, *Staten og Den norske kirke*, 27.
[28] "Den evangelisk-lutherske Kirke er den danske Folkekirke og understøttes som saadan af Staten."

C. Hansen, National Assembly in 1848, *oil on
canvas, 1860.
[Hillerød, Det Nationalhistoriske Museum på
Frederiksborg Slot]*

in §80: "The Constitution of the Folk Church is regulated by an Act".[29] At the time,
it was the clear intention of the responsible cabinet minister, D.G. Monrad, that the
church should have a separate constitution, with a synod being established able to
speak on its behalf.[30] Such a piece of legislation, however, has so far not been passed,
although discussed, from time to time, ever since. In legal terms, the Danish parliament is still today the synod of the Danish Church, since the church itself does not
have its own representative body on the national level. Unlike in Norway, however, the
church was recognised as a separate body distinct from the state. The constitution also
included freedom of conscience for all citizens (§81) and the assurance that nobody
could be deprived of their civil and political rights or evade their civic duties by reason
of their confession (§84). Interestingly enough, the intention of §80 was to disen-
gage the absolute state church from the state and at the same time §83 ("The affairs
of religious communities diverging from the Folk Church are regulated by an Act")[31]

---

[29] "Folkekirkens Forfatning ordnes ved Lov."
[30] Schwarz Lausten, *A Church History of Denmark,*
230-232.

[31] "De fra Folkekirken afvigende Troessamfunds
Forhold ordnes nærmere ved Lov."

indicated that 'the other religious communities' needed help to engage with the state.[32] Such a piece of legislation has not been passed either.

The official translation of the constitution into English which is on the website of the Danish parliament has translated "*den danske Folkekirke*" as "the established Church of Denmark", probably because even the government knows how difficult it is to explain the concept of '*folkekirke*'. According to the Norwegian historian Dag Thorkildsen, '*folkekirke*' can be defined in a democratic sense, meaning an inclusive church, which includes and serves almost all citizens (regardless of the extent to which they are actually involved in the church) and is governed by elected representatives. It can also be defined in a cultural national sense and be seen as an expression of the special history, language and faith of a certain people or nation.[33] The first definition was probably close to the mindset of 1849, since nobody then could imagine the Evangelical Lutheran Church as other than the majority church. Only approximately 0.4% of the population was outside the church (most of them Jews) in 1850. In 1901, after fifty years with freedom of religion, 98.65% of the Danish population were still members of the folk church. The later definition largely expresses the ecclesiology of Grundtvig and his followers, and it not only influenced the legislation applying to the Danish Church in the second part of the nineteenth century, but also, as mentioned above, the way in which nation and religion were linked in Norway.

The ecclesiology of N.F.S. Grundtvig was based on his "peerless discovery" (1825) that the one true church was to be found in the testimony of the Christian congregation, where the Lord's Prayer, the apostles' creed and the words of institution of the sacraments have always been present in the celebration of baptism and Eucharist.[34] This oral testimony of Christ, he asserted, was far older than the dead pages of the Bible. In 1829-1832 Grundtvig made three trips to England and was greatly impressed by the situation of the free Dissenting churches. He came to believe that the ideal was "a free state church with a free congregation" with as much freedom as possible for the laity (to choose their own minister) and the clergy (to preach freely). The consequence for the institutional church was, in the words of the English scholar A.M. Allchin, that Grundtvig "saw the institution of the Church at the national and diocesan level as providing a framework, a civil structure of no religious significance in itself, in which the true Church, in the shape of believing, worshipping congregations, could find a place to shelter. The institutional Church was like a tree and the congregations like birds who came and made their nests in its branches".[35] Allchin concludes that this ecclesiology is the reason why the Danish Church has not yet been able to establish a national synod, because it has been opposed by powerful Grundtvigians in church politics. This was certainly the case in the end of the nineteenth and the beginning of the twentieth century.

216

---

[32] This observation has been made by Lene Kühle, cf. note 6.

[33] Thorkildsen, "Stat og kirke", 119-120.

[34] Schwarz Lausten, *A Church History of Denmark*, 210.

[35] Allchin, *N.F.S. Grundtvig*, 68.

In the day-to-day administration of the church, the new constitution did not change much. The state administration was reorganised and ecclesiastical affairs were handled in the Ministry of Church and Education (*Ministeriet for Kirke- og Undervisningsvæsenet*). The continuity was assured by the head of the department, J. de Jonquières (1815-1890), who had learned his business as a young public servant under the absolute rule and who now ruled the church until 1890 under no less than twenty secretaries of church affairs. Interesting enough, de Jonquières himself belonged to the French-Reformed congregation in Copenhagen, but his impeccable qualities as a civil servant meant that this was never raised as an issue, even though he had the practical responsibility for the appointment of all the clergy in the Evangelical Lutheran Church.

Religious Freedom and Establishment

The majority church was challenged in the second half of the nineteenth century by revival movements and different free churches. However, Norway and Denmark answered the challenge in different ways, perhaps because there was a different balance of power between the different factions. In both countries (and unlike Sweden) the pietistic revival movements mainly remained loyal to, but critical of, the church and developed a secondary culture of revival meetings, associations, activities and publications in their own *missionshus* (mission halls) in Denmark or *bedehus* (prayer halls) in Norway as a supplement to the Sunday church service. 217

In Denmark, there was rivalry between the pietists and the Grundtvigians, who also had their own *forsamlingshuse* (assembly halls). When it came to church politics, the two groups seemed to keep each other in check. The second generation of lay pietists had organised themselves in a society for *Den indre Mission* (inner mission) in 1853, but had a limited success until the minister Vilhelm Beck (1829-1901) in 1861 involved himself and altered the central committee giving it a clerical co-opting majority and the name to *Den kirkelige Forening for Indre Mission* (The Ecclesiastical Society for Inner Mission). Even though Beck himself had been an admirer of Grundtvig as a young man, he brought about the mission's conclusive break with the followers of Grundtvig in February 1869. This happened basically because the two did not agree on the importance of the Bible as opposed to the Creed, on the importance of conversion as opposed to baptism, on understandings of nationalism and Christianity after the defeat at the hands of Prussia in 1864 and, finally, on legislation for voluntary, independent congregations.

The law for voluntary, independent congregations (*valgmenighedsloven*) in 1868 was so far the high point of Grundtvig's aim to secure as much freedom as possible to the individual congregations within the church. The first victory had been the abolition of the home parish principle in 1855, meaning that the parishioners were no longer obliged to avail themselves exclusively of the services of their parish minister (*sognebåndsløsning*). With the new law, a minimum of 20 households was allowed to form a free congregation and pay for their own minister, who was nevertheless ordained

A. Londborg, Nikolaj Frederik Severin Grundtvig,
photograph, 1872.
[Copenhagen, Grundtvigsk Forum]

and supervised by the bishop of the folk church. Consequently, the congregation and the minister remain members of the national church, but make all their own decisions. Initially, it was stipulated that congregations had to build or buy their own church building, but this was relaxed in 1903 with the passing of a law which gave the voluntary, independent congregations the right to use the parish church for worship. The law of 1868 met with fierce opposition from the bishops who were sure it would create chaos to let in "parasites sponging off the folk church" as the bishop in Copenhagen delicately put it. The ecclesiastical opposition was reflected in parliament, but in the end the prime minister, Count Frijs, declared that the cabinet would resign if the bill was not accepted - so, reluctantly, it was. At the end of the century, only nineteen such congregations (inside the folk church), along with twelve free congregations (outside the folk church) within the Grundtvigian tradition, had been established. So the situation did not evolve quite as chaotically as had been envisaged. In most cases, such congregations used the rite and liturgy of the *folkekirke*, but they also tended to sing a lot of Grundtvig's hymns.

These laws established a new interpretation of §80 of the Danish constitution; the church could no longer expect a single comprehensive legislative act which would regulate the government of the church and establish a synod. Instead, it had to settle for particular acts passed in the ordinary course of parliamentary legislation.[36] They also established the principle that parliament could and would rule, despite massive resistance from among the ministers and bishops of the church (a later example was passing the law allowing female ministry in 1947). In 1876 the Norwegians also had a law on '*sognebåndsløsning*', but a proposal on voluntary, independent congregations was refused in 1882.

The Tangled Web of Finance

219

The economy of the churches was closely intertwined with the state.[37] Roughly speaking, the king had expropriated the property of the bishoprics in Denmark and Norway at the Reformation, but left the parishes and their properties undisturbed. The tithes or fees paid to the church were tripartite; a fee towards the maintenance of the church building, a fee to the minister and a fee to the bishop. The tithe for the bishop was revoked by the king and became a royal tax; in return the crown paid the salary of the bishops (still today, the episcopal salaries in Denmark are paid directly from the Treasury as instalments of this old debt). The two other tithes laid the ground for a financial separation of property and capital used for church buildings and churchyards (called *fabrica ecclesia*) and property and capital used for the clergy (called *mensa presbyterii* or *pastoris*). It was clearly stated in the law code, *Danske Lov* (1683) and has characterised the finances of the church ever since. In the seventeenth century, many churches were sold by the Crown to private persons, who were allowed to receive the tithe against an obligation to keep the building in good repair. During the nineteenth century the churches drifted back into the hands of local congregations. Clerical income was also based on different kinds of offerings from the congregation at Easter, Pentecost and Christmas and payment for church ceremonies like baptism and weddings. This gave a considerable variation in the salaries of the clergy according to the size and wealth of the local population.

In Norway, the local councils assumed the responsibility for the church buildings already in 1837 and became the economic manager for the congregation, gradu-

---

[36] Schwarz Lausten, *A Church History of Denmark*, 232.

[37] This section is built on the articles by Dübeck, Elstad and Stenbæk.

ally resulting in the church being funded primarily through taxation (levying taxes on the basis of the civil taxation list). An important contributory factor was the law on regulation and standardisation of clerical salaries in 1897, which ended the system of tithing and donations, so the minister was now on the pay list of the local municipalities. At the introduction of parish councils in 1920, the local municipal councils retained the economic responsibility for the church buildings and salaries (including clerical wages).

In Denmark, a great many arrangements for administration and financing were in place, depending on whether it was a rural or town parish or Copenhagen, which had its own special scheme. The paying of tithes and offerings was gradually changed to a levy tax during the nineteenth century, collected by the local councils. The municipalities did not however, control the money, but passed them along to a 'church inspection council' (usually the minister and one or two local government officials). The Commutation Act (*tiendeafløsningsloven*) in 1903 ended the system of tithing. Only in 1915 did the parish councils assume the economic responsibility for church buildings and all non-clerical staff. At the same time (1913) clerical remuneration was reformed and standardised, so offerings and payments for ceremonies were abolished in favour of a tax on all members of the church. At first, the system was in balance, but already in 1919 it became necessary for the state to subsidise the salaries of the clergy and introduce a national church tax. The reason was also that the state in 1919 expropriated most of the land belonging to the benefice - vicarages in the countryside were until this juncture usually farms - to create smallholder properties.

The economic reforms in the period from the late eighteenth century to 1920 adapted the churches to a modern economy. The consequence, however, was that their financial and administrative dependency on the state or local municipalities grew.

Continued Debate on Church Order

The liberal constitutions did not settle the debate on the state-church relationship for long and the debates continued from mid-century onwards. Two main topics were on the agenda, the possibility of a national synod and the influence of the laity through representative parish councils.

In Norway, an official reform committee was set up in 1859-1870 (*Kirkekommisjonen av 1859*), but the practical results were few.[38] Parliament voted for a law on parish councils in 1869, but the king refused to sanction it and instead parish meetings were established in 1873, mainly to decide which hymnbook the congregation should use. It came after a period in which there were voluntary organised meetings in parishes and dioceses around the country to discuss reforms, but the reform movement more or less fizzled out in the late 1880s, without any significant results. In 1886 a new proposal on

---

[38] Oftestad, *Den norske statsreligionen*, 130-133.

parish councils was submitted to parliament, but for the reform-minded in the church, it did not change enough, because it did not include a synodal structure 'all the way'. At the same time it was not democratic enough for most politicians, due to a clause about loyalty to the teaching of the church as stipulation for the right to vote. It was crushed with only a single member of parliament voting in favour.[39] The parish meetings slowly gained more responsibility to decide on the rites and liturgy to be used locally and were put on the statute book in 1897.

Another committee was appointed in 1908-1911 (*Kirkekommisjonen av 1908*). It emerged that while a minority was in favour of disestablishment, the majority only wanted reforms within the existing church order. The minority spokesperson was the law professor Absalon Taranger (1858-1930), who was a founding member of a political party (*Det norske kirkeparti*) working for disestablishment, but it had little success and was dissolved in 1920. The party suffered a fatal blow when a proposal to change the constitution was totally rejected when it was presented in parliament in 1916. The government had decided to poll the people in 1914 and made a survey of different local administrative bodies, among them parish meetings. The votes from the parishes showed that 17% wanted a free church, 14% wanted status quo - and 51% wanted reforms within the established church, such as parish councils. These were established in 1920 as the main result of the reform process.[40]

In Denmark, a commission with fourteen members of parliament and nine church ministers was appointed in 1868 (*Kirkekommissionen af 1868*) and after many compromises, an agreement on a proposal for a synod (but not parish councils) was reached in 1870, but never came before parliament for a decision. In 1883, the government quite unexpectedly set up a rather ineffective Ecclesiastical Council (*Det kirkelige Raad*) with all the bishops, a professor of law and a professor of theology in 1883, probably to devise moderate reforms with the aim of warding off more wide-ranging wishes for freedom. The conservative stand of the bishops (also the new ones elected by the government in this period) combined with a difficult parliamentary situation meant that ecclesiastical legislation was stagnant until 1901 when the council was dissolved and parliamentarianism implemented.

From the 1880s a new political voice was heard as the newly-formed Labour parties declared that "religion is a private matter" and demanded the separation of church and state in their manifestos. The Danish Labour Party (*Socialdemokratiet*) was founded in 1871 and gained seats in parliament in 1882. Even though their numbers were small, their voice was loud, not least when the former student of theology, Frederik Borgbjerg (1866-1936) was the social democrat spokesman in parliamentary debates on the church 1900-1922. The Norwegian Labour Party (*Det norske Arbeiderparti*) was founded in 1887 and gained its first four parliamentary seats in 1903, the most prominent among them being the clergyman, Alfred Eriksen (1864-1934) from Karlsøy.

221

---

[39] Molland, *Norges Kirkehistorie*, II, 31-37, 65-71; Oftestad, *Den norske statsreligionen*, 152, 154-56.

[40] Oftestad, *Den norske statsreligionen*, 185-187.

In 1916, the party alienated the church by demanding the abolition of religious instruction in schools. However, in both countries, the parties were too small to set their own mark on ecclesiastical politics until the interwar period when they formed governments, in Denmark in 1924-1926 and from 1929, in Norway two weeks in 1928 and again from 1935. As popular majority parties in countries with an overwhelming membership of the national church, they then took a softer line on the disestablishment issue and seemed more concerned with the role and form of religious education in schools.

The Church of Democracy

The Danish Church was fundamentally changed with the passing of a law on parish councils in May 1903. The proposal was based on the democratic ideals of the Secretary for Church Affairs, J.C. Christensen (1856-1928). His case was that ordinary people were not much interested in the church as things stood, but if they were given scope for involvement they would learn to love it. He argued that the church had to be democratised along with other public institutions in society. It took two years of heated discussions and public debate to get the law through parliament. It was widely opposed in the church, partly because on one hand many ministers wanted the whole question of an independent constitution for the church dealt with and not just on the parish level; two thirds of the ministers signed a petition to that effect. On the other hand, many ministers feared what would happen if the laity had influence on the appointment of ministers and their future wages.[41]

When the law was passed, Danish women got their first chance to vote in an official election and it seems that many of them did. They did not gain the right to participate in parliamentary elections until 1915, while Norwegian women had already done so in 1913. These parish councils had only limited responsibilities, but foremost they were involved in choosing new ministers for the parish, something the revival movements had wished over decades to see. Even so, many conservative theologians were not in favour of the law, because the right to vote was solely based simply on membership of the church and no additional involvement in its life was required. This conservative reservation was also found in the Norwegian debate some years later, but in both cases the conservatives then decided to take advantage of the law and work to put their own people in the councils.

In 1922, two important changes took place in the legal framework of the Danish Church. It was caused by the need to harmonise the legislation of the Danish Church in 'the mainland' with the church in North Schleswig, when the region was reunited with Denmark in 1920. In the period since 1864 the church in Schleswig had been ruled according to local German ecclesiastical law, which from 1878 included a synodical structure, with representatives on three levels (parochial councils in each parish and

---

[41] Malmgart, *Vilkår for liv*, 20-28.

222

deanery, and a synod for Schleswig-Holstein). Only one of these was accepted in the Danish legislation, an elected council in each deanery, responsible for approving budgets, but with no other functions. Another important invention was a democratisation of the election of bishops. In the period 1849-1922 the Danish bishops were appointed directly by the Secretary of Church Affairs (formally acting for the Crown according to Lex Regia). After 1922 the candidates were nominated by groups within the dioceses, and elected by ministers and parish council members in the dioceses. The majority candidate was then appointed by the Secretary of Church Affairs and the government as such was not involved.

The procedure for electing bishops in Norway had developed rather differently. Until 1841, candidates had to put themselves forward and the choice was then made by the Secretary of Church Affairs, to be confirmed by the Crown. In 1841 the procedure was changed as the deans (in the whole country, not just the diocese) and in 1848 also the bishops and theological professors were asked to nominate and prioritise three candidates; however, the king was not bound by the prioritisation. In 1882, all ministers in the relevant diocese were also drawn into the election, strengthening the democratic and the local element. But still, the government was not bound by the nomination and could choose, for instance, to appoint some candidates who had not won the election (Wexelsen in Trondheim, 1905 and Hognestad in Bjørgvin, 1916), mainly because they were supporters of 'Norwegian *Nynorsk*'.[42] When parish councils were introduced in Norway in 1920, the laity also gained influence in the elections of bishops. The bishop, however, is still appointed in the Ecclesiastical Council of State, and there have been cases where the candidate with the majority vote has not been appointed. This was the case in 1993 when Rose Marie Köhn was appointed the first female Lutheran bishop in the Nordic countries, despite coming third in the election. Thus the election of bishops actually shows a nuance in the church-state relationship in Denmark and Norway, which in so many ways resemble each other.

223

Conclusion

In 1920, the Evangelical Lutheran Churches in Denmark and Norway were no longer a function of the absolute state, but they remained close and intertwined with it. They were recognised as independent bodies, but were not autonomous or self-supporting. Liberty for dissenters and democratic elements in the structure of the churches had been introduced, but many decisions were made by political representatives in parliament. In Norway, the establishment of parish councils in 1920 was part of a continued development of the church and its structure in the twentieth century. The Norwegian Church has since expanded the synodal structure with diocesan councils (1933), the

---

[42] This information has kindly been supplied by Professor Dag Thorkildsen, Oslo.

National Council (1969), diocesan synods (1984) and the General Synod (1984) and thus the road has been paved for changing the Norwegian constitution and the church-state relationship in the near future. For Denmark the laws in 1922 marked the end of parliamentary configuration of the folk church. The only change in the Danish Church structure since 1922 has been the adoption of diocesan councils with a consultative purpose in 2009 and other changes are not expected. In general, therefore, one may conclude that, in comparison with some other countries considered in this volume the ecclesiastical-political relationship in 1780 had not changed radically by 1920.

Political Reform in Sweden

Anders Jarlert

The End of the Mediaeval Parliament

On 22 June 1866, Archbishop Henric Reuterdahl of Uppsala (1795-1870), Speaker of the Estate of Clergy in Parliament, faced with the fact that the four-estate parliament was to be abolished and replaced by two elected chambers, gave vent to his feelings about this step - the greatest political change of the position of the church in Sweden since the Middle Ages: "When I say that our work is forever ended, I say this without delight, but without sadness as well. I cannot delight in changes which interrupt the whole development history of an old people to start a new one. And still less can I delight if it would be the obvious or veiled purpose of the new order to separate from state affairs all direct influence of positive Christian religion and its guardians. [...] The Lord has allowed this to take place. In this He has had His ends. If He thereby would let some blessing reach our people - and who would deny the possibility of this? - why should we then feel sadness? And if He thereby wants to discipline and punish, let us be submissive and grateful. Discipline and punishment do not come undeserved."[1] In Reuterdahl's view, "State and Church in Sweden formed an indissoluble unit, and in this inherited system he found indispensable values. He felt almost physically sick at the thought of some people considering themselves to be better Christians than others, more virtuous than others, and in consequence deliberately cutting themselves off from the community of the ordinary parish."[2]

---

[1] Quotation translated from Jarlert, *Romantikens och liberalismens tid*, 211. This whole chapter is built on the recent multi-volume history of Swedish Christianity: Lenhammar, *Individualismens och upplysningens tid*; Bexell, *Folkväckelsens och kyrkoförnyelsens tid*; and Brohed, *Religionsfrihetens och ekumenikens tid*.

[2] Österlin, *Churches of Northern Europe*, 172.

The consequences of the parliamentary reform were more far-reaching for the clergy than for the aristocracy since, over the decades that lay ahead, many of the latter managed to get themselves elected to the new First Chamber. As a result of the Reformation, bishops had been required to vacate their places on the King's Council. However, since the Estate of the Clergy had been preserved, the bishops and the higher clergy had still kept their influence on political matters at the national level. Now this changed. Under the new system, only a couple of bishops were elected to parliament, though those few were very influential. Archbishop Anton Niklas Sundberg was elected Speaker of the Second Chamber (1867-1872) and of the First Chamber (1878-1880), and in the early twentieth century Bishop Gottfrid Billing chaired the State Committee.

The change had an impact on another level as well. The ideal concept of a bishop was remoulded. During the years 1809-1862, demands for the abolition of the bishop's office had been discussed at eleven different parliamentary sessions. These demands did not so much have an anti-clerical as economic basis, and - especially from the estate of the farmers - bishops were criticised for being absent from their dioceses and spending most of their time in parliament. It was claimed that the salary of one bishop was equivalent to the pay of 400 elementary school teachers. After the parliamentary reform, most of the bishops stayed resident in their dioceses for the whole year, and their interest in pastoral inspections and other ecclesiastical matters increased. So did their impact as theologians. Before 1865, it was a self-evident matter that a professor in, say, mathematics, could be elected bishop. Now, theological knowledge and pastoral experience were more appreciated. However, the bishop's position as *eforus* (supervisor) for the grammar schools in the diocese continued, and the senior masters of the grammar schools in the diocesan centres were still members of the *domkapitel* (diocesan chapter), together with the bishop and the dean.[3] After the Reformation, the *domkapitel* ceased to be a cathedral chapter and was turned into an ecclesiastical board for the diocese. The dean was rector of the cathedral parish, but simultaneously deputised for the bishop in the whole diocese. With regard to marriage, until 1918, all divorces required the authorisation of the *domkapitel*. The bishops retained their leading position in the grammar schools for a further four decades, and, in legal terms, the *domkapitel* remained a public authority directly under the government until 2000.

The Church Assembly and the Bishops' Conference

The attempts to establish a Church Assembly were separate from the parliamentary reform of 1865. To radical reformers, the Free Church of Scotland (1843) was an ideal model. They wanted to break up the episcopal system and establish an elected general synod. The planned parliamentary reform made it necessary to institute a separate

---

[3] Jarlert, *Romantikens*, 63.

The Swedish bishops Anton Niklas Sundberg and
Gottfrid Billing, *photographs. Both were elected
to parliament and were very influential in Swedish
politics.*
[Private collection]

representative body for the Church of Sweden in 1863, and it assembled for the first
time in 1868. The division between secular and ecclesiastical matters, newly introduced at the local level in 1862, was repeated at the national level. The spheres of
parliament and Church Assembly were regulated in detail. Only those issues especially defined as ecclesiastical were to be discussed in the Church Assembly. This body
consisted of the bishops and elected clergymen (totalling 30) matched by 30 elected
laymen from all the dioceses, with the archbishop of Uppsala presiding. Since it met
only every fifth year, the initiative in ecclesiastical matters was in the hands of the
Cabinet, the parliament, and the bishops.

Before 1862, one and the same council, the *Sockenstämma* (Parish Meeting)
had taken all decisions concerning both secular and ecclesiastical affairs.[4] The division between secular and ecclesiastical matters at the local level meant that church
parishes got a 'communal' status with the right to assess the amount of taxation to
be paid to the parish by the individual church members, a system that with some
changes worked until 2000. This 'communal' status gradually gave the local parishes,
or the united parish councils (in Göteborg from 1883), a political character in parallel

---

[4] Österlin, *Churches of Northern Europe*, 171.

alongside existing communal political institutions. The formal and practical influence of the local clergy on the elementary schools, which were made compulsory for the parishes in 1842, was considerable and continued far into the twentieth century. A general right to vote, for both sexes, was first granted, in some privileged town parishes in the elections for clerical positions decades before such a right was introduced in society at large. In the countryside, however, the right to vote still depended on financial status. Unmarried women, on the supposition that they had independent means of their own, could speak publicly at local parish meetings in the 1890s. In 1909 all men were given the vote, though it was still related to wealth. Ten years later voting rights for men and women were put on an equal footing - the first women voting in 1921. It may be noted that in Finland, under its constitution within the Russian Empire, men and women were given equal voting rights in 1906 - the first country in Europe to do this. It was a step which calls into question the assumption of an automatic connection between political liberty and political reform. In Sweden while it can be said that while churches and denominations in some ways pioneered democratic values on a local level, in most ways they remained connected to older social patterns, and were conservative in their political opinions.

228

Until the late 1920s no sharp conflicts occurred between parliament and Church Assembly. In 1893, a Crown proposal, prompted by liberals in parliament, to limit the authorised *symbola* (creeds) of the Church of Sweden to the three confessions of the Ancient Church, the Augsburg Confession of 1530, and Luther's Small Catechism - instead of mentioning the whole Book of Concord of 1580 - was narrowly rejected by the Church Assembly by only two votes. In 1898, a conflict over whether pastors and laymen, largely from the *Missionsförbundet* (Covenant Church) were entitled to carry out baptisms was settled by a gloss which the bishops placed on the decision of the Cabinet.

The church took steps, though only gradually and slowly, to move beyond the limited sphere of operation which had been accorded by the distinct line between political and ecclesiastical matters drawn in the 1860s. It did so at the local level, for example, when deaconesses from the 1890s were permitted to be paid out of the local church taxes. It did so at the national level when Archbishop Nathan Söderblom (1866-1931), after the World War, set out his international, ecumenical vision as a political strategy for the Church of Sweden.

Because, since 1865, all the bishops no longer met regularly in parliament they lacked a common conference. An informal bishops' conference was instituted to fill this hole in 1898. Thereafter, when the government asked the Church of Sweden for advice and opinions, the question was put to the archbishop, who in turn presented it to this informal conference. On another level, the bishops' conference was to play an active part with regard to ecumenical matters - something with political implications. Starting with the Lambeth conference in 1908, going on to the meeting in Uppsala in 1909, and then, especially with Nathan Söderblom as archbishop of Uppsala (from 1914), the negotiations with the Church of England continued at Lambeth in 1920 and in Uppsala in 1922. Such contacts were a necessary preliminary to the leading bridge-building role which Söderblom played in the emerging international ecumeni-cal movement, particularly in the work of post-war reconciliation, and at the Stock-holm 'Life and Work' Conference in 1925. It was on his initiative that a Nordic bishops' conference was set up in 1919. His bridge-building role was part of a political pattern, characteristic of and significant for Swedish neutralism from the First World War onwards and associated with the premiership (1914-1917) of Hjalmar Hammarskjöld (1862-1953), the father of the later UN secretary-general Dag Hammarskjöld (1905-1961). Söderblom spoke of the three great centres of Christianity, besides Rome, as Constantinople, Canterbury and Uppsala. Uppsala should lead the North European block, which he called *corpus evangelicorum*, a terminology used in Swedish history in the context of Gustav II Adolf's plans following his victory over the German emperor at the battle of Breitenfeld in 1631.[5]

A New Constitution and a Reduced Nation

As a consequence of the 'revolution' of King Gustav III (1746-1792) in 1772, the parlia-mentiarism of the so-called 'Liberty' period came to an end. Indeed, after the assas-sination of the king in 1792, autocracy was still further strengthened. However, in the revolution of 1809, his son, Gustav IV Adolf (1778-1837) was forced to resign as a consequence of the defeat in the war in Finland. He was succeeded by his childless uncle, Karl XIII (1748-1818). After his death, Napoleon Bonaparte's field marshal, Jean Baptiste Bernadotte (1763-1844), succeeded to the throne in 1818 under the style Karl XIV Johan, having been elected as crown prince in 1810.

229

The new constitution of 1809 prescribed a balance between king and parlia-ment, and guaranteed liberty of conscience. This meant in practice that the Lutheran religion was still the only publicly recognised religion, with an exception being made for foreigners and their children, but privately, every citizen was given the right to think freely. Religious censorship was maintained, but the last successful trial took place in 1821. In the very last case of religious censorship, in 1841, the editor concerned was found not guilty. In 1810-1811 a new Church Agenda and a new Catechism were imposed, followed in 1819 by a new Hymnal. But the old Common Law of 1734 was still in force, and in the province of Finland, which had been lost to Russia in 1809, the old 'Gustavian' constitution and the old ecclesiastical books were also still maintained. The political union with Norway (1814-1905) did not affect either the constitution or religious administration in Sweden.

As a result of the loss of Finland - one third of the country's area, with a quar-ter of its population - the national identity of Sweden changed. The former glorious picture of Sweden as a European power, which had been faltering since 1721, defi-nitely passed into history in 1809, or at least in 1812, with the adoption of a friendly

---

[5] Österlin, *Churches of Northern Europe*, 247.

policy towards Russia. It followed that Finland, as the poet and later bishop of Växjö, Esaias Tegnér (1782-1846), described it in the second version of his poem *Svea* could not be reconquered and be reabsorbed politically. Rather, the objective should be to 'incorporate' it in a spiritual sense. A further consequence of this vision was that the reduced Sweden should concentrate on its own internal economic and industrial development rather than hanker after greatness by trying to get Finland back. In all conscience there were problems enough in that respect. Between 1850 and 1910 more than one million Swedes emigrated to the United States where, working on the land or in industry, they could find a better standard of living that they could expect at home.

Religious Toleration for 'Foreigners'

Since the closure of the Birgittine convent in Vadstena in 1595, practice of Roman Catholicism in Sweden had been confined to occasional visitors as well as the foreign legations and their chapels. A restricted, but common religious tolerance for foreign Roman Catholics and Jews was decided by parliament in 1779, and introduced by the royal Edict of Toleration in 1781, placing them under the supervision and inspection of the state. The Vatican appointed a special vicar apostolic for Sweden as early as in 1783. This reveals the efforts from both the Swedish government and the Holy See to release Catholics from their dependence on the foreign legations. J.L. Studach (1796-1873), the private chaplain of Queen Joséphine (1807-1876, queen from 1844), herself a Catholic, became vicar apostolic in 1833 and was made bishop in 1862. Studach built the church in both a spiritual and physical sense. In 1836-1837, St Eugenia Church in Stockholm was erected as the first Roman Catholic church in Sweden since the Reformation.[6]

For Jews, religious tolerance had been regulated by a special provision in 1782. However, in 1815, some members of parliament tried to restrict their freedom, a move which had an economic basis, but which also represented a reaction against enlightenment ideas of toleration. The Edict of Emancipation (1838) abolished the 1782 regulation. Now, the Jews were defined as 'Mosaic believers' and those who had become Swedish subjects were in most senses treated on a basis of equality with other Swedes. The services, education and administration of the Jewish congregations were regulated by a royal circular, in force until 1951. The Edict of Emancipation led to anti-Jewish demonstrations and campaigns even in liberal newspapers. The consequence was that the Jews' right to settle was limited to four cities - Stockholm, Göteborg, Norrköping and Karlskrona. During the 1850s, the attitude changed to a more liberal one. In 1854, Jews were allowed to settle in all cities, and in 1860 to own property everywhere in the country. In 1863, Jews were allowed to marry Christians in civil ceremonies.[7] In 1908, every subject was given the right to choose between an ecclesiastical and a civil

[6] Jarlert, *Romantikens*, 70 ff.   [7] Ibid., 200.

The synagogue in Göteborg built in 1855, *postcard,*
c.1905.
[Private collection]

marriage ceremony, although the church ceremony was still popularly regarded as normal and a civil right which every Swedish citizen possessed.

By the Dissenter laws of 1860 and 1873, conversions from the Lutheran Church to Catholicism were legalised. As late as in 1858, six Swedish women had been compelled to leave the country for having converted - an action observed and criticised in the press all over Europe. Catholics on the continent gave them financial and moral support. Popular opinion in Sweden changed. The "Church of Sweden" was introduced as a political term in the Dissenter law of 1860. Before that date, the unity between church and state had been self-evident, and the "Church in Sweden" had been sufficient to distinguish this church from the national churches in other countries. Now, there was a need to distinguish the church also from other denominations within the country.

Tolerance within the Lutheran Church

Religious toleration inside the Church of Sweden was quite another matter. The severest of the edicts against conventicles, that of 1726, was intended to check and suppress the pietistic movement, forbidding all public gatherings for worship except under the parish priest. It was not repealed till 1858.[8] The leaders of conventicles were severely punished with high penalties, and, on a second offence, resulted in two weeks in prison on bread and water only.[9] However, during the last half of the eighteenth century, the edict had fallen into oblivion, and it was not until 1810 that it was used again. The severe regulations were in fact difficult to enforce since cases could not be brought before local courts without the consent of higher authorities and the whole proceedings could be declared null and void if not reported to an appeal court. It often happened when conventicle leaders were judged by the lower courts, their cases were dismissed by higher courts on technical grounds.[10] Even so, this edict has been regarded as a symbol of intolerance and oppression, and emphasis both on the cruelty of the police and the eagerness of the clergy to dissolve the meetings has loomed large in the picture of the Church of Sweden in the first half of the nineteenth century presented in historiography. The new conventicle regulations in 1858 changed the locus in dealing with them from the local police to the local church councils, a step which indicates that private religious meetings were ceasing to be regarded as a political matter.

In Northern Sweden, village prayer meetings had been allowed since the seventeenth century in districts where the long distances made it impossible for the inhabitants of distant villages to go to church on ordinary Sundays. For the big festivals, the villagers went to church, and stayed for several days in the so-called 'church villages'.

232

---

[8] Wordsworth, *The National Church of Sweden*, 324 ff. Its perspectives reflect its age, but Wordsworth's book still gives the best overall view of Swedish church history in English. See also Jarlert, "Schweden II".

[9] Lenhammar, *Individualismes*, 58 ff.

[10] Jarlert, *Romantikens*, 90 ff.

Here they encountered people from other villages. News - both secular and religious - spread quickly, so the very act of staying in the 'church villages', intended to strengthen the position and discipline of the Church of Sweden, in fact often introduced the villagers to new religious currents and movements.

Lay protests in the north concerned preaching and teaching in church, but still more the new Prayer Book of 1811, and especially its baptismal rite. Those children, who were not baptised according to its formulae but by their parents according to the old order, the Prayer Book of 1693, were then sometimes transported by the local police to have their baptism confirmed by the parish priest according to the new order. In some cases, these children were then re-baptised by their parents according to the old Prayer Book, since the new forms were regarded as legalistic, baptising (or confirming) the children not to Christ, but to Moses, as the critics put it. They did not oppose Lutheranism as such, rather they regarded themselves as the only strict Lutherans. These conflicts are interesting also from a social point of view, since the critics did not, as the later Baptist movement did, question the baptism of children as such, but only the particular rite of infant baptism. Some of them criticised the rites for common confession and Eucharist as well. In placing themselves outside the common church order, these critics also separated themselves from social communion.

233

The later conflict about the Baptists' refusal to baptise their children showed how far, with the Church of Sweden, the views of Christians differed. Church and state clearly did not want to abdicate from their responsibility to maintain the 'right' doctrine. Some children were forcibly taken by police from their mothers to be "transported to baptism", others were baptised on the spot, while their Baptist parents made it clear that in their opinion the priest was simply washing the hair of the child. However, at least one clergyman refused to baptise a Baptist child by force. Bishop J.H. Thomander (1798-1865) of Lund tried to act in a more pastoral way when he proposed prayers for the conversion of the Baptists in his diocese, but the Baptists answered with prayers for the conversion of the clergy, "not excluding the bishop". Thomander was the leading advocate of a synodal Church Assembly, of the abolition of the Conventicle Edict, and other liberal reforms. He was liberal in politics, though conservative in dogmatics. He was Low Church when it came to matters of lay influence and activities, and was in many ways influenced by Romanticism, being the first important Swedish translator of the dramatic works of William Shakespeare. The English combination of High Church and political liberalism was unknown in Sweden.

When formal conversion from Lutheranism was accepted by the state in 1860, only the Roman Catholic and the Methodist Episcopal Church, together with a solitary Baptist congregation, used the possibility to be registered as publicly recognised denominations. The other Baptist congregations did not want to be registered, and, thus their marriages were still not officially recognised by the state. Baptists were officially regarded as coupling together without marriage. This meant that their self-interpretation as being persecuted by both state and church was confirmed by their own conscious denunciation of any cooperation with the state. A consequence was that up till 1951, most Baptists were formally members of the Church of Sweden, and as such, from the point of the state, regarded as Lutherans.

When the Lutheran Home and Foreign Mission Movement, the *Evangeliska Fosterlands-Stiftelsen* (Swedish Evangelical Mission), split in 1878, and the *Svenska Missionsförbundet* was established, this split occurred mainly in the ecclesiastical area, concerning the teaching on the atonement, preaching as restricted to the ministry and the distribution of the Eucharist by impious priests or to ungodly people. From a political point of view, one has to observe that despite their critical attitude towards the Church of Sweden and its orders, the people of the *Missionsförbundet* were loyal to the monarchy and the state, and were even over-represented in parliament.

When publicly recognised, the Catholic, Methodist and Jewish congregations also got the right to compile and be responsible for the civil registration of their members. However, this was abolished in 1910, when parliament decided that every citizen should be publicly registered by the Church of Sweden only. This meant a limitation of the rights of the 'foreign' denominations, but also entailed a political instrumentalisation and secularisation of the parish registers of the Church of Sweden, and remained in force until 1991. Secularisation showed another side in the reform of religious teaching in lower schools in 1919, proposed by the liberal-social democratic coalition government. Liberal and radical interests changed the basis of religious teaching from the Small Catechism of Martin Luther to the ethical teaching of the Sermon of the Mount. In future, the Christian religion was to be taught in schools in a more general or common way.

The Swedish situation differs from both the Danish and the Norwegian one. In Sweden, we do not encounter any equivalent to the religious liberty provided in Denmark in 1849. The Church of Sweden was never a state church in the same, total meaning as the Danish Church before 1849, and there was no transformation into a '*folkkyrka*' (People's Church) as in Denmark. The Swedish '*folkkyrka*' is a much later concept, theological more than political, emanating from German High Church Lutheranism, and with its peak during the first three decades of the twentieth century. Sweden has no analogy to the freedom allowed in Denmark for congregations to be formed within parishes on an individual basis but remaining within the unity of a national church. One consequence might be the much stronger position of the free churches in Sweden. The popular saying that we speak about the Church of Sweden, the congregations of Denmark, and the Christians of Norway has something important to say not only about the ecclesiastical organisation of these three countries, respectively, but also about the political reforms of the nineteenth century.

Social Reform, Church Building, and Financial Reform

In Sweden, political reform took a different form from what took place in Denmark and Norway, but in social reform similar patterns can be discerned. Many church people were inspired by Danish efforts. This was especially clear in the efforts to build new churches in the big cities, where the church building movement in Copenhagen inspired a continuing work in Stockholm at the end of the nineteenth century. The Swedish capital passed 100,000 inhabitants in 1856 and reached 300,000 by 1900. At the turn of the century, one clergyman in Stockholm served 10,000 individuals, compared to 2,000 in the rest of the country. Two Stockholm parishes had more than 50,000 inhabitants. With the exception of revivalist chapels, Ersta Church for the Deaconess Home, and a couple of military churches, only one single church had been built for the use of the Church of Sweden in Stockholm during 1800-1890. The matter had been discussed in parliament without result. In 1891, the ecclesiastical authorities in Stockholm proposed a reorganisation, with six new parishes, five new church buildings, and eighteen more priests. The process was delayed, and the parishes were not divided until 1905-1906. Simultaneously, the *Sällskapet för kyrklig själavård* (Society for Ecclesiastical Care of Souls), founded 1893, collected money to fund a priest who would serve the poor. The Society argued that without voluntary work of this kind the people would be left to the free churches or the socialists. This voluntary society built several churches or chapels, which were later handed over to the local parishes.[11]

235

The German so-called Elberfeld system for the relief of the poor was introduced in the 1880s. It was built on voluntary visitors, each caring for three or four families in their district. Personal contact with the poor was a cornerstone. In the 1890s, the Elberfeld system was applied in some towns by the political authorities, in some by the ecclesiastical. During this period, many conservative church leaders reacted sharply against liberalism and the consequences of capitalism, emphasising the social responsibilities of the well-to-do classes. Both in the Church of Sweden and in the free denominations, social democracy was regarded as a godless enemy, distancing many workers from the church and gradually contributing to the secularisation of society.

The whole financial system of the Church of Sweden was built on an old agrarian structure. Until 1910 parish priests could and some did work the land themselves. The land was owned by the local church. The reform of priests' salaries in 1910 changed this situation. It required that such land be always leased out and in turn stipulated the salary that was to be paid to all priests. In order to produce financial equalisation of such salaries across the country, the *Kyrkofonden* (Ecclesiastical Fund) was set up and administered by the state. Simultaneously, a state pension at the age of 75 was introduced for parish priests. The new system did not make the clergy civil servants,

---

11 Brohed, *Religionsfrihetens och ekumenikens tid*, 211-216.

236

The coronation of King Karl XV of Sweden in 1860
in the cathedral in Trondheim (Norway), *engraving
published in* The Illustrated London News, *7 June
1860.*
[*London, British Library*]

since they were still paid by the church out of its land and tax income, but since it was regulated by the state, the government was very reluctant to institute new clerical posts, even though they were to be paid for by the church. Due to this reluctance to change the ecclesiastical structures regulated by the state, the Church of Sweden slowly built up its own complementary organisation in each diocese, voluntary in its character, but based on parish councils and comparable bodies, rather than on separate societies.[12]

Loosening Ties but still Together: Oaths, Universities, a Diocese - and no Coronation

The development of political reform in Sweden was not straightforward. While the ties between church and state were in many ways successively loosened, they were simultaneously also tightened in some other areas. The late-nineteenth-century political scene in itself contributed to this complexity. After the parliamentary reform, the general opinion in the aristocratic First Chamber was that party systems were dangerous. This could be supported by religious motivations. In the Second Chamber, where farmers were in the majority, parties were accepted. The *Lantmannapartiet* (Farmers' Party) was founded 1867 (though it had no national organisation, that began later, in 1904). It was conservative, with a tight economic policy, hostile to heavy administrative and defence expenditure. This rural, conservative, and anti-bourgeois group formed the majority after 1868 in the Second Chamber (in which there was also a competing neo-liberal party). The conservative King Oscar II was influenced both by developments in Victorian Britain and Wilhelmine Germany. The restored *Lantmannapartiet* (1895-1911) took a moderate position, while the *Liberala samlingspartiet*, founded in 1900, organised nationally in 1902. In the 1905 elections, liberals and social democrats, following a somewhat anti-clerical line, won a majority in the Second Chamber. The 'unpolitical' Church Assembly, like the First Chamber, had a conservative majority.[13] This concluding section offers a brief consideration of four different cases which illustrate how difficult it is to consider church-state relations in Sweden at this juncture in terms of a straightforward dichotomy.

Oath-taking became a source of both political and religious conflict. Every candidate for priesthood had to swear an oath which combined theological loyalty to the doctrines of the church with allegiance to the king. These oaths were repeated before entering office as rector or bishop. They illustrated the close union between church and state. During the last decades of the nineteenth century, the ecclesiastical oaths were questioned, and then successively mitigated and changed into solemn

237

---

[12] Bexell, *Folkväckelsens och kyrkoförnyelsens tid*, 13-17.

[13] Carlsson, *Tiden efter 1718*.

promises. This was due both to modernisation of society, where all other oaths, except for judges, were successively abolished, but also demonstrated a new emphasis on the individual conscience. This emphasis took different forms. Sometimes it was an expression of radicalism or liberalism. Sometimes it stemmed from a 'biblical' standpoint which opposed such swearing in church. The formal ties between church and throne were therefore being loosened, but informally they remained in practice.

Another area where tradition came in conflict with modernity was the bishops' positions as chancellors of the universities at Uppsala and Lund. These conflicts in the early twentieth century revolved around the appointments of professors - in theology, but also in natural sciences - if the candidate was known for radical moral principles. Both freedom to conduct research and personal 'private' freedoms were discussed (for example whether a professor might live together with a woman without formal marriage). If theology was to be treated as any other academic discipline, this would have consequences for the membership of the theological professors in the *domkapitel* in Lund and Uppsala, where they by oath were bound to defend the same doctrines of the church that they sometimes criticised in their teaching at the university. In these conflicts, bishops took a political position that was severely criticised as backward looking. The result was, perhaps significant in Swedish politics, a compromise. Universities were secularised, but the composition of the *domkapitel* was not to be reformed until 1936.

In former times, new dioceses had been instituted mostly for pastoral reasons, though political and cultural 'Swedification' had sometimes played an important part. Such a mixture of motivation still obtained to the joint benefit of state and church. The case of Luleå, in the far north of Sweden, is an example of one such meshing of political and ecclesiastical imperatives. One factor in the institution of the diocese in 1904 was a political need to strengthen 'the Swedish presence' on the border with Finland so as to counteract the Russian influence and the supposed plans to expand westwards.[14] Simultaneously, both Samis and Finnish-speaking children were forced to speak Swedish at school. A political condition for the institution of the new diocese was the amalgamation of the dioceses of Växjö and Kalmar in the south in 1915. Mostly for economic reasons, it was not until 1942 that the number of bishops was allowed to exceed the apostolic number of twelve.

At least since 1210, the reigning kings and queens of Sweden had been crowned by the church. After the death of Oscar II (1829-1907), his successor, Gustaf V (1858-1950), decided he did not want a coronation ceremony, mostly because, reacting against his pompous father, he thought it would be too expensive. Coronation was widely regarded as old-fashioned, but some conservatives criticised the king's decision - which meant that an important symbolic link between church and state, with the church performing on the national stage, was broken. This development was the

---

[14] Bergman, "Luleå stifts inrättande och Kalmar stifts upphörande".

more remarkable in that, when the political union with Norway was dissolved in 1905 - in a peaceful way, uncommon in European history - the new king of Norway (a Danish prince) was crowned by the church.

In short, taken in conjunction with the other issues considered in this chapter, these concluding examples illustrate the way in which political and legal reform in the state, and with it a process of secularisation, proceeded in a distinctive and puzzling way in Sweden, partly in conjunction with the church, partly against it.

239

Bibliography

Denmark and Norway

Allchin, A.M. *N.F.S. Grundtvig. An Introduction to his Life and Work*. Aarhus, 1997.

Amundsen, Arne Bugge, ed. *Norges religionshistorie*. Oslo, 2005.

Balling, J.L. and Lindhardt, P.G. *Den nordisk kirkes historie*. Copenhagen, 1973³.

Bregnsbo, Michael. "Clerical Attitudes Towards Society in the Age of Revolution: Points of View on Government, Freedom, Equality and Human Rights in Danish Sermons, 1775-1800". *Scandinavian Journal of History*, 16 (1991) 1, 1-25.

Bregnsbo, Michael. "Præster under pres. Den danske statskirkegejstligheds reaktioner på udfordringen fra Oplysningen i 1790'erne". *Den Jyske Historiker*, 105 (2004), 94-108.

Departementet for Det Indre, ed. *Resultaterne af Folketællingen i Norge i Januar 1866*. Christiania, 1868.

Det statistiske Centralbureau, ed. *Folketællingen i Kongeriget Norge 3 December 1900*. Christiania, 1904.

Dübeck, Inger. "Kirchenfinanzierung der nordischen Länder". *Zeitschrift für evangelisches Kirchenrecht*, (2002), 47, 369-394.

Ellingsen, Terje. *Fri folkekirke. Den norske kirkes forfatning under debatt 1906-1916*. Oslo, 1973.

Elstad, Hallgeir. "Lønn som fortent. Endringar i det geistlege lønnssystemet på 1800-tallet". *Norsk Teologisk Tidsskrift*, 97 (1996), 35-43.

Hope, Nicholas. *German and Scandinavian Protestantism 1700-1918*. Oxford, 1995.

Jensen, Jens Toftegaard. "Sekularisering af tiden? - Den danske Helligdagsreduktion 1770". *Den Jyske Historiker*, 105 (2004), 73-93.

Knudsen, Tim. *Dansk Statsbygning*. Copenhagen, 1995.

Kühle, Lene. *Out of Many, One: A Theoretical and Empirical Study of Religious Pluralism in Denmark from a Perspective of Power*. PhD dissertation. Aarhus, 2004.

Malmgart, Liselotte. *Vilkår for liv og vækst. Menighedsrådsloven 1903-2003*. Aarhus, 2003.

Molland, Einar. "Problemet religionsfrihet i norsk politikk og lovgivning 1814-1964" in: Per-Olav Ahrén, ed. *Kyrka Folk Stat. Till Sven Kjöllerström*. Lund, 1967, 143-158.

Molland, Einar. *Norges Kirkehistorie i det 19. Århundre*. Oslo, 1979, 2 vols.

NOU 2006:2. *Staten og Den norske kirke*. Utredning fra Stat-kirke-utvalget, avgitt 31 januar 2006 (Report of the State-Church Committee, 2006). <www.regjeringen.no/nb/dep/kkd/dok/NOUer/2006/NOU-2006-2.html?id=156177> (13 April 2010).

Oftestad, Bernt T. *Den norske statsreligionen. Fra øvrighetskirke til demokratisk statskirke*. Kristianssand, 1998.

Schwarz Lausten, Martin. *A Church History of Denmark*. Aldershot, 2002.

Schwarz Lausten, Martin. *Oplysning i Kirke og Synagoge*. Copenhagen, 2002.

Stenbæk, Jørgen. "Folkekirkens ejendomsforhold og økonomi - historisk belyst". *Kirkehistoriske Samlinger*, 2002, 123-148.

Statistiske Bureau. *Befolkningsforholdene i Danmark i det 19. Aarhundrede*. Copenhagen, 1905.

Thorkildsen, Dag. "Church and Nation in the 19th Century" in: Ingmar Brohed, ed. *Church and People in Britain and Scandinavia*. Lund, 1996, 249-266.

Thorkildsen, Dag. "Stat og kirke i historisk og nordisk perspektiv". *Norsk teologisk Tidsskrift*, 103 (2002) 2-3, 113-124.

Thorkildsen, Dag. "Da den norske kirke ble nasjonal". *Nytt Norsk Tidsskrift*, (2005) 4, 406-415.

Thuringer, Rune P. "Jesuitter i Norge på 1700-tallet". <www.katolsk.no/ordener/sj/a_sj_1.htm> (1 March 2010).

<www.ft.dk/~/media/Pdf_materiale/Pdf_publikationer/English/My_Constitutional_Act.ashx> (8 November 2009).

<www.kirken.no/english/engelsk.
  cfm?artid=5730> (8 November 2009).
<www.stortinget.no/en/In-English/
  About-the-Storting/The-Constitution/
  The-Constitution> (8 November 2009).

Sweden

Bergman, Martin. "Luleå stifts inrättande
och Kalmar stifts upphörande. En stifts-
reglering, dess motiv och orsaker". *Kyrko-
historisk årsskrift*, 101 (2001), 67-100.

Bexell, Oloph. *Folkväckelsens och kyrkoförnyelsens tid*. Sveriges kyrkohistoria 7.
Stockholm, 2003.

Brohed, Ingemar. *Religionsfrihetens och
ekumenikens tid*. Sveriges kyrkohistoria 8.
Stockholm, 2005.

Carlsson, Sten. *Tiden efter 1718*. Svensk histo-
ria 2. Stockholm, 1980[4].

Jarlert, Anders. "Schweden II" in: *Theologi-
sche Realenzyklopädie*. Vol. 30. Berlin-
New York, 1999, 649-671.

Jarlert, Anders. *Romantikens och liberalismens tid*. Sveriges kyrkohistoria 6. Stockholm, 2001.

Lenhammar, Harry. *Individualismens och
upplysningens tid*. Sveriges kyrkohistoria 5.
Stockholm, 2000.

Österlin, Lars. *Churches of Northern Europe
in Profile: A Thousand Years of Anglo-Nordic
Relations*. Norwich, 1995.

Wordsworth, John. *The National Church of
Sweden. The Hale Lectures*. London, 1911.

Index

243

Authors

Stewart J. Brown, professor of ecclesiastical history and head of the School of Divinity, University of Edinburgh. Research interests: religion, politics and society in Britain and Ireland since 1680 and in Western Europe, c 1650-c 1850.

Heiner de Wall, professor of ecclesiastical law, constitutional and administrative law at the University of Erlangen-Nuremberg, director of the Hans-Liermann-Institut für Kirchenrecht. Research interests: state-church law, law of the German Protestant churches, history of church law, German constitutional law, political thought in early modern Germany.

Andreas Gestrich, professor of modern history at the University of Trier (on leave) and since 2006 director of the German Historical Institute London. Research interests: history of childhood, youth and family, social history of religion and religious groups, and history of poverty, poor relief and philanthropy.

Anders Jarlert, professor of church history at Lund University and member of the Royal Swedish Academy of Letters, History and Antiquities. Research interests: early modern and modern church history, including Scandinavian revivalism, church and state, modern historiography, church and National Socialism, law and religion, theology and biography.

James C. Kennedy, professor of Dutch history since the Middle Ages at the University of Amsterdam. Research interests: political and cultural developments in Dutch postwar history and Dutch religious past.

Emiel Lamberts, emeritus professor K.U.Leuven, honorary president of KADOC-Documentation and Research Centre for Religion, Culture and Society/K.U.Leuven. Research interests: conservatism and Christian Democracy in contemporary Europe (nineteenth and twentieth centuries).

Liselotte Malmgart, professor at the Department of Church History and Practical Theology, Faculty of Theology, Aarhus University. Research interests: Christian social work, Danish church history (nineteenth and twentieth centuries), Scandinavian church-state relations.

Keith Robbins, emeritus vice-chancellor, University of Wales, Lampeter. Research interests: British/European nineteenth-twenty-first-century political, cultural, church and diplomatic history.

Colophon

Final editing
Beatrice Van Eeghem (UPL)
Luc Vints (KADOC)

Copy editing
Lieve Claes (KADOC)

Lay-out
Alexis Vermeylen (KADOC)

Printing and binding
Lannoo Printers, Tielt (Belgium)

KADOC
Documentation and Research Centre for Religion, Culture and Society
Vlamingenstraat 39
B - 3000 Leuven
http://kadoc.kuleuven.be

Leuven University Press
Minderbroedersstraat 4
B - 3000 Leuven
http://upers.kuleuven.be